THIEVES OF STATE

ALSO BY SARAH CHAYES

The Punishment of Virtue:
Inside Afghanistan after the Taliban

THIEVES
OF
STATE

*Why Corruption
Threatens Global Security*

Sarah Chayes

W. W. NORTON & COMPANY
New York · London

For information about permission to reproduce selections from
this book, write to Permissions, W. W. Norton & Company, Inc.,
500 Fifth Avenue, New York, NY 10110

For information about special discounts for bulk purchases, please contact
W. W. Norton Special Sales at specialsales@wwnorton.com or 800-233-4830

Manufacturing by Courier Westford
Book design by Brooke Koven
Production manager: Julia Druskin

Library of Congress Cataloging-in-Publication Data

Chayes, Sarah, 1962–
Thieves of state : why corruption threatens global security / Sarah Chayes.
pages cm
Includes bibliographical references and index.
ISBN 978-0-393-23946-1 (hardcover)
1. Political corruption—Case studies. 2. Security, International—Case studies. I. Title.
JF1081.C43 2015
364.1'323—dc23

2014031700

W. W. Norton & Company, Inc.,
500 Fifth Avenue, New York, N.Y. 10110
www.wwnorton.com

W. W. Norton & Company Ltd.,
Castle House, 75/76 Wells Street, London W1T 3QT

1 2 3 4 5 6 7 8 9 0

For my Sainted Mother
Antonia Handler Chayes

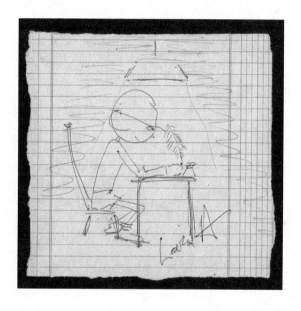

CONTENTS

THIEVES OF STATE

CHAPTER ONE

"If I See Somebody Planting an IED . . ."

Afghanistan, 2009

T he man before me—young, passionate, brilliant, difficult—was transfigured with a barely contained rage.

"I called the chief of police," he plunged on with his story. "And you know what he said? He asked me, 'Well, did he die of it?' Think about that! You call that law?"

Nurallah and I and perhaps a half-dozen others were sitting behind the stout mud-brick walls of the compound that served as our workshop, tucked away on one of the unpaved backstreets of Kandahar, Afghanistan. I can't remember now what we were doing—eating a breakfast of spiced tea and our own almond butter on flat bread, or else packaging bars of the handcrafted soap we lovingly manufactured there. This would have been early 2009.

Nurallah was telling me what had happened to his brother.

We were always doing this—sharing stories as we worked. It took hours each day just to process it all. Improvised bombs would rattle our windows as they detonated, pounding the air like thunderclaps, or like great objects falling in the next room. I used the formal Arabic word for "explosion": *infijar*. The guys had trouble pronouncing it. The Pashtu was so much more intuitive: *pataw*. We'd climb up to the roof to look for the smoke, or else not, for fear of presenting a target. We'd try to guess the direction of the sound and think of someone to call on that side of town.

We'd listen avidly to stories of the Taliban's rule a few dozen miles away in the flat, vine-studded village where Abd al-Ahad's brother tended his land—the makeshift mines the militants buried to keep people indoors at night, the taxes they collected, the "telephone tree" where they hung the carcasses of cell phones they confiscated from passersby and broke with rocks. They didn't hang the people there; they hung the people at the former schoolhouse.

Just as often, the horror stories were about the Afghan government. An Albany man whose father was blown up in a 2005 explosion during a funeral at a mosque had to pay a bribe to get provincial clerks to fill out the death certificate. Big, gutsy Nargis from the wild country in the north, with her gypsy air, was married to the garbage man—a wizened white-beard who heeled a little to the right as he trundled his wheelbarrow from house to house on our well-kept dirt street. They, like so many other Kandaharis, lived in the graveyard, in a hovel built over somebody's tomb. Now Nargis was in a panic, because the mayor had announced he was bulldozing the squatters out, in line with the five-year plan. Thousands of them. In the middle of an insurgency.

One day, weathered elders from Hijran Karez, a village over the rocky ridge to the east of town, came and knelt on our floor to tell their story. President Hamid Karzai's younger half-brother Ahmed Wali had claimed dozens of acres in the watershed of their precious spring as eminent domain—and then proceeded to subdivide it and sell it off like his own private property. Bulldozers protected by police brandishing AK-47s and driving U.S.-supplied Ford Rangers had carved up the land.

That was the kind of story Nurallah was telling.

His brother Najib owned an auto-parts store at bustling Shikarpur Gate, the mouth of the narrow road linking their village to the city—an ancient byway that had once led southward through the passes all the way to India. At dusk it is clogged with a riot of vegetable sellers' handcarts beset by shoppers, Toyota pickup trucks, horse-drawn taxis, and three-wheeled rickshaws clambering around and through the throng like gaudy dung beetles.

Nurallah's brother Najib had gone to Chaman, just across the border in Pakistan, where the streets are lined with cargo containers serving as shops, and used motor oil cements the dust to the ground in a glossy tarmac, and every variety of automotive organ or sinew is laid bare, spread out, and strung up for sale.

He had made his purchases and set off back to Kandahar. "He paid his customs dues"—Nurallah emphasized the remarkable point—"because that's the law. He paid at every checkpoint on the way back, fifty afghanis, a hundred afghanis." A dollar or two every time an unkempt, underage police boy in green fatigues slouched out of a sandbagged lean-to into the middle of the road—eight times in the sixty-six miles when last I counted.

"And then when he reached the entrance to town, the police there wanted five hundred afghanis. Five hundred!"

A double arch marks the place where the road that swoops down from Kabul joins the road leading in from Pakistan. The police range from one side to the other, like spear fishermen hunting trout in a narrows.

"He refused," Nurallah continued. "He said he had paid his customs dues—he showed them the receipt. He said he had paid the bribes at every checkpoint all along the way, and he was not paying again."

I waited a beat. "So what happened?"

"They reached into his window and smacked him."

"They *hit* him?" I was shocked. Najib might be a sunny guy, but Kandahar tempers are strung on tripwires. For a second I thought we'd have to go bail him out. "What did he do?"

Nurallah's eyes, beneath his widow's peak, were banked and smoldering. "What could he do? He paid the money. But then he pulled over to the side of the road and called me. I told him to stay right there. And I called Police Chief Matiullah Qatih, to report the officer who was taking the bribes."

And Matiullah had scoffed at him: *Did he die of it?*

The police buzzards had seen Najib make the call. They had descended on him, snatched the phone out of his hand, and smashed it.

"You call that law?" Now Nurallah was ablaze. "They're the police! They should be showing people what the law is; they should be enforcing the law. And they're the ones breaking it."

Nurallah was once a police officer himself. He left the force the day his own boss, Kabul police chief Zabit Akrem, was assassinated in that blast in the mosque in 2005.[1] Yet so stout was Nurallah's pride in his former profession that he brought his dark green uniform into work and kept it there, hung neatly on a hook in his locker.

"My sacred oath," he vowed, concluding: "If I see someone planting an IED on a road, and then I see a police truck coming, I will turn away. I will not warn them."

I caught my breath. So maybe he didn't mean it literally. Maybe Nurallah wouldn't actually connive with the Taliban. Still, if a former police officer like him was even mouthing such thoughts, then others were acting on them.

Afghan government corruption was manufacturing Taliban.

WHEN THAT conversation took place, I had been in Afghanistan about seven years. I had entered Kandahar in December 2001, on the heels of the fleeing Taliban, as a reporter for National Public Radio. Before long I resolved to set aside my journalism career and stay, to help Afghans rebuild their shattered but extraordinary society—and discover in this crisis, I hoped, an unanticipated opportunity.

My focus was on economic reconstruction, not rule of law. Yet within weeks I was hearing stories of shakedowns by thugs in uniform, the private militia of Kandahar's warlord governor. As early as 2002, Kandaharis were pointing anxiously to the presence of notorious criminals in their new government.

Years later, due to my long experience in country, I was asked to serve as an adviser to the U.S. military. By then I had watched that early chaotic warlordism take hold and solidify. I had listened to hours of my neighbors' anguish about it. And so, given the opportunity, I spent much of my energy trying to persuade international officials to take corruption seriously. I was sure that unless they recognized the danger it presented and addressed it head on, they would never win the war.

That 2009 morning, in other words, was hardly the first time I had considered that kleptocratic governance—acute and systemic public corruption—was fodder for an expanding insurgency. Nurallah's tale was just the most striking demonstration. Corruption, it made plain, was not solely a humanitarian affair, an issue touching on principles or values alone. It was a matter of national security—Afghan national security and, by extension, that of the United States.

And if corruption was driving people to violent revolt in Afghanistan, it was probably doing likewise in other places. Acute government corruption may in fact lie at the root of some of the world's most dangerous and disruptive security challenges—among them the spread of violent extremism.

That basic fact, elusive to this day, is what this book seeks to demonstrate.

CHAPTER TWO

"Lord King, How I Wish That You Were Wise"

Mirrors for Princes, ca. 700–1516

The Prince ought to inspire fear in such a way that, if he does not win love, he at least avoids hatred. . . . This he can always do if he abstains from the property of his citizens and subjects, and from their women.

—NICCOLÒ MACHIAVELLI, *The Prince*

In the fall of 1513 and into the winter, on a small property lapped by gently rolling Tuscan hills, where December's chill brought mud not ice, a disgraced former Florentine civil servant named Niccolò Machiavelli wrote some pages of practical advice on how not to lose a principate. His rigorously unromantic approach to the subject has become eponymous.

That Machiavelli's everlasting fame should have been connected with cunning, self-interested autocratic rule is something of an achievement. Mere months before he put pen to paper, he had been arrested and tortured and had barely escaped beheading by the very family of the prince for whom he wrote *The Prince*.

In fact, Machiavelli was an ardent believer in representative government and had spent more than a decade in the service of Florence's short-lived republic. When the Medici family invaded the city at the head of a papal army, toppled the republic, and (re)took power themselves, Machiavelli was dismissed, suspect for his prior loyalties. Within months, his name showed up on a list in the pocket of a harebrained conspirator against the Medici restoration, and Machiavelli was clapped in irons and carried off to Le Stinche prison, where interrogators broke his arms, by hanging him up by the wrists bound behind his back. He made light of the screams in a sonnet for Cardinal Giovanni de' Medici.

Machiavelli survived by fluke: Giovanni was elected pope and, in thanksgiving, set all the felons free. Confined to his rural family estate, Machiavelli apparently decided the one way to return to the intoxicating tumult of his beloved politics was to prove he had forsaken his former ways and was now a reliable supporter of Medici rule. That was part of his objective in writing *The Prince*.[1]

To court Medici approval, he went so far as to challenge the timeworn list of virtues that members of budding rulers' entourage traditionally served up in books of advice addressed to their lords. Piety, for example, fear of God, mercy, and generosity were predictable—if perhaps unappetizing—fare. Machiavelli deliberately played the contrarian. It was acceptable, he wrote, even beneficial, to be mean, not generous, to be harsh, not merciful. Those more bitter qualities, he contended—if properly understood and embodied—could keep realms secure and princes from perdition.

But there was one vice that Machiavelli admonished his reader to shun if he cared to prolong his reign: theft of his subjects' possessions. In other words, corruption. "Being rapacious and arrogating subjects' goods and women is what, above all else . . . renders him hateful," he wrote.[2] And widespread hatred of a ruler was conducive to conspiracy. And conspiracy reliably brought down governments.[3]

Machiavelli knew *The Prince* was vying with long tradition.[4] The rich and well-known body of advice literature was referred to collectively as "Mirrors for Princes." Hundreds had been written and copied and traded across continents by the time Machiavelli wrote his.[5] An anonymous Irish "mirror," addressed in verse to a mythical king, was composed around A.D. 700—and was as poetic and primeval as any of that island's literature.[6] Clerics and courtiers wrote them, even monarchs, for their heirs. James VI of Scotland, for example, who would become James I of England when Queen Elizabeth I died childless, penned one for his son Harry. His *Basilicon Doron* endures as one of the signal expositions of divine right monarchy.[7]

> *Lo heere (my Sonne) a mirrour vien and faire,*
> *Which sheweth the shaddow of a worthy King.*
> *Lo heere a Booke, a patterne doth you bring*
> *Which ye should preasse to follow mair and maire.*[8]

I first encountered this body of literature decades ago, while studying history—medieval Islamic history, in fact. For Muslim scholars and statesmen wrote mirrors for their princes, too. I perused several while considering writing a dissertation on systems of justice—a dissertation I ultimately discarded, and with it my studies.

But one day, browsing the shelves of the bookstore at the Institut du Monde Arabe, on a Parisian break from Afghanistan, I happened upon a remembered text, translated from the Persian in one of those voluptuous laid-paper softcovers that French publishing houses still put out. *A Treatise on Government*, it is titled, or *Siyasat Nameh*—literally, "Book of Politics." I bought it and brought it back to Kandahar.

Its author, Nizam al-Mulk ("Organizer of the Realm"), was one of the greatest, most thoughtful and foresightful administrators in the Muslim world. Born around 1018 in what is now eastern Iran, he was the son of a provincial tax collector for the Ghaznavid Empire, whose capital was the city of Ghazni—about three hour's drive up the Kabul road from our workshop in Kandahar, where I was reading Nizam al-Mulk's text.

His world flourished at the confluence of three powerful human currents: a millennial Persian-speaking tradition of letters and administration, a crystallizing Muslim orthodoxy expressed in Arabic and nominally represented by the caliph in Baghdad, and an increasingly separate secular power wielded by Turkic sultans and their seminomadic troops.

Nizam al-Mulk was chief minister to two of those sultans in turn. Coming from the Persian tradition himself, he wrote *Siyasat Nameh* not just to help his second master keep his principate but to show him how to consolidate, organize, and expand it. Nizam al-Mulk contributed to that effort by overhauling and streamlining a complex land-grant system for paying military commanders, and by expanding—in order to ensure a supply of competent civil servants—an educational innovation: residential institutions of higher learning, otherwise known as colleges, or in Arabic, *madrassas*.

When, around 1090, Sultan Malik Shah asked "his peers, elders, and men of science to reflect upon the constitution of his government," the aging Nizam al-Mulk produced a manual that, while full of colorful anecdotes, is at least as practical as *The Prince*. Its chapter headings catalog the administrative functions required in a sophisticated empire: "Of financial inspectors and their means of subsistence." "Of envoys sent out from court for important matters." "The necessity of maintaining supplies of forage at way-stations." "The necessity of a racially integrated army." "Of civil servants."[9]

Alerted as I was, by then, by the frustrations of my Afghan neighbors, I found myself increasingly spellbound by the book's admonitions against various forms of corruption:

> Only what is just should be exacted from God's creatures, and it should be requested with gentleness and consideration. . . . If an official assesses a farmer more than is due to the authorities, the sum he unjustly raised should be demanded of him and returned to the farmer, and if the official has any property, it should be confiscated as an example to other agents, so they refrain from tyrannical acts.

Now *there* was an anticorruption measure that would make an impact. If the police officer who had shaken down Nurallah's brother had lost his house over it, others might think twice.

Stories of land grabs, like the ones taking place in Kandahar, come up again and again in the *Treatise*.

> It is reported that [the powerful eighth-century governor of Basra] Umara b. Hamza attended Caliph Wasiq's audience on the day the caliph was meting out justice for those complaining of arbitrary conduct. A man . . . rose and accused Umara in these

terms: "Umara b. Hamza forcibly commandeered a property that belongs to me."

According to the legend, Umara, thus shamed in public, renounced the property on the spot.[10]

Half a dozen pages are devoted to the tale of an aged widow who gleaned a bare subsistence from a parcel of land that the governor expropriated, and the legendary Persian king Anushirvan's investigation and redress of the grievance. Another monarch of Persian fable, Bahram Gur, comes to suspect his most powerful minister of corrupt practices. To learn more, Bahram Gur decides to question detainees in the main jail. "I had," said one, "a beautiful and pleasant garden. [Minister] Rast Revish possessed a domain nearby. One day he entered my garden and was enchanted by its beauty, and voiced his desire to buy it. I refused to sell, and he had me arrested." The man had been in prison for four years.[11] Other stories follow in a similar vein.

This Persian fable's narrative device would sound perfectly contemporary to residents of present-day Kandahar, where arbitrary detention to extort a fat payment (or, looked at differently, official kidnapping) is a frequent event. Say the man is a Talib, and few would question his arrest.

Nothing preoccupied Nizam al-Mulk so much as justice. "The salaries and emoluments accorded to judges," he wrote, "assure their independence and keep them from unfairness. This point is extremely important and extremely sensitive, for judges . . . dispose of the lives and fortunes of Muslims."[12] One king is described descending from his throne to kneel down in public audience if a subject has a complaint against him, and warning the judge of judges to rule without favoritism on pain of death.

By including such tales, in so many variations, Nizam al-Mulk was hammering home a point: that a government's ability to administer justice—and especially to hold its highest officials to account—was indispensable to its very survival.

One story about Umar ibn al-Khattab, an early caliph whose name became synonymous with justice in Islamic literature, has him promise on his deathbed that he will return to visit his heir in a dream within three days of passing. But it takes twelve full years for the new caliph to dream of his father. When the young man complains about the delay, Umar explains he was too busy to come earlier. "A bridge in the region of Baghdad fell into disrepair because local officials neglected its maintenance," Umar tells his son in the dream. "A sheep's hoof got caught in a hole in the bridge and broke. From the day of my death till today, I've been discharging my responsibility for that accident."[13]

OUTSIDE KANDAHAR, beyond the arched city gates in the direction of Pakistan, a long bridge straddles the shallow, winding bed of the Tarnak River. That bridge, rebuilt and paved with international development funds in 2003, was always coming apart. Inching past the latest hole in its surface, colleagues and I would peer down at the stony river through a tangle of steel reinforcing rods denuded by the missing concrete. Often the bridge would be closed altogether, and we would join the rest of the traffic—gaudily caparisoned cargo trucks with their skirts of jingling chains, taxis and minivans, police trucks, white Toyota Corollas with their bouquets of children peering out the back window—and jump the banks of the road, angle downward through the talcum powder dust till we reached the river floor, and navigate a route across the shallowest stretches of water.

That bridge was a constant affliction to Kandaharis. People would trade figures on how much money had been allotted for the repair. They knew how the scam worked: the well-connected outfit that had won the contract would transfer it to a subcontractor—pocketing a percentage. That subcontractor would hand the deal off to a sub-subcontractor, also minus a cut, till the company actually doing the work received only a fraction of the initial contract and threw something together with shoddy materials and underpaid workers. Meanwhile cocky young employees of the companies up the line would thrust around town in slick SUVs worth years of an ordinary farmer's harvest.

"We know all this money is coming in," a man from the orchards north of town once told me. "We just don't know which hole it is spilling out through." That bridge kept springing holes. And the foreigners kept paying more money for more repairs. And no one, so far as we knew, was called to account.

PREFIGURING A MODERN judicial notion known as "command responsibility," Nizam al-Mulk emphasized rulers' ultimate accountability for the doings of their subordinates. He repeatedly warned Sultan Malik Shah that his reckoning would come: "May the king—God render his reign eternal—understand that when on Judgment Day he is examined about all the creatures that were placed in his power, should he try to point out another to answer in his place, that person's testimony will not be heard."[14]

This strong emphasis on the accountability of those who wield power for the actions of their underlings—"because the good and the bad that they do reflects on the prince and his government"—is equally explicit in today's Kandahar.[15]

As Afghans, beginning around 2005, found the international presence in their country increasingly offensive, it was not because of their purported age-old hatred of foreigners. Nor did puritanical horror at the presence of unbelievers in their land enter our conversations, or outrage about Afghan sovereignty trod underfoot. My neighbors pointed to the abusive behavior of the Afghan government. Given the U.S. role in ushering its officials to power and financing and protecting them, Afghans held the international community, and the United States in particular, responsible. My neighbors wanted the international community to be stricter with Afghan government officials, not more respectful. "You brought our donkeys back," one man put it in 2009. "You brought these dogs back here. You should bring them to heel."

"The government is your face," Nurallah told me a year later. "If it's pretty or ugly, it's your face."[16]

Rereading Nizam al-Mulk's nearly thousand-year-old political treatise, I was struck by how specific and detailed its relevance was. The point, for me, was not so much that corruption has always existed—as many who aim to downplay the problem helpfully point out. Remarkable to me was the clarity with which a great statesman of the Islamic Middle Ages linked the problems of corruption and injustice, and perceived the danger they posed to organized government.

And I found myself wondering as I finished his book: Did other writers of manuals of advice for monarchs see it the same way? Did they too pinpoint corruption as a critical threat to the stability and security of the realm?

MIRRORS FOR PRINCES stud the literature of the Western Middle Ages. In the Carolingian period, for example, several were addressed to Emperor Charlemagne's turbulent offspring. Around the year 831, one Jonas, bishop in the graceful Loire Valley town of Orléans, addressed *Of the Royal Institution* to the emperor's grandson, Pepin I. High among the recommended virtues that fill the book's pages is, once again, justice: "He, who is the Judge of Judges, must introduce into his audience the cause of the poor, and diligently inform himself, so it does not come about that those whom he has delegated to take care of the people in his stead allow . . . the poor to be victims of oppression."[17]

As in the Islamic text, accountability for iniquitous officials lies with the king: "When dishonest judges are placed over the people of God, the fault lies with him who appointed them." Across the religious divide, Jonas depicted a God who will be just as terrible as the later Nizam al-Mulk's in calling the king to answer for the "ministry that he has received."[18]

Jonas was even more explicit about the likelihood that injustice perpetrated by governing officials would lead to rebellion, or "rupture of the peace between peoples." The title of his sixth chapter spells it out: "The Equity of Judgment is the Consolidation of Royalty, and Injustice its Ruin."[19]

During a later chapter in the epic European struggle between church and state, one that rocked England to its foundations in the twelfth century, another churchman, John of Salisbury, wrote a mirror for King Henry II. The book, called *Policraticus* (an invented word), is full of keenly observed and bitingly rendered anecdotes about various categories of official misbehavior. John displayed an equal talent for theorizing. He suggested a broad category—and a loaded one—within which the forms of misconduct he portrayed might fall: tyranny.

In Kandahar today, the same word is used to describe the same type of deeds—an Arabic loan-word into the local Pashtu: *zilm*, "tyranny" or "oppression." I heard that word every day.

A prince, John of Salisbury explained, differs from a tyrant in that a prince "obeys the law, and rules his people by its dictates, placing himself at their service, and administers rewards and burdens within the republic under the guidance of law." And law, John construed, is the instrument of equity, "which compares all things rationally and seeks to apply like rules of right and wrong to like cases."[20]

As for a tyrant, John hazarded a revolutionary doctrine: "That by the authority of the divine book, it is lawful and glorious to slay public tyrants, so long as the killer is not bound to the tyrant by [an oath of] fealty."[21]

It is not clear that a later English text, the *Mirror of King Edward III*, written around 1330 by a country vicar named William of Pagula, ever made it into the hands of the prince to whom it was addressed. Less taken with offering instruction than with leveling criticism, the book would have tried the king's patience.

Fueling William's rage was King Edward's resuscitation of an ancient royal right to requisition goods and services from his subjects, in order to help fund his wars.

And men of your court—not men, precursors of the Antichrist— seize many goods by violence from the owners of those goods, namely, they seize bread, beer, fowls, cocks, beans, oats, and many other things, for which practically nothing is paid.[22]

Woven as he was into the daily lives of his parishioners, William was painfully acquainted with the spiraling consequences of such shakedowns:

A poor man comes to the market with one ox [which he plans to sell to discharge a debt.] He has to pay one mark on a certain day or lose his own land. His ox is seized by your ministers and nothing is paid to him, because of which he loses his land [and] incurs per- jury, excommunication, and a reputation as a dishonest person.[23]

Like other mirror writers, William of Pagula held the king respon- sible for his men's conduct and warned of the national security consequences should the corruption continue: "And for you, Lord King, unless you ordain otherwise, the loss of your kingdom must be feared."[24]

In 1332 William sat down and wrote another whole book, whose language echoes the spluttering frustration of the first. Four chapters in, right there on the page, he dissolves into what can only be described as a howl:

> O woe! O shame! O disgrace! O infamy! O affliction! O ambition! O struggle! O compassion! O outcry! O damnation! O sadness! O error! O falsehood! O fraud! O theft! O plunder! O infidelity! O ingratitude! O instability! O labor! O tears! O lamentation! O martyrdom! O lying! O perjury! O danger! O fear! O scandal to you, King![25]

'The man,' I thought when I read this, 'is screaming.'

And his screams sounded like those of Afghans I knew. "How can we work with this government?" one elder from Shah Wali Kot district challenged me in May 2009. "The government doesn't hear our voices. The government doesn't do anything. It's just there to fill its own pockets. Oppressors! Tyrants! Liars! Bribe-takers! If the government administration in this country isn't reformed, it doesn't matter how many soldiers the Americans bring, the situation will never improve."

Afghans were screaming. And like fourteenth-century William of Pagula, they were going unheard.

The Renaissance saw a spate of mirror writing. One author whose fame almost rivals that of his contemporary, Machiavelli, was the Dutch humanist Desiderius Erasmus. Just three years after *The Prince* was completed, Erasmus dedicated his own *Education of a Christian Prince* to the future, enormously powerful Holy Roman Emperor, Charles V.

Though Erasmus supported monarchy and would oppose the heretical wildfire of religious reform that shortly exploded across Europe, his conception of the people—bound in an organic relationship to their prince—is strewn with the radical seeds of modern democratic arguments. "Nature created all men free," he opened one section, which admonishes against reducing "free citizens into slaves."[26] In another, he argued not only that laws should not favor the mighty, but that their application should actively help redress power imbalances:

The whole purpose of the law should be to protect everyone, rich or poor, noble or humble, serf or free man, public official or private citizen. But it should incline more towards helping the weaker elements, because the position of humble men exposes them more easily to danger. The law's indulgence should compensate for the privileges denied them by their station in life.[27]

Erasmus warned of acute economic inequality, seeing in it a potent danger to the health of the empire—a concern that led him to the brink of advocating a redistributive income tax.[28]

Within this context, he defined corruption. Corrupt princes

pick out from the mass of their subjects a wicked few who use cunningly chosen pretexts and constantly changing excuses to drain off both the strength and the wealth of the people and then convert it to their own account. . . . It is as if the prince were the enemy of his people, not the father, and the prince's best minister the man who most effectively thwarts the well-being of the people.[29]

And people so thwarted, as Erasmus's pragmatic Italian contemporary warned, would bear violent grudges. "He who is threatened, and sees himself constrained by necessity either to act or to suffer, becomes a most dangerous man for the Prince," wrote Machiavelli (not in *The Prince* but in reflections on the writings of the ancient Roman author Livy). "Those injuries of possession and honor are matters that harm men more than any other offense, and against which the Prince ought to guard himself, for he can never despoil one so much that he does not leave a mind obstinate to vengeance."[30]

Thus did these two great, but very different, sixteenth-century political thinkers come together on one point: not just the moral evil, but the danger to the realm—and to the stability of the region around it—of acute public corruption.

Indeed, nearly all the mirror writers, Christian and Muslim alike, divided by the centuries and by different systems of government, seem to have shared a consensus that eludes many of today's policy makers:

that acute, abusive government corruption prompts extreme responses and thus represents a mortal threat to security.

THERE IS just a slight problem with this whole body of literature, reiterating down the ages thoughtful, often detailed, and colorfully phrased warnings against corrupt practices. Other than threats of divine punishment in the afterlife, these manuals fail to suggest any systematic means of redress against corrupt governance. What if their royal readers were to ignore their advice? What would happen then? Disaster—collapse of the state through tyrannicide or revolt—hangs behind their words like a dark thunderhead. For what other options remain for the aggrieved people? To whom should they appeal?

CHAPTER THREE

Hearing the People's Complaints

Kandahar to Kabul, 2001–2009

In Afghanistan, my neighbors—barred as they were from U.S. bases that grew more fortified with every passing year, with taller walls, more loops of barbed wire, increasingly complex screening procedures—were on a similarly fruitless search for appeal. Often they came to vent their frustrations to me—the only American within reach.

My presence in their midst had not resulted from any preexisting logic. I had no family roots or professional background in Afghanistan. I first came to consider the place half a continent away in the legendary but painfully dilapidated blue and white Mediterranean port city of Algiers.

It was 1998. Algeria was in flames. A decade earlier massive popular protests (much like the 2011 "Arab Spring" that erupted in neighboring Tunisia) had forced the autocratic and self-serving government to open the political process and allow multiparty elections. A religious movement with a burning sense of purpose, grassroots organization due to its access to neighborhood mosques, and a reputation for honesty conferred by the presumptions of a devout population was the chief beneficiary of the pent-up protest vote.[1] During Algeria's first-ever free parliamentary elections, in 1991, this Islamic Salvation Front trounced the ruling party in the initial round of voting.

Then the army stepped in, canceled the election, pushed the prime minister from office, and seized direct rule.

What resulted was a protracted civil war, whose death toll is still uncertain but is believed to top 100,000. Massacres were visited on sleeping villages at night. Hundreds were slaughtered, knife to throat, in hours-long orgies of killing. Infants' brains were dashed out against walls. And through it all, a horrifying doubt persisted about the role of the government itself. Algerians I met suspected then, and more believe today, that the security forces facilitated some of the butchery, to scare the population away from Islamist movements, back into the fold of the single party. Neither the army nor the militants seemed concerned with giving the people a stake in their future.

As the violence reached its paroxysm, in 1997 and 1998, I covered Algeria for National Public Radio. Visas to the police state were hard to obtain and were delivered arbitrarily and on very short notice. Trips to the countryside, where survivors stood stupefied amid the wreckage of their ordeal, were orchestrated by Algerian gendarmes. Most of the local journalists we were permitted to meet were ferociously anti-Islamist. My idiomatic Arabic helped break the ice, but I had the nagging sensation I was missing the crux.

Still, I learned something about political Islam during those years. I was brought to consider, for example, the garb that its adepts affected: square-cut tunics or monotonous headscarves tied under women's chins, modeled on styles from the Gulf or Afghanistan, where many Algerian men had traveled to work as laborers or to fight. These clothes contrasted with the equally modest but quite different traditional local dress, which could vary from village to village by a hem of lace or the hang of the drapery—communicating geographical origins or personal taste.

"It's a uniform," a local historian explained to me. "This clothing has nothing to do with piety. This is about advertising adherence. And like any uniform, military or school or Boy Scouts, it removes a person's individuality; its wearer becomes a faceless member of a mass movement, whether he lives in Algeria or Egypt or Saudi Arabia."

Even without the violence, I realized, this burgeoning political Islam was not just an expression of devotion. It was a militant, doctrinaire response—to something.

One day one of the Algerian journalists, whose almost impossible working conditions were the topic of my next radio report, mentioned Afghanistan. "Here, the story is over," he commented matter-of-factly. We were chatting in the sun on the cement stoop of the press center where he and his threatened colleagues had their offices, under the watchful eyes of their police protection. "The rise of militant political Islam," he clarified. "That story has moved on to Afghanistan." I nodded, silently, not entirely sure what he meant.

LESS THAN FOUR years later, on December 11, 2001, I was clinging to the backseat of a yellow taxi, whose color and license plates trumpeted its Pakistani origin, in the company of a burly but terrified driver, an equally terrified interpreter, and a euphoric teenager from the Afghan border town of Spin Boldak, proud bearer of a Kalashnikov and a couple of pistols, whose militia commander had lent him to me as a bodyguard. I had my mike out and tape rolling, trying to capture the teenager's comments above the remonstrances of the taxi as it negotiated the river of rocks and dust that passed for a road. We shimmied down the last spiny crest above the Afghan city of Kandahar.

Two days earlier the battened-down, earth-colored city had been the stronghold of America's new enemy, the Taliban. Now anti-Taliban militia in turbans and flowing tunics, rocket launchers lashed to the struts of their pickup trucks, were charging through the streets on patrol. And already, through their relief, nervous residents were voicing fears that the warlords—a haunting memory from the early 1990s—would return to replace the now-hated Taliban. Tribal elders in the nearby province of Farah appealed for UN peacekeepers to come and disarm the people— not just Taliban remnants but U.S.-armed government-affiliated militias too.

I was covering the fall of the Taliban for an American public (including my NPR editors) that was still too badly rattled by the earth tremor of the 9/11 terrorist attacks to think clearly about the events, their significance, or the mix of underlying motivations that might have led men to perpetrate them.

Within another month, I had made the abrupt decision to drop my journalism career and stay behind in Afghanistan to try to *do* something.

To me, this staggering crisis seemed to provide a once-in-a-generation chance to reimagine the world—to try to contribute to one where the people of two different but deeply interconnected, culturally rich and diverse civilizations might examine and take account of each other's perspectives. It was time to stop talking and roll up my sleeves.

For my first two and a half years in Kandahar, I worked for President Hamid Karzai's older brother, a Baltimore businessman named Qayum. I was hired to launch the activities of an NGO of unclear mission that he and his wife had registered in permissive Delaware. Neither we, nor my older sister who gallantly leaped into the endeavor, knew much about what we were doing. We blithely combined a sister-school program with a radio station, a women's discussion group on the drafting of a new Afghan constitution with rebuilding a village that had been flattened in the U.S. bombing, and a socioeconomic study on the potential impact of repairs to a canal system in a neighboring province. While perhaps dysfunctional, that unorthodox diversity did provide a broad-spectrum exposure to the realities of Afghanistan's chaotic transition.

It took me a while to realize that I had better acquire some notions of accounting, for I was never asked for a budget or reckoning to submit to the Delaware tax authorities.

I dodged a suggestion of Qayum's that we hit up the U.S. Agency for International Development for funding to help Qayum's brothers develop a housing project outside Kandahar. That place, built on public land that the Karzais obtained for the equivalent of a symbolic dollar an acre, grew to be a fantastically lucrative, city-sized gated community whereby they and their partners profited from the violence that came to reign in Kandahar, by selling coveted building plots for a fortune in cash.

For a while, Qayum insisted that our NGO should organize armed village watch groups and serve as the intermediary between these militias and the interior ministry. That did not seem an appropriate activity for a U.S. 501(c)(3), and I balked.

At first I believed Qayum's description of himself as constituting a "loyal opposition" to his younger brother the president. His analysis of events was mesmerizingly brilliant and has shaped, to this day, my understanding of his country. Not for years would I begin systematically comparing his seductively incisive words with his deeds. Welded to his brother's interests, he behaved in ways that contradicted his language so starkly that for a long time I had difficulty processing the inconsistency.

Throughout those same early years, I replicated at my own level the very blunders I berated American officials for committing.

THE CLASSIC ERROR that outsiders make in Afghanistan is to single out a proxy in whom to repose trust and through whom to interact with most other locals. Over the years of intrusions by outside powers, some Afghans have grown adept at capturing this privileged position and exploiting it to advance and enrich themselves, while disempowering (and thus incensing) their neighbors.

In an early 2013 conversation in Brussels, a Hungarian NATO official described almost the identical process at work in Eastern Europe after the fall of the Iron Curtain. Western democracy promoters, he explained, would arrive with little experience with or intuition for local dynamics, then get captured by self-promoting "political activists," who had learned to speak their language. "The Westerners weren't to blame, really," he told me. "These people are very clever. They figured out how to express just what the Westerners expected to hear." Their objective being the seizure of power rather than the midwifing of democracy, these individuals corralled the transition: "If the rules of the new game were 'democratic,' they would play by those rules—well enough to get their grip on power."

The outcome, he concluded, was the profound corruption of the resulting polities, to the point that the very notion of democracy is now discredited among much of the post-1989 generation in places like Hungary or Bulgaria. There many young people call for the return of a "good dictator" to deliver rule of law and a modicum of social justice.

In my case in Kandahar, the self-interested intermediary was a balding, dour-faced Karzai retainer named Abdullah, who called himself an engineer, and whom President Karzai's younger half-brother, the late Ahmed Wali, recommended to me in the following terms: "If I put a million dollars in a storeroom and gave Abdullah the key, and I came back in ten years, I'd find every penny of that money still locked inside." I hired the man.

In late 2002 I departed Kandahar for an extended flurry of talks and meetings in the United States. Before leaving Abdullah in charge of the NGO, I walked him through my system for keeping track of petty cash expenditures: marking each outlay on the back of the envelope in which I carried the money, along with the date and the purpose. For an engineer, he seemed to have trouble catching on.

I returned, after several weeks, to find not a single new mark on the back of that now-empty envelope. Not one receipt, not a record of a single purchase, did Abdullah turn over. We were building schoolrooms. He had made deliveries of bricks and sand and gypsum, had paid weekly cash wages, bought the food our cook prepared for our employees . . .

Swallowing my panic, I demanded receipts. Abdullah went scurrying around to gather some. Sweating, I pieced together forensics that could tell a semicoherent tale.

Years later another employee recounted Abdullah's derisive comments about "Western accounting" and "Afghan accounting"—in which I was obviously unversed. I heard painful stories of suppliers who had never been paid. I reconsidered the probable reasons we'd been forced to leave a school building unfinished for lack of funds.

I had, in other words, been an accessory to fraud.

I have reflected on those suppliers, no doubt furious—and bitter and humiliated at their lack of recourse, their helplessness to make good their claims in the face of the Karzai name. Maybe their anger was initially aimed at Abdullah. But known in town as a Karzai retainer, he must have stood in for the Afghan government in their minds. And I, working for the Karzais alongside him, an American who had shown up on the heels of the fleeing Taliban, represented the new Afghan government too, not to mention its U.S. and international backers. It would have been hard to credit my negligence. I suspect most of the victims figured I had planned the heist and split the proceeds with Abdullah.

How many such episodes would it take, I have wondered, before one of those suppliers decided to shutter his store and pick up a gun? Or look the other way when his son did? Or tell his wife, her skirts tucked back in the fold of her knees as she crouched by the gas cooking ring, to fix a meal for the clutch of outlaws, his distant relatives, who had come down from the hills in the north to plan an attack?

One way Abdullah kept me in thrall was by cultivating fear: by convincing me that Kandaharis were unabashed murderers and thieves. Himself a transplant from near Kabul, he professed a pious horror of the people among whom he was living. They would, he insisted, dismember me in a second were it not for his watchful protection.

A further technique was to keep me from interacting with anyone else face to face, without his presence in the room. Abdullah could get temperamental. Once when I decided to eat lunch with the rest of the staff, instead of separately with him, he threw a violent tantrum, refusing to speak to me for three days. I put it down to jealousy or made excuses for his psychological fragility. How rational would I be after more than two decades of war? Besides, I needed Abdullah. He got things done. What if he were to quit? What would I do?

And so did I commit—at my own humble level—one of the signal errors that many mirror authors warned their august readers to avoid. I lost touch with the people I was purporting to serve.

Writing to Sultan Malik Shah in 1091, Nizam al-Mulk described how Persian monarchs, "according to the books of our ancestors," would hold court out of doors, seated on horseback, atop

> a tall platform . . . so as to distinguish from among all the people gathered in the plain those who were suffering oppression, and to give them justice. The reason for this custom was that once a prince retires to a residence where doors abound, and barriers and vestibules and hallways and gates, men of ill-will and perversity can bar people's entrance, and keep them from lodging complaints with him.[2]

In a contemporary *Book of Counsel for Kings*, Abu Hamid Muhammad al-Ghazali, one of the most distinguished thinkers of the medieval Muslim world, warned that

> nothing is more damaging to the subjects and prejudicial and sinister to the king than royal inaccessibility and seclusion; and nothing impresses the hearts of the subjects and functionaries more than ease of access to the king. For when the subjects know the

king is easily approachable, it will be impossible for the officials to oppress the subjects and the subjects to oppress one another.[3]

An anonymous mid-twelfth-century Persian-language mirror called *The Sea of Precious Virtues* ranks such approachability at the apex of a king's etiquette: "First, he should not conceal himself from subjects and petitioners; for when the king conceals himself the people are ruined, wrongdoers become powerful, and the sin of that is on his head."[4]

The sin of that is on his head. Command responsibility, once again.

"The sovereign," Nizam al-Mulk summed up a string of legends along these lines, "must listen himself, without intermediary, to what his subjects have to say to him."[5]

I was hardly a sovereign. But I did wield a lot of power over the people I employed. And I made it impossible for them to get to me to raise legitimate complaints about the conduct of my subordinate, Abdullah. I denied them any avenue of appeal.

In other words, just as the U.S. government has so often done on a grander scale, I had enabled the development of a corrupt system under my very eyes. However good my intentions may have been, they were not effectively detectable to the sufferers. As a result, I discredited not just myself, but the country and especially the principles I professed to be representing, and I provided fodder to the extremist arguments I had come to help Afghans rebut.

LATER I WOULD devote considerable energy to encouraging senior U.S. officials to "listen themselves, without intermediaries," to what Afghans had to say to them. I was taken aback at the resistance I encountered—not just from sidelined Afghan intermediaries, but from within the U.S. government structures I thought I was assisting.

When Representative Jane Harman of California wrote me in March 2009 that she was leading a congressional delegation to Afghanistan with Senator Jon Kyl, and what could I suggest they do, I offered to get them together with some tribal elders. For several years, a self-appointed council had been trying—sometimes clumsily and often self-interestedly but against ridiculous odds—to serve as a clearinghouse for the concerns of a disenfranchised population. "We want to be a mirror," the council leader told me when I visited them in late 2007, "to reflect to the government how it should be working, how it should solve the people's problems."

But what obstacles U.S. embassy and military officials threw up in their scramble to derail that encounter! The State Department "control officer" shepherding the delegation warned Harman against it. The elders could be anyone; it might not be safe. Jane Harman is a tenacious woman. The embassy must have laid it on thick, because she wrote to ask if I was *sure* this meeting was well advised.

Next it was Regional Command South (RC-South), the international military headquarters in charge of Afghanistan's four southern provinces. This wasn't going to work, a major on the deputy commander's staff e-mailed me. It was too big a group; the logistics were impractical. I replied that we were talking about a dozen men. I could ask them to arrive early. The major countered with an insoluble security problem. Whenever the command had tried to bring elders on base, they had objected to being searched at entry.

"They can strip us naked if they want," laughed Hajji Bacha, when I called to ask him if his cohorts might demur. I soon discovered that this RC-South command had not invited any delegations of Afghan elders on base yet, let alone tried to wand them. The search issue was a sham, a last desperate salvo to try to torpedo the meeting.

Representative Harman insisted. And those two hours were among the most memorable of my years in Afghanistan. U.S. senators and representatives, awkward in their store-fresh cargo pants and stiff boots, connected with the weathered Afghan graybeards, whose turbans and shawls and well-worn prayer beads were like superficial props that merely embellished a worldliness and experience the American politicians could recognize. A precious, friable aura of mutual trust settled over the exchange, for which I acted as interpreter, to assuage any fears the elders might have that their words would get back to people in power.

"You want the truth?" one of them burst out toward the end of the session, after a moment's pause to gather his courage. "There *is* no government here. They don't even control their official buildings."

The occasion lodged in the minds of its congressional participants for years, altering their perspectives and in many cases their votes. Never had they glimpsed such a raw, unfiltered take on the impact of U.S. action in Afghanistan.

A few months later I tried it again—and failed. General Stanley McChrystal had been appointed to command the international troops in Afghanistan, known as the International Security Assistance Force (ISAF), where I now worked as an adviser. He was planning a trip to Kandahar. I submitted a list of elders I thought he should meet, including several who had been at the Harman-Kyl session.

At seven in the morning on the day we were to depart, McChrystal's "executive officer" ordered me to the general's office, where I found the assembled command staff waiting. And upon crossing the threshold, was seared to ash by McChrystal's molten rage.

How could I have exposed him to conflict with the governor? he blazed. How could I have been so unconscious?

McChrystal's team, it transpired, had shared my list of elders with the command of RC-South, which had vetted it with the governor—a close Karzai confidant, a key node of precisely the corrupt and abusive network the elders were likely to criticize. I had somehow failed to learn from the Harman saga to plan for this eventuality. And just as Abdullah had done when I had tried to have lunch with the junior staff, the governor had thrown a tantrum to prevent McChrystal from meeting other Afghans alone.

The event was canceled—with the effect of undermining, instead of buttressing, the elders who dared take a stand. Like so many before him, including myself, McChrystal got captured by corrupt intermediaries, whose abuse was driving Afghans into the arms of the very extremist insurgents his soldiers were fighting. He had refused to "listen himself, without intermediary," to what the elders wanted to say to him.

REALIZING THAT the terms of this equation were still unclear to the new general and his command staff, I resolved to try repackaging it in a form they might understand: a PowerPoint presentation, the military's favorite mode of ingesting and transmitting information.

According to the counterinsurgency theory that McChrystal espoused—and that had the merit of recognizing the existence and relevance of an Afghan population—our efforts were supposed to be directed toward what we called "the 80 percent." That is, the vast bulk of Afghans who supported neither the government nor the Taliban. "Fence-sitters," as some put it. In my experience, few were neutral or undecided—they viewed both government and Taliban insurgents with equal disgust. Both treated them abusively, as sources of money or goods or services or obedience but not as citizens. Our aim, according to the recently articulated counterinsurgency approach, should be to win this 80 percent over to the government.

The problem, as the image I devised sought to depict, was that we were badly positioned to do that, because an explicit part of our mandate was also to "work with" the Afghan government.

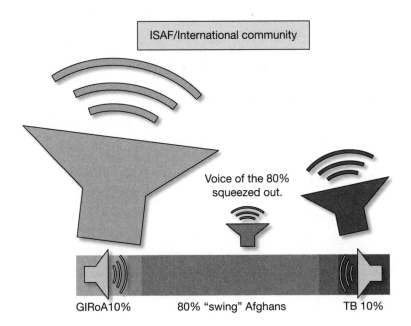

We—represented by the horizontal bar at the top of the diagram—had situated ourselves off-center from the swing Afghans we were supposedly trying to attract. We had aligned ourselves with our partners in "GIRoA" (our shorthand for the Government of the Islamic Republic of Afghanistan). We communicated almost exclusively with government officials, delivered development resources through their agents, hired their relatives and cronies, bought gravel and T-walls and gasoline and intelligence from them, and often used their armed thugs—known as private security companies—to protect our convoys.

And we provided our GIRoA partners, in turn, with the real or implicit shield of our presence by their side. We even let them use us as their enforcers. For, by frequently acting on their intelligence—killing or capturing Taliban suspects they pointed out to us—we allowed them to credibly threaten to punish dissenters with a U.S. Special Forces night raid. We were affording venal officials near-perfect impunity.

To protect its monopoly over these valuable relationships, GIRoA aimed a powerful loudspeaker in our direction. Not only did most officials, unlike the vast majority of Afghans, speak English, they picked up our vocabulary, our technical terms, our acronyms, the latest fashions in interagency jargon for whatever it was we were trying to accomplish. In the words of that Hungarian NATO official, speaking of a different people at a different time, "They figured out how to express just what the Westerners expected to hear."

The Taliban, depicted in black ("TB") over to the right of the diagram, were also using loudspeakers, though most of their messages were directed at Afghan citizens and were spelled out not in words but in actions—attacks or scrawled warnings pinned to the clothes of a murdered schoolteacher.

Amid this clangor, the voice of that crucial 80 percent, the Afghan people who were caught in the middle, was nearly drowned out. In fact, it had grown increasingly dangerous for the 80 percent to speak out at all. The government could, and did, deride them as marginal, or unearth some indication of Taliban affiliation to spread fear of them—the way Abdullah got me to fear Kandaharis. Or it could intimidate them, or find a pretext to arrest them. Or get them killed.

Taliban violence, meanwhile, was also designed to sever Afghans' contacts with international officials.

So that representative of the 80 percent, clutching his skinny loudspeaker, was caught in a withering crossfire. A civic-minded, outspoken, unaffiliated Afghan was perhaps the most vulnerable person in the country. "The Taliban hit us on this cheek," an elder once put it, striking himself in the face, "and the government hits us on that one," another blow. As it stood, he—or she—enjoyed no cover, certainly not ours.

No wonder the mirror writers so insisted on the pains that a good prince should take to connect with the people. We should have been deploying the equivalent of witness protection measures just to ensure open and safe channels.

But a structural rigidity, not just in Afghanistan but in foreign affairs more generally, impedes that approach. Governments are set up to interact with governments. Officials present their credentials, spend much of their days in meetings and at functions and events with their counterparts—when they're not locked in secure conference rooms with their own colleagues. They lack the time and energy to learn local languages. They let a concern not to impinge on host-nation sovereignty compound the difficulty of building authentic relationships with ordinary people. Too often they come to see the local environment through the eyes of their opposite numbers. This legitimist reflex distorts U.S. understanding and its conduct of foreign policy.

Take Egypt, for example. In mid-January 2011 Christopher Schroeder, an Internet entrepreneur and angel investor I know, was in Cairo for a competition for Egyptian start-up businesses that he had helped mentor. Afterward he was invited to dinner at the U.S. embassy. The room was abuzz with news of the overthrow, a day or two earlier, of Tunisian president Zine el-Abidine Ben Ali.

Popular dissatisfaction with the regime of Egyptian president Hosni Mubarak had been smoldering for months by those first days of 2011. In fact, for half a decade, some Middle East watchers had been highlighting the acute need for political reform in the Arab world.[6] But U.S. ambassador Margaret Scobey seemed unaware of the gathering crisis. "It could *never* happen here," Schroeder quotes her as insisting that night. "Egypt is not Tunisia. Mubarak is not Ben Ali."

Schroeder then turned to two young Egyptian entrepreneurs among the dinner guests, for their view. "Egyptians are polite," he later told me. "They defer to age and experience. Those kids cocked their heads and shrugged and said, 'Maybe she knows something we don't. But it's hard to see why we're so different.'" A week later Cairo erupted.

Time and again U.S. officials are blindsided by major developments in countries where they work. Too often they are insensible to the perspectives and aspirations of populations. Focused on levers to pull, on people who "get things done," they overlook or help enable networks that are bent on power and private enrichment and are structured to maximize both, at the expense of the citizenry. And they formulate reasons why doing so is, unfortunately, necessary to the U.S. national interest.

As a U.S. embassy official in Kabul put it to me in January 2003, "We work with governments. And lots of them aren't savory."

SLOWLY PROCESSING what I was seeing and hearing those first years, I gradually learned how the system worked in Kandahar. During a week of heart-wrenching candor in August 2003, Abdullah himself explained how the Karzais had operated in the 1980s, when he had been the chief engineer of their "NGO" EAFA. "They were taking in a hundred thousand dollars a month," he told me. "At least. I remember one project. They got a contract to build a hundred and seventy *kishmish khanas*," fortlike mud-brick structures for drying grapes into the region's prized raisins, whose yard-thick walls are pierced with slits to let the dry air circulate. "We built about twenty. And paid the workers fifty bags of wheat. The people spent their own money on that project. No one saw the cash that was meant for the builders' wages."

Even with such tutoring, it took me another year to truly catch on. But when at length I grasped who and what I was taken up with, I broke from the Karzais and set out on my own. I had finally learned, through the lacerations of shattered illusions—which by then I shared with millions of Afghans—how self-serving those brothers were.

In May 2005, after several months' absence, I returned to Kandahar to try providing some economic opportunity, which Afghans kept calling on foreigners to generate. Armed with a book on the chemistry of soap making, a precision-cast seed-oil press, and $25,000 from Oprah Winfrey, I founded a soap factory.

The objective was to demonstrate the possibilities for productive economic activity offered by Afghanistan's world-class horticulture— pomegranates and apricots and almonds and aromatic seeds like cumin and anise, dye roots that had furnished rug makers for centuries, and walnut hulls, and the wild pistachios that Kandaharis snack on in winter, whose fragrant, copper-colored oil became the base for one of my favorite body lotions.

And I learned to say all that in Pashtu.

We called it the Arghand Cooperative, borrowing part of the name of the river that watered the pomegranate orchards north of town. The women, most of whom were struggling single-handedly to provide for their families, were natives of Kandahar city. The men hailed from villages scattered around it, their extended families cultivating a few acres of grapes or fruit trees.

Now living on the economy, trying to build a business in this outlandish environment, I came to experience corruption from a new angle—the receiving end.

For nine months, we attempted to register our cooperative, making weekly trips to the provincial department of agriculture on the edge of town. But each time we would find the cooperatives director absent, or the registration forms suddenly out of stock. At length, we were ready to dispatch our unflappable administrator, Pashtoon Atif, to complete the last formality. He had to deposit a sum in the national bank. Several of us, and the two dogs, trailed out into the street to see him off.

An hour later my cell phone rang. Not even Atif could keep the frustration from his voice. The bank clerk wanted a bribe.

I wheeled and strode over to our battered red pickup truck, clambered aboard, and roared off to the bank.

Atif and I joined forces outside and then went to find the impediment. The man had to sign five different receipts out of his little book, didn't I see? He paged through them. He would be needing twenty afghanis each to do that, or a total of about two dollars.

"Fine," I replied, with a sunny grimace. "I'd be happy to give you the money." I extracted a crumpled bill from my pocket. "The only thing is, I need a receipt. We have a board of directors. They look at our books. They demand amounts and accounts."

The clerk snorted at the idea of a receipt for his baksheesh. I suggested we talk it over with his manager. The three of us trooped into an office, and I explained the case: delighted to give the man a hundred afghanis, but I needed a piece of paper to justify it to my board. The manager conceded it was a fair point, and we trooped back out.

"Come back tomorrow," the clerk commanded sullenly.

The scene could have been plucked directly out of *Policraticus*, John of Salisbury's twelfth-century mirror for Henry II. "See how Cossus completes your documents," John wrote.

> If you are permitted to pay a visit to him, consider this great luck. If you have not brought your transit papers, you approach him in vain. Yet if you have brought them, it is still of no use, for he will not acquiesce to dishonour noble hands with your vile parchment. What more? It is necessary to buy his efforts, since neither work nor pen nor the various inks come without price. If you do not make him favorable to you, he will so twist the very syllables and strokes of the letters as to write war for peace and quarrel for quiet. If perhaps a handsome belt is yours, or a suitable knife, or anything else in the way of attractive small possessions, count it among his goods, if you do not wish to lose all your trouble and expense. For it will be wrung from you by direct requests if you do not forestall these by your own generosity.[7]

I'm not sure I can reconstruct the physics of what happened next. Suddenly I was seated cross-legged atop the man's desk, amid the file folders and the stray papers, severe faces stapled passport-sized to some of their corners. "Okay," I declared. "I'll just sit here till you sign for our money." I folded my arms across my chest. "As long as it takes."

After a stunned second, a bustle commenced. The man got up from his chair. Ten minutes later another clerk delivered our booklets, duly signed and stamped. Atif and I thanked him and descended the stairway, trying not to exult too openly. We had won. We had obtained an administrative service without giving in to corruption.

But something about that encounter has bothered me ever since. Another man had been waiting with us most of that morning. He was a weathered old graybeard, in a turban and tunic, perched on one of the black vinyl chairs with a heel tucked under him, out of long habit of sitting cross-legged on mats on the floor. Like us, he was trying to accomplish some formality. He had paid his bribe—ten afghanis, I think he told us—but he was still waiting.

And I hadn't done a thing to help him. As a foreigner, I could afford to bluster and bluff. A lowly bank employee was unlikely to take the risk of dragging an American to jail or smacking her in the face. That creased old Afghan farmer had no such standing.

On this and later occasions, I let officials treat me as an exception. I'd get my problem solved—the concern of most businesses operating in acutely corrupt environments—and then go away, leaving the system unbolstered by a bribe, but also unchecked. What impression must it have made on Afghans, as they waited through a blistering afternoon in the dusty customs yard, to see an American get preferential treatment at the hands of venal administrators?

IN 2007, my friend Paula Loyd,[8] a former U.S. Army staff sergeant and civil affairs officer, asked me to share such perspectives with incoming Dutch, British, Canadian, and other officers who traded off command of RC-South every nine months. She recommended me, as a civilian subject-matter expert, for NATO training exercises.

To speak effectively to these officers, I had to learn yet another new language. I ingested a lot of specialized vocabulary and acronyms, which seemed to change from one year to the next. But I never managed to gain control of my style. Epiphanies, once they hit, seem so *obvious*. I forgot what the fog was like. I lost patience, because time was passing and the grace period Afghans had accorded us was running out. I couldn't contain my shrill frustration as I watched successive Western officials make precisely the mistakes I had made, and their predecessors had made. Corruption networks were solidifying and growing more brazen by the day. There was no more time to give them the benefit of the doubt, or to prioritize some short-term security imperative, like moving matériel up a road, over a tough-minded approach to the Afghan police officer whose men patrolled it.

I must have sounded as repetitive as William of Pagula, railing at Edward III in the 1330s.

But my NATO training audiences could not, or would not, see how self-defeating the conventional approach was. If the very Afghan officials by whose side they planned to combat extremists were generating those extremists themselves—by having their men shake down travelers and taking a cut, or leaving bills unpaid, or by providing judiciously selected "intelligence" to engineer a night-raid against a rival trafficking network—it was too big a paradox to take in. NATO officers did not want to know.

ONE INTERNATIONAL OFFICIAL who did seem to get it was deputy NATO senior civilian representative Nicholas Williams, whom I had met when he held a different job in Kandahar. In 2008 he invited me to ISAF headquarters to meet some senior officers. "Sally the Soapmaker Gives an Ops Brief" was how I jokingly came to refer to my main presentation.

It was received with interest. So I began a routine that took me to the Afghan capital once every couple of months, to do the rounds. In early 2009, I requested a meeting with the ISAF commander, General David McKiernan. Steeling myself for a hedgerow of star-studded officers and guarded interest at best, I found it was just the two of us—bound, I realized with a start, by an inconvenient love for this impossible place. McKiernan asked me to join his staff. I accepted on the spot. From that perch, I might at last be in a position to help force some change.

The inauguration of a new U.S. administration in Washington infused me with hope. It would be led by a constitutional lawyer, no less, who could be expected to understand the importance of good governance. It might even launch a wholesale policy revision.

During those months, indeed, I had also been traveling to Washington to try to put some imprint on the still-wet cement there. One meeting led astonishingly to another, and on a January day, I found myself ushered in to see the chairman of the Joint Chiefs of Staff, Admiral Mike Mullen.

I was a long way from Kandahar, on the oak-paneled "E Ring" of the Pentagon. But just the look of his inner office set Mullen apart. Instead of the standard-issue dark furniture, the framed mementos and photos of handshakes jostling for space on the walls, it was blond wood everywhere: a sweep of curved desk standing light on its legs, a matching table with webbed ergonomic chairs, and a bookshelf against the opposite wall cut so it tilted—a glint of silent humor on the part of a navy guy presiding over two land wars.

Mullen listened intently, head cocked. He took notes in a spiral book with misshapen fingers. But it wasn't that meeting that lodged in my memory. It was something that happened afterward, when we crossed paths in a paneled hall. He called me over, almost trapping me against a wall, and launched into a lecture about my security. I tried to wave his concerns away. This was the chairman of the Joint Chiefs of Staff. "I know you have more important things—"

"This is important," he cut me off. "I call mothers. I don't want to have to call your mother."

That brought me up sharply. I looked at him. "If you're serious . . ."

"I am."

"Then there are two things you can do that would really help."

He raised an eyebrow.

"Next time you see President Karzai, and next time you're in Pakistan to visit the chief of the army staff, General Kayani, let it slip that I'm a friend of yours. That will reduce the threat to me by about seventy percent."

I'm not sure Mullen entirely followed my logic, but he promised he would do it. My point was this: as feckless as both countries' governments might look, they operated as networks, with a lot of vertical reach. Many of the bad things that happened at ground level could be traced to the top.

NOT THREE MONTHS after I moved to ISAF Headquarters from Kandahar, in late spring of 2009, my boss General McKiernan was recalled and replaced by the emaciated bundle of torqued nerves that was General Stanley McChrystal—a different man entirely.

CHAPTER FOUR

Nonkinetic Targeting

Kabul, 2009

The team of General Stanley McChrystal tore into the international military headquarters in Kabul in June 2009 like a summer twister, knocking down trees, pulling tiles off roofs, scrubbing clouds of dust out of back corners. I had gotten to know most of the tight-knit group during my D.C. visits and had loved their incandescent energy and sense of purpose. But I had underestimated the accompanying arrogance.

The day after McChrystal formally took command, I sent him a first e-mail: "drafting an anti-corruption strategy." I was intent on using my position to design policies I had been mulling over for years and to see them tried out in practice. The effort to do so, over the next seven months—and the resistance it encountered from both Afghan and international officials—taught me a great deal about systemic corruption and all the reasons that can be dreamed up for ignoring it.

McChrystal's reply to my e-mail came back a seemingly eternal four days later: "Concur we need to get on the anti-corruption policy—let's do it."

A phalanx of colonels bustled from office to office, during those heady first weeks, with the latest version of some PowerPoint diagram they were building, determined to encapsulate everything in one visual blow. Civilians from Washington think tanks descended to conduct an assessment of the campaign. In meetings with these groups, in whirlwind trips to the regional commands, around conference tables in window-less plywood rooms, earnest conversations were had about how the force was explaining the war to itself, the true nature of the threat. Brigade and battalion commanders felt empowered to reframe the problems they were facing in ways they hadn't dared to before. And corruption kept coming up.

"I believe we could do all the things we need to do in a counterinsurgency strategy, but we won't succeed if we don't change the political environment."

"What would be a game changer? We have to show we are willing to tackle corruption. We have to drop GIRoA and focus on the people."

Drop the government and focus on the people. The prospect still raises anxiety inside many embassies and international organizations. The World Bank recently began formulating the radical notion that its end user might perhaps not be developing-nation governments, as previous policy had it, but rather their people.

At ISAF headquarters in 2009, the very concept was revolutionary. Implementing it would have required a rupture with years of mission statements framed around such objectives as "building and reinforcing GIRoA" or "connecting the people to the government." It would have called upon sophisticated political judgment at every echelon. It would have required strategic direction from Washington, and explanations to allied governments, many of which had sold the Afghanistan mission to voters by arguing that their troops would be supporting a democratically elected government against religious fanatics. A new narrative, with the Afghan government sharing the role of villain, would have made for some complicated talking points.

But a growing number of us were convinced that any hope for success in Afghanistan depended on just such a transformation.

The first occupant of a newly minted anticorruption post—a jointed-at-the-waist, stubborn, benevolent giant of a Dutch lieutenant colonel named Piet Boering—became an inseparable partner. The two of us, together with Nick Williams and others, started from earlier recommendations on how to enhance the credibility of the upcoming Afghan presidential election. Karzai was visibly working to rig it. Vietnam and Algeria provided examples of insurgencies that had triumphed in the wake of blatantly stolen elections. With such a clear rationale for action, we gambled, approaches might be tested in the electoral context that could later be used against corruption more generally.

Officers, however, balked at the prospect of reducing their "distance from local and international politics," as one brigadier general put it in an e-mail to the command group. Surely managing elections was the United Nations' role, many argued, not the military's. Our security mandate was understood to mean protecting Afghans from violence perpetrated by insurgents only—not from violence perpetrated by the government.

The problem with this logic was that Afghans were threatened by both—as are so many populations, caught between the abuses of a predatory government and the violence of extremists claiming to combat it. Soldiers, moreover, had more contact with the Afghan population than did their civilian counterparts—they stopped to speak to villagers or drink tea with elders during patrols. Why not add a few queries about electoral intimidation to their standard questionnaires? What about allocating some of the flight time of all those satellites and drones and blimps floating above military installations to observing polling places? Even a general picture of voter density, provided to oversight bodies for comparison to reported turnout numbers, might help.

It was military officers, moreover, who carried on the bulk of interactions with Afghan officials—and who were seen by those officials to constitute the international community that mattered. The logic holds in other countries, too, where the military-to-military relationship constitutes the backbone of U.S. ties. In Afghanistan, forty-year-old battalion commanders were closeted with provincial governors every week. Troops were training the Afghan army and police. Special operations officers were often the only foreigners far-flung district officials encountered. If those officials were engaged in flagrant political corruption and their ISAF interlocutors ignored it, they—and ordinary Afghans—took the silence as approval.

"Wherefore one who does this is guilty," the strident fourteenth-century William of Pagula would have concluded. "For, one who permits anything to take place that he is able to impede, even though he has not done it himself, has virtually done the act if he allows it."[1] In contemporary American jurisprudence, the principle is called "conscious disregard" or "willful blindness." And it is considered a sign of criminal intent.[2]

In the end, none of our election recommendations was implemented. Afterward I asked ISAF's intelligence chief, General Michael Flynn— among the most sympathetic officers to the anticorruption agenda—if any surveillance satellites had been assigned to monitor turnout. He seemed startled, as though we had never discussed the idea. Oh no, came his answer. They were too busy tracking insurgents.

The fraud perpetrated in the 2009 Afghan election was so egregious and widespread as to stun even seasoned election monitors, several of whom declared it the most pervasive they had ever seen. Later, U.S. officers who spoke to Taliban detainees found that the election had generated a spurt in support for the insurgency, as Afghans lost faith in a "political process that only seemed to strengthen power brokers and maintain the status quo," as one put it.

And the sin of that is on his head.

ONE GROUP at ISAF headquarters was receptive to the premise that systematic corruption was discrediting the Afghan government in the eyes of the people and tainting the international community by association. It was the civilian assessors who had been called in from universities and Washington think tanks to analyze the Afghanistan campaign. The strategic assessment that resulted from their work—whose leak to the *Washington Post* irrevocably poisoned the relationship between the Obama White House and the military—was the only major document to pinpoint poor governance as a key driver of the conflict in Afghanistan.[3]

Boering and I hosted a governance brainstorming session for those outside experts, with participants from several embassies, the UN, the European police-training mission, and key Afghan agencies. Fragile bubbles of enthusiasm pearled the mood that day, as these disparate professionals, devoted to the rule of law, came together for perhaps the first time, daring to hope that the issue they thought mattered most was finally commanding attention.

By the end of June 2009, with the help of such discussions, ISAF's budding anticorruption team had elaborated both a conceptual argument and practical recommendations for why and how to tackle corruption.

Criticizing the "corrupt, questionable, and unqualified leaders [placed] into key positions," the argument rested on the principle of command responsibility: "The international community has enabled and encouraged bad governance through agreement and silence, and often active partnership."

Moving the issue away from the humanitarian terrain where it often resides, we made corruption relevant to war fighters by explaining its centrality to prospects of victory. "Afghans' acute disappointment with the quality of governance . . . has contributed to permissiveness toward, or collusion with," the Taliban, we wrote, laboring to stultify our language with a credible amount of jargon.

In plain English: why would a farmer stick out his neck to keep Taliban out of his village if the government was just as bad? If, because of corruption, an ex-policeman like Nurallah was threatening to turn a blind eye to a man planting an IED, others were going further. Corruption, in army-speak, was a force multiplier for the enemy.

"This condition is a key factor feeding negative security trends and it undermines the ability of development efforts to reverse these trends," our draft read.

The great eleventh-century thinker Ghazali made just such a link between poor governance and insecurity—in that order and not the reverse—in his *Book of Counsel for Kings*: "Whenever Sultans rule oppressively, insecurity appears. And however much prosperity there may be, this will not suit the subjects if accompanied by insecurity."[4]

But Western officials, military and civilian alike, habitually flipped the sequence: first let's establish security, then we can worry about governance.[5] Like Ghazali, the anticorruption team saw the vector the other way around: poor governance *caused* the insecurity, so it was fruitless to try to reduce violence without addressing corruption.

Our questioning—again echoing Ghazali—of the likely impact of development efforts ("prosperity," in his formula) also flew in the face of received wisdom. For years, the notion had prevailed that the best way to sway Afghan "hearts and minds" was by giving away stuff: blankets, bags of wheat, wells for drinking water, schoolrooms. Among the conditions fueling extremism, commentators and policy makers often repeat, is economic malaise, aggravated by demographic shifts or such externals as drought. Foreign assistance is seen as a palliative to those ills. Evolving U.S. military doctrine even referred to "money as a weapon system."

But examination of extremist leaders' sociological backgrounds casts doubt on these presumptions. Studies by such analysts as Andrew Wilder have found that in Afghanistan, infusions of development resources often exacerbated local conflict rather than reducing it, by providing new prizes for opposing groups to fight over.[6]

I had observed a more systemic problem with the way aid was delivered. Afghanistan is a country made smaller, in human terms, by its convivial and relationship-based culture. In a town like Kandahar, everyone knew who was securing the juicy development contracts and who their patrons were. Everyone discussed the quality of the work, who benefited, or the new cars the chief implementers were driving. In other words, development resources passed through a corrupt system not only reinforced that system by helping to fund it but also inflamed the feelings of injustice that were driving people toward the insurgency.

Laboratory experiments over the past several decades have demonstrated humans' apparently irrational revolt against such unjust bargains. The experiments, known as "ultimatum games," allocate a sum of money to one player, with instructions to divide it with another. If the recipient accepts the offer, the deal goes through. If she rejects it, both players get nothing. Economists had presumed that a recipient, acting rationally, would accept any amount greater than zero. In fact, in experiment after experiment—even with stakes as high as a month's salary—roughly half of recipients rejected offers lower than 20 percent of the total sum.[7]

These experiments apply almost directly to development work. I frequently heard the very same numbers come up in the arguments of Western officials. 'Let's say 80 percent of the humanitarian aid money is skimmed off,' they would postulate. 'At least the people are getting *something*. More than they would if we weren't funding the projects at all.' But ultimatum game experiments show that many recipients would in fact prefer to walk away empty-handed than accept such an unfair deal.

This pervasive human reflex might help explain why development projects kept getting attacked in Afghanistan. Perhaps it was not just the projects' association with non-Muslim foreigners that angered the attackers. Perhaps it was also the unjust distribution of resources—especially when the benefits to ordinary people were indirect, as in the case of a road or a school, while the much greater payoffs to corrupt officials and their cronies came in the form of cash in hand. Perhaps Afghans, in line with subjects of experiments conducted in the United States or Indonesia or the Slovak Republic, would rather foul a well so no one could use it than watch most of its water irrigate a corrupt village elder's land.

So much for the argument. Next came recommendations. The anticorruption team was still up against a widespread and debilitating presumption. 'Corruption is part of the culture in a place like Afghanistan,' we kept hearing. 'What can really be done about it?' I have always been perplexed at the sham regret, and authentic eagerness, with which so many embraced helplessness as a rationale for inaction.

What can be done? Lots, it turns out. But a serious anticorruption campaign has to make use of the plentiful leverage carefully—craftily, even—and with foresight and stubborn fortitude.

The first recommendation we put forward that summer was to repair a startling deficiency: knowledge. Despite the thousands of intelligence professionals spread throughout the country, not to speak of the hundreds of diplomats and development practitioners, the international community knew almost nothing useful about the government officials or local contractors we were dealing with.

Any battalion- or brigade-level intelligence shop could produce a sophisticated "network diagram" for the main local Taliban group, featuring a photo of the commander—or a baleful black silhouette complete with turban—and lines spiking out to other known members. The eager but respectful twenty-something officer who would brief such a slide would be legitimately proud of the detective work.

But where were the network diagrams for the district governor or the provincial police chief? What tribe was he? Who were his associates? Who did he pay kickbacks to? Which construction companies belonged to his family members? How was he facilitating the traffic in chromite or timber or opium? Did he have Karzai on speed dial? Who had he fought with during the last war?

No one knew.

A similar ignorance reigns in other regions where the United States and like-minded governments operate. In a dozen years of obsessive focus on terrorism, the CIA and other intelligence agencies have mushroomed. Data collection has exploded. Yet new blood, talented veterans, and most of the focus have been aimed at identifying and targeting individual terrorist suspects.[8] Those individuals' environments, the social structures of their communities, and the grievances or aspirations that might animate them or their neighbors, have excited less interest.[9]

The sixteenth-century humanist Erasmus instructed the future Holy Roman Emperor to gain an intimate knowledge of just such details: "It seems necessary to the prince to . . .get to know his kingdom, and this achievement will be most effectively brought about by three things: the study of geography, the study of history, and frequent tours of towns and territories."[10]

On the Afghan battlefield, we recommended adding questions about local governance to the cards that soldiers consulted when chatting with villagers, and sending the information up the line, assigning intelligence officers to study government officials, and setting up tip lines or drop boxes for Afghans to use anonymously. And we called for officers to meet regularly, no officials present, with ordinary Afghans.

The sovereign must listen himself, without intermediary, to what his subjects have to say to him.

Next we listed concrete actions that officers in the field could take at their own level to deter corrupt behavior. Cease actively contributing to it, for starters. Avoid meeting with corrupt officials in ways that raise their status: Don't visit their offices, for example, because in Afghan culture, it is the social superior who hosts, and the inferior who visits. Don't renew contracts with businesses owned by their cronies. Stop paying Western-level salaries to their personal staff, or letting them control the distribution of humanitarian aid. In extreme cases, halt development projects altogether, while explaining the reason to the local population.

Where an official was just too disruptive or too powerful, or his misdeeds too egregious, we recommended that his case be passed up the chain of command to ISAF headquarters, where senior officials could take it up with President Karzai or launch law enforcement action.

Eventually these suggestions were drafted into the official military language of a FRAGO—a fragmentary operations order, spelling out what units were commanded to do in the field. After some fancy footwork by the oversized Boering, who proved remarkably nimble in dealing with military bureaucracy, the order was issued.

We illustrated the dry phraseology with a diagram based on an early ballpoint sketch by the command's affable legal adviser, Rich Gross. "Soft COAs" were courses of action that could be implemented directly by subordinate commanders. "BN" stands for battalion, "TF" for a brigade-level task force, and "RC" for the five regional commands. At higher echelons, serious cases should be referred to the High Office of Oversight, for prosecution by the Anti-Corruption Unit in the attorney general's office, or the ministry of interior.

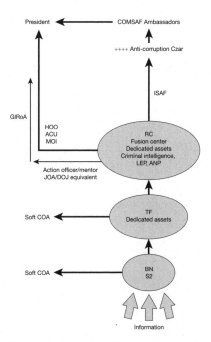

Many officers objected that the effort amounted to launching a two-front war. Not only were they engaged in a bloody standoff with the Taliban, they complained, now we were asking them to fight our allies in the Afghan government too. It would multiply the risks to their men.

As we cataloged those risks at the time, we did not dwell on the probable countermoves by Afghan officials. What worried us most was ourselves.

Some countries in the international coalition had historic relationships with criminal power brokers that they were reluctant to break. Concern for troops' safety, we believed, led others to strike deals with corrupt officials or even insurgents. Most problematically, officials whose abusive behavior poisoned relations with the population were the favored "assets" of some Western intelligence agencies.

Rigorous pursuit of an anticorruption approach would expose these conflicting agendas. Savage internal battles might result, or public embarrassment, or nonparticipation or even obstruction by some NATO organizations. And Afghan frustration would only rise.

We suspected the profound and self-defeating internal contradictions that lurked beneath the awkward surface of this war. But we didn't know the half of it.

ON JULY 5, 2009, McChrystal's top brass and incoming U.S. embassy officials gathered for their first joint meeting. Acting Ambassador Tony Wayne ran down a list of priority action items. Number two, after opium, was corruption. The military, he conceded, had "been thinking about it, and we haven't." It was a candid observation on the lack of diplomatic attention paid to the issue, nearly eight years into the war.

Wayne convened an anticorruption strategy group meeting, calling in officials from a handful of civilian agencies. U.S. embassy staff and the new ISAF Anti-Corruption Task Force began working together. I remember the moments of slightly dazed discovery. It was as though some people had made their separate ways to a park and, meeting there, had decided to spread out a single blanket and share a picnic. Baskets came open, and everyone craned for a glimpse of what the others had brought to the table.

The State Department's Bureau of International Narcotics and Law Enforcement Affairs was sending rule-of-law advisers to Regional Commands East and South. U.S. attorneys had stood up a counternarcotics court, with its own state-of-the-art facility on the edge of town. Now they were mentoring anticorruption prosecutors too. The British government had developed a special Afghan criminal investigations unit, called the Major Crimes Task Force (MCTF), whose remit included corruption. The FBI was helping support it. A "Threat Finance Cell," manned by DEA, Treasury, and FBI officers, whose job was to trace terrorist funding, was nurturing its own Afghan team, the Sensitive Investigations Unit (SIU). These officers' third priority, the heavyset director informed us in a deceptively bored monotone, was public corruption. The special investigator general for Afghan reconstruction was, diffidently, attempting to track misspent U.S. dollars. The anticorruption lead at the headquarters in charge of Afghan army and police development told us international trainers were instructed to pass reports of police corruption to the Afghan interior ministry. "The issue," he conceded wryly, "is what happens once the report is turned over."

Those picnic baskets were well stocked, in other words. But what did it all add up to? "We're supplying things," one participant summed up. "But are we achieving things?"

Not everyone around the table was enthusiastic about a more energetic anticorruption effort. One civilian who worked outside Kabul feared attacks by disgruntled Afghan officials. Another urged a careful cost-benefit analysis before doing anything at all. "Just collecting information sends a political signal," he worried.

And we heard a notion that would shape the State Department's approach to corruption in the years ahead. There should be a triage among different varieties, argued one embassy official. Anticorruption efforts should be focused on those that were most "meaningful to the people."

This thinking segmented the corruption phenomenon, shaving off "high-level" misdeeds (corruption that was so politically sensitive, and presumably so removed from the people and their concerns, that it was best ignored) and "petty corruption" (the daily palm greasing that many Westerners thought was the only way to get things done in a place like Afghanistan and should therefore also be left alone). Such a formulation profoundly misunderstood the character, impact, and structure of acute corruption.

It took us quite some time to understand what our collective capacity was. Until then, for example, the two mentored Afghan police teams had been autonomous and self-directed. Their mentors aimed mostly to improve the officers' technical proficiency. The complex investigations, requiring locally unfamiliar techniques, like judicial wiretaps and seized bank records, ate up the young units' bandwidth. They could handle only one case each, it turned out: a crushing bottleneck. Afghan criminal prosecution could not be counted on as a significant element of an anticorruption campaign.

"We have got to think harder about nonjudicial approaches." Sarah Peck led the charge. She was the U.S. embassy's anticorruption officer—a former prosecutor, sparkling, determined, invariably elegant, with her short copper hair and long black skirts. "We have to make the ground burn under their feet. Let's find other ways."

We considered the absolute minimum: symbolic gestures against Afghan officials whose behavior was off-the-charts unacceptable. We came up with three. No accepting gifts from them. No inviting them on fancy visits overseas. No publicized high-level meetings with them. We envisioned a flagging system that would allow for a concerted international approach.

The point was not to end all interactions with these officials. It was to break with the prevailing binary thinking. "Working with" corrupt officials seemed always to mean writing them a blank check. And the only alternative seemed to be cutting all ties—a move that was rarely possible. We thought there was room for nuance, some specificity in the manner, degree, and purpose of "working with" these complex and ultimately counterproductive men.

We did think through stronger options, as well, like steering development funding away from businesses connected to corrupt officials, refusing them or their children visas to visit Western countries, raising the priority level of their insurgent friends on the list of Taliban to be killed or captured.

But we needed an objective system for ranking priorities—for choosing which provincial governor to ask President Karzai to remove first, or which Afghan National Army officer ISAF should cease supplying with ammunition, or against whom the MCTF should build its next, lone case.

A disciplined procedure existed for putting suspected insurgent leaders on the kill/capture list.[11] It was a bottom-up vetting process. Via secure videoconference, each regional command would argue its case against the militants it judged the most dangerous. A single-screen "targeting packet" informed the discussion, featuring such elements as the likely impact on his network of killing him, potential conflicts with other military operations, the quality of the intelligence on which the recommendation was based, or legal considerations.

The Anti-Corruption Task Force used that targeting process as a model for its own. We had to weigh a different set of considerations, of course—the level of public outcry about the official's corrupt behavior, for example, whether theft of international funds was involved, his political affiliations, his connivance with the insurgency, or his involvement in drug trafficking. Our process differed, too, in that our weapons were less lethal.

Yet ironically, the prospect of turning off aid or denying a visa to someone was more complex than the prospect of shooting him. The potential unintended consequences were dizzying. Since international officials were in daily contact with potential targets, leaks were likely. And while Taliban targets could either be killed or captured, ours were subject to a far more varied menu of actions, requiring a custom-tailored selection for each case.

This complexity, and our own diversity, kicked up squalls of mistrust. U.S. law enforcement was adamant against inviting Europeans to our meetings. Stockholm syndrome, the Americans were sure, or plain naïveté would impel Europeans to warn Afghan officials of investigations, ruining months of painstaking work.

I didn't mind the Europeans so much; I minded the CIA. I remember standing in the doorway before one meeting, chest inflated with a held breath, to bar an uninvited "regional affairs officer" from entering the room. The CIA was paying one of my prime targets—I had seen it with my own eyes—Karzai's younger half-brother Ahmed Wali, who pulled the strings to most of southern Afghanistan, who stole land, imprisoned people for ransom, appointed key public officials, ran vast drug trafficking networks and private militias, and wielded ISAF like a weapon against people who stood up to him. The inhabitants of three provinces hated him.

But the CIA had been paying him for years. I had watched officers hand him a tinfoil-wrapped package of bills when I was over at his house for dinner one 2003 night. I never understood what they thought they were getting, but Ahmed Wali Karzai was an "asset." The CIA was not joining our meetings to help, I knew it. Its aim was to learn our moves and protect its people.

I lost that battle. The CIA retained its seat at prioritization meetings, its silent representative taking meticulous notes, and never volunteering a shred of information.

ISAF HEADQUARTERS, shielded behind periodically heightened blast walls from the dusty, smog-choked, cacophonous welter that was downtown Kabul, boasted a garden. The whole compound had once been the Afghan National Army officers' athletic club, until the international community came and plunked down steel containers fitted with bunk beds and collective bathrooms, put combination locks on all the doors, and converted one of the gyms into a chow hall. The garden, with its stately trees and corner gazebos where staff sections held barbecues on Thursday nights, was a reminder of the bygone elegance of the place—and, by extension, of Kabul itself.

I used it as my conference room.

That summer I got together regularly with Steve Foster, the unassuming Scotland Yard detective who had personally launched, and was nursing into autonomous life, one of the special Afghan police investigation units, the Major Crimes Task Force (MCTF). Foster had reason to favor ISAF's involvement in the anticorruption effort and the protective support it might bring. His fledgling Afghan unit had just taken an episode of political interference right in the teeth. I had to make him spell out the details a couple of times, before I could glimpse—through his diplomatic suggestion that the Afghan interior ministry might perhaps not be entirely trustworthy—a flash of the reality.

The MCTF had concluded its first case a month or so earlier, a counternarcotics case. Unlike corruption, drug trafficking had galvanized international concern, resulting in a heavily fortified counternarcotics judicial complex on the edge of town, staffed by designated judges and prosecutors. No such structure yet existed for anticorruption. Foster chose a maiden case for his MCTF that would fit with the counternarcotics mission, so his officers could benefit from these facilities.

"They arrested our man on Kandahar Airfield," Foster recounted. That was the sprawling base I had watched grow like a tumor over the years, devouring the dust-choked plain that stretched into the desert east of Kandahar. "Atmar didn't take it terribly well."

Hanif Atmar I knew. Minister of interior, former minister of education, before that minister of rural development, clipped beard shaped to a point, hooded eyes, walked with a pronounced limp, spoke with a broad, condescending English accent. One of the international community's darlings.

"He called the head of the detention facility onto the carpet. Threatened to sack him on the spot."

I had to mull that one over to let the implications sink in. The Afghan minister of interior had nearly relieved a senior officer for doing his job: for providing temporary detention, at the behest of U.S. and U.K. officials and his own superior, of a duly arrested suspect, who happened to be a border police officer.

In the U.K. embassy's negotiations to preserve the case and the Afghan officer's job, Foster and the MCTF were stripped of one of their key assets: stealth. Henceforth, the U.K. officials had agreed, the MCTF would inform Atmar ahead of any planned arrest. These arrangements could be made to sound perfectly reasonable. After all, why shouldn't an interior minister be kept abreast of criminal investigations proceeding under his watch?

During one of these late-summer conversations, Foster shared his planning for the next MCTF arrest. Another border police official was in the cross hairs—in fact, the titular commander for the critical four provinces that make up the southeastern corner of Afghanistan. One hundred thousand dollars of police money had gone missing—including from the widows' and orphans' relief fund. Bank records and judicial wiretaps had three accomplices nailed. The lead suspect's name was Sayfullah.

MY MIND darted back to the last time I had seen him. Sayfullah, a soft man, a bit lost in his police uniform, whose clean-shaven face lacked much of a chin, had offered me a lift in his green police Ford Ranger, when I was in Kandahar just weeks before.

General McChrystal's whole command team had descended on Kandahar Airfield for a daylong election update. The proceedings, begun soporifically enough, were shattered, as if a bomb had exploded in our midst, when an aide had bent over by McChrystal's ear: Provincial Police Chief Matiullah Qatih had just been assassinated.

Matiullah Qatih, the man my cooperative member Nurallah had called the day his brother had been shaken down by the cop at the gates to Kandahar. The one who had asked Nurallah, with weary sarcasm, "Well, did he die of it?"

Pacing hard, my blood oddly cold, phone welded to the side of my head, I quested for facts. What I got back was more stunning and perturbing even than the event itself. This had been no roadside explosion, no Taliban suicide bombing. Afghan soldiers had gunned the police chief down. The Kandahar Strike Force had done it, a special unit that worked for and lived with the CIA. The circumstances of the shooting were almost unbelievable: a full-blown commando raid on the chief prosecutor's office, snipers on the roof. The strike force was purportedly trying to spring a friend out of jail. The beleaguered provincial prosecutor had called Police Chief Matiullah, who had driven over and walked into the ambush.

The details did not compute. The jailed man wasn't even being held at that location. The phone call seemed like a setup. All Kandahar put the shooting down to the CIA. Command responsibility.

Then another call refreshed a detail that lay stored somewhere in the folds of my memory: Ahmed Wali Karzai had provided every member of the Kandahar Strike Force to the CIA, personally guaranteeing them all. The shooters had been his men. The potential implications—the move this murder might represent on one of several chessboards—outpaced the ability of dull-witted international officials, myself included, to keep up.

Command responsibility, indeed. But who was in command?

A team was dispatched from Kandahar Airfield to the governor's palace downtown, and I had flinched at the thought of driving through what amounted to my hometown in a U.S. Army Humvee. I looked around, and Sayfullah, local chief of the Afghan Border Police, offered me room in his green pickup truck. He was a nobody in this drama, a placid sort of figurehead from out of town, unconnected with Ahmed Wali Karzai and his coterie. Gratefully, I accepted.

FLICKING MY HEAD to scatter the memory, I looked back across the brown wooden table at Steve Foster and studied a response to his project of going after Sayfullah. "Are you sure?" I ruminated, skeptical. "I know the guy. He actually doesn't amount to much." In the complex pattern of Afghan politics, Sayfullah didn't matter, despite his rank. "He's kind of a front man. I'm wondering if getting him will send the right message."

Foster did not disagree with my analysis. Still, his fledgling investigators *had* the evidence. They had worked so hard, and it was good evidence. It seemed hardly fair to ask them to abandon it now and start afresh on some new quarry. I could see his point. "Besides," I offered. "Maybe it's not such a bad idea to start small. We can stress the system, see how it responds, and be better prepared for the next one."

Plans for the Sayfullah arrest went ahead.

Interior Minister Atmar's immediate reflex, upon being informed some days after that meeting in the garden, was to "kick the issue into the long grass," as Foster put it. He demanded a detailed review of the evidence—though the attorney general had already sworn out an arrest warrant. At our request, ISAF's intelligence chief, the frenetically energetic General Mike Flynn, visited Atmar one evening and spelled out why it would not be a good idea to stand in the way. Atmar got the message—and began bargaining. Sayfullah's arrest, he insisted, should be a dignified affair, no handcuffs.

It took place on October 19, 2009. Sayfullah was invited to Kabul to attend an official ceremony, and as it concluded, he was quietly led out a side door. I noted the success with complacent satisfaction. One down—now we could get on to serious business.

A few evenings later I got a call—from quite a different kind of Afghan police official, my friend Hakim Angar, whose career I had followed for years. He was phoning from a plane on a runway; it was hard to make out what he was saying.

Slowly, I pieced it together. Angar was aboard a flight to Kandahar.

He had an official paper in his pocket. Beside him on the seat were bouquets of plastic flowers, congratulations gifts from dozens of visitors to his office the previous day. He had been appointed to replace Sayfullah—a stunning departure from the Karzai government's habit of exchanging one corrupt official for a more corrupt one.

But as the plane began revving its engines, Angar's phone had rung. It was Atmar's deputy. "Get off the flight," he had ordered. Angar's appointment had been suspended. He should stand by for further instructions.

For the next three months, I worked that aborted appointment. ISAF intelligence chief Flynn told me he raised the issue with Atmar. The three-star operational commander confronted the chief of the Afghan Border Police. In January 2010 Angar's appointment was on General McChrystal's list of talking points for a meeting with President Karzai. But nothing moved. Angar remained in limbo.

Nor was this the only interference that plagued the Sayfullah case. A search warrant had been signed out for Sayfullah's office. Who knew what would be revealed about the doings of the border police? But at the last minute, the interior ministry called the search operation off, Foster, the MCTF, and ISAF reluctantly acquiescing.

Atmar, the story went, had consulted President Karzai about the advisability of this search; Karzai had called Ahmed Wali in Kandahar to get his view. And Ahmed Wali had warned of potential "tribal unrest," should the warrant be executed. Karzai had told Atmar to call off the search. With the safety of officers potentially at stake, international officials had opted not to fight the cancellation order.

I closed my eyes to quiet the boiling in my ears as I listened to this fairy tale. There was no threat of tribal unrest. Sayfullah had no tribal allies in Kandahar; he wasn't even from Kandahar. And Karzai, a Kandahar native, didn't need to make any calls to get the picture. The Afghan officials had shrewdly selected a pretext they knew would strike a chord with their untutored international counterparts.

The Sayfullah case, in other words, had proved to be a more instructive test than I had imagined. It had stressed the system, all right. And the system had responded with a lightning sequence of calibrated blocking maneuvers.

The question was, why deploy all that skill and effort on behalf of a mere Sayfullah? Why would Interior Minister Hanif Atmar, a man who basked in considerable international credibility, risk his luster by throwing himself across the tracks for some two-bit border police boffo like Sayfullah? Why not sacrifice a Sayfullah and retrench around people who mattered? It did not add up.

CHAPTER FIVE

Vertically Integrated Criminal Syndicates

Kabul, Garmisch, 2009–2010

"Sarah, do you have a minute?" It was Colonel Chris Kolenda aiming toward me on a gravel path that simmered in the reflected heat from the prefab metal buildings around it. A former reconstruction team commander tangentially interested in corruption, Kolenda was one of McChrystal's phalanx of colonels. "I want to show you something we've been working on." I followed him up to his office, on the second floor of one of the steel boxes that posed as work space. Three factory-fresh black desks on spindly metal legs and some tables shoved together in the middle of the room did not yet convey an inhabited feel.

Kolenda clumped over to a whiteboard in a corner. He sketched a rough triangle in black marker, a circle at the top. "So here's how traditional Afghan government used to work," he launched. "Patronage flowed downward." He drew an arrow pointing down from the circle.

"Wait a second, wait a second," I cut in, already irritated. This was romantic bunk, constantly regurgitated by Westerners discussing Afghanistan. It discounted the sophistication achieved by the 1960s and 1970s. The country was a constitutional monarchy then—a national assembly and local elders gathered in traditional structures affording a further check on executive power. Citizens expected a decent education from their government, health care, even employment in state-owned industries. Afghanistan had been a favored tourist destination and the envy of its neighbors. The Afghan government had *not* been a patronage system.

"Stop," Kolenda interrupted in turn. "Let me just finish." I clamped my teeth together. "Here's how *this* Afghan government is operating." He started on a new triangle, a new circle at its summit. "Here's GIRoA," he said, the Afghan government. An array of smaller circles formed the triangle's midsection. They represented subordinate officials—governors or provincial chiefs of police. At the bottom of the triangle was a row of stick figures: the people. Kolenda drew an arrow between the levels of officials again, indicating the flow of money.

But this time, rather than pointing downward to signal a distribution of resources from patron to client, the arrow was pointing upward, from the subordinate official to the superior. Money, Kolenda argued, was moving up the chain of command in today's Afghanistan, in the form of gifts, kickbacks, levies paid to superiors, and the purchase of positions.

Much of the cash garnered this way didn't even stay in country. It was being transferred offshore, to places like Dubai in the United Arab Emirates.

I didn't snap a picture of that whiteboard sketch. I wish I had. It has structured my understanding of Afghan corruption, and of acute corruption in general, ever since. And incidentally, it pierced the mystery of Interior Minister Atmar and Border Police Chief Sayfullah. I've been perfecting that diagram for years, adapting it to fit different countries. I've confirmed the behaviors it predicts in hundreds of conversations with Afghans and people living under other kleptocracies. I've briefed it dozens of times.*

The critical feature is the directionality of the arrows indicating the money flow. Their upward motion contradicts a widely shared preconception about how the Karzai government operated. Karzai was not, as conventional wisdom had it, doling out patronage.[1] He wasn't distributing money downward to buy off potential political rivals.[2] If anything—with exceptions especially before elections—the reverse was true. Subordinate officials were paying off Karzai or his apparatus. What

---

* Please see the Appendix for versions of these sketches, as they have now evolved.

the top of the system provided in return was, first, unfettered permission to extract resources for personal gain, and second, protection from repercussions.

And *that* explained the contortions Atmar had put himself through to shield Sayfullah. The whole system depended on faithful discharge, by senior officials, of their duty to protect their subordinates. The implicit contract held, much as it does within the Mafia, no matter how inconsequential the subordinate might be. Every level paid the level above, and the men at the top had to extend their protection right to the bottom. The Sayfullah arrest—like any legal challenge—represented a test case. How well the regime defended even its lowliest officials would broadcast a message throughout the system about the strength of the protection guarantee. If Karzai failed to uphold his end of the bargain, the whole edifice would collapse.

Thinking about the Afghan government this way abruptly solved other puzzles too. I could now decode two subsequent episodes in the Sayfullah saga, which many of my ISAF and rule of law colleagues found baffling.

The first was Interior Minister Atmar's flat refusal to call a press conference to announce the arrest. "You do it," he shot back at U.S. officials, who had expected him to leap at the chance to pose as a champion in the battle against corruption. They could not understand why a member of the sovereignty-conscious Afghan cabinet would let foreigners speak in his place.

But Atmar was contemplating the signal that would be transmitted to members of the network. The last thing he wanted them thinking was that he was behind Sayfullah's arrest. That would violate the protection deal. He needed it known that he had opposed the move—that the foreigners had made him do it. And the best way to get that message across was to have an international official make the announcement.

The press conference never happened.

President Karzai did hold one, just two weeks later, his first speech as declared victor of the August presidential election. It was a virtuoso performance in conveying different cues to different audiences.

Karzai dwelled on corruption. "Afghanistan has been tarnished by the scourge" of it, he conceded. And he vowed, "I will launch a campaign to clean the government." Many international observers applauded his change of course.

Standing on either side of Karzai as he made this pronouncement, however, were his vice presidents, Karim Khalili and Muhammad Qasim Fahim, two of the most notorious war criminals in all Afghanistan. They symbolized, for most Afghans, the yawning justice deficit of the post-Taliban government.

That bit of stagecraft—putting them on display that way—was aimed at members of the Mafia system. So was Karzai's answer to a reporter's question: would he be removing any key officials as part of this new anticorruption campaign?

"These problems cannot be solved by changing high-ranking officials," Karzai replied. "We'll review the laws and see what problems are in the law, and we will draft some new laws."[3] He was promising just the sort of busywork that would occupy earnest international officials. And simultaneously, he was signaling to members of the corrupt networks that they could relax—and to the Afghan people that they could swallow their frustration. No one was going to be held accountable.

So there were answers to one set of questions. The solution of more nagging riddles followed.

A perplexing discrepancy existed between my experience of the Afghan government and many other Americans' characterizations of it. "Weak," "incapable," and "absent" were the words Americans typically used, evoking a void that the Taliban, according to the standard narrative, were filling. But that was not the government we lived with in Kandahar. Kandaharis were up against an arbitrarily powerful, abusive entity—as noxious to many of them as the Taliban themselves.

The differing depictions, I now understood, had to do with where the observer was located with respect to the country's main revenue streams. Most Americans were stationed in zones where intelligence indicated Osama bin Laden and other Al Qaeda leadership might be hiding. Terrorists on the lam were expected to cling to infertile, sparsely populated terrain, far from frequented road systems. And at least until late 2009, most U.S. troops were deployed along the eastern fringes of Afghanistan, where steep crags and a lack of water, soil, and roads kept economic activity to a minimum. Afghan government officials were sparse there too.

The presumption was that the Afghan government just couldn't reach those uncharted tracts. Americans (and other international observers) presumed that GIRoA *aimed* to govern, but was failing, due to its lack of human capital and the monumental physical and institutional challenges facing a country that had suffered more than two decades of war. Secondarily, they presumed that this feeble government was also plagued by corruption—almost a side issue.

But what if the Afghan government wasn't really trying to govern? What if it was focused on another objective altogether? What if corruption was central to that objective and therefore to the government's mode of operation?

Perhaps GIRoA could best be understood not as a government at all but as a vertically integrated criminal organization—or a few such loosely structured organizations, allies but rivals, coexisting uneasily—whose core activity was not in fact exercising the functions of a state but rather extracting resources for personal gain.

If GIRoA's main objective was siphoning riches, then why should it waste manpower on the impoverished east? It did well to leave that forbidding terrain alone and deploy its personnel, effort, and force in places like Kandahar, a city situated in the heart of opium country, near important deposits of marble and alabaster, the principal entry point to southern Afghanistan, and a major node at the intersection of transcontinental land routes.

No executive decree would be required—no edict penned by President Karzai—to enforce these personnel policies. The system's internal economy would weight the distribution. Officeholders who had to recoup the money they'd spent buying their jobs would request assignments in zones where cash flowed. And senior officials, anticipating the sums to be collected from subordinates, would not try too hard to fill billets in impoverished rural districts.

I was often asked, moreover, why it was so hard to find honest people to serve in government. If that government was actually a crime syndicate in disguise, the dearth of good people was no surprise. Mafias select for criminality, by turning violation of the law into a rite of passage, by rewarding it, by hurting high-minded individuals who might make trouble. An absence of integrity within this system did not mean

Afghans as a people were intrinsically or culturally corrupt. This late in the game, constructive men and women had been stripped out—and by now might prefer to stay clear. "No one would dirty his clothes getting near this government," a Kandahar-area farmer exclaimed to me once.[4]

Twelfth-century John of Salisbury recognized this tendency of corrupt systems to distill and purify their own criminality. Acts of corruption, he wrote in his mirror *Policraticus,*

> are done publicly, and neither governors nor proconsuls check them, because . . . the raven rejoices in the works of the wolf, and the unjust judge applauds the minister of injustice . . . in lands whose princes are infidels and companions of thieves; they hasten to embrace those whose misdeeds they observe, thus adding their own share of iniquity in the hope that they may gain for themselves some portion of the spoil.

The resulting entity is almost unassailable, John continues, quoting Job:

> Their "body is like a shield made of cast and tightly packed scales which have been joined together; one is connected to the other, and not even a breathing space comes between them; one has been glued to another and, holding fast, they will not be separated from each other."[5]

That was the Afghan government. It was not incapable. It was performing its core function with admirable efficiency—bringing power to bear where it counted. And it was assiduously protecting its own. Governing—the exercise that attracted so much international attention—was really just a front activity.

Such an analysis might well be applied to other "failed" or "failing" states. They are failing at being states. That is because the business model their leadership has developed has nothing to do with governing a country. But it is remarkably effective in achieving its objective: enriching the ruling clique.

In Afghanistan, faced with such moral and material depravity, a brutal and tenacious insurgency was serving up its idea of an antidote: a narrow reading of religious devotion. Many Afghans were swayed by the argument that government integrity could be achieved only through religious rectitude. Some appreciated the outlet that militancy provided for their anger. Still others just laid low, unwilling to take risks on behalf of a government that treated them almost as badly as the Taliban did. And it was all U.S. troops could do to keep that insurgency at bay.

IN THE WINTER of 2009, the ISAF Anti-Corruption Task Force—with its evolving procedures for prioritizing "malign actors" and its still-tentative back channels for sharing information and planning joint action—was something like that airplane Hakim Angar had boarded, anticipating his new duties in the border police. The machine was on the runway. Its engines were turning. But it was not off the ground.

Even the simple notion that the international community should refrain from actively showering the most egregiously corrupt Afghans with honors was proving hard to implement.

One day I got a call from the U.S. embassy's creative and determined anticorruption officer, Sarah Peck. "You'll never believe it." Her voice seethed with exasperation. "Guess who they've invited to Germany—to a counternarcotics conference. Daoud Daoud!"

Daoud Daoud was Afghanistan's young and, to many, appealing minister of counternarcotics. He was also, according to multiple, separate strands of information, one of the biggest drug traffickers in the country. At ISAF we would soon be digging through indications that he had influenced the dispatch of an Afghan National Army unit into a pointless skirmish in order to protect his control of a major smuggling route on the border with Tajikistan.

"Oh, you're kidding." The ironies kept exceeding even our jaded expectations. "Who's inviting him?"

"The Marshall Center."

Attached to the U.S. European Command, situated among the trapezoidal Alps of Garmisch, Germany, the George C. Marshall European Center for Security Studies holds courses and seminars for members of

Eurasian and other foreign defense establishments. And a good friend of mine, who had left Kabul only months earlier, now worked there.

"The Marshall Center?" Grinning, a bone in my teeth. "I might just be able to get this turned off."

Thanks to some bureaucratic moves by my friend, the invitation was canceled, a victory of sorts—though ad hoc, achieved by means of our own network of personal contacts, not the impartial application of an across-the-board rule.

A few days after the change was finalized, I got a call from Germany. My friend just had one problem. The Marshall Center's counternarcotics conference was now out a speaker on Afghanistan. Did I have any ideas for someone to plug the hole?

I thought about it. The last thing I needed right then was to drop everything and run the teeth-gritting gauntlet of the Kabul airport on my way to Dubai, then Germany, just to give a talk. But my friend was in a jam. And I did know a bit about narcotics. I lived in the middle of the opium economy in Kandahar; my cooperative was designed to compete with it. I would watch baskets appear in the bazaar each spring, filled with the specialized tools used in the harvest—the wooden rods with tiny needles at the end for scoring the pods, and the snub, triangular, trowellike scoops for collecting the thick sap. Arghand couldn't hire laborers to pick the wildflowers we needed in May and June, because the manpower of two provinces was drained off to the poppy fields in buses and taxis that left from the outskirts of town. I knew a dozen people who had planted, or had taken a job harvesting, opium. We had discussed their reasons. At trainings, I had briefed incoming NATO commands on the Afghan opium economy.

"I could probably do it," I offered.

So on a January day in 2010, I found myself in the pit of an auditorium-style classroom, looking up curving ranks of seats at about two hundred military and police officers from forty-plus countries. I had put together a few slides depicting general trends in Afghan opium trafficking. I explained how it was largely the inaccessibility of credit that was driving people to poppy—not Taliban coercion or even the high price (which was not all that competitive against the sums the region's legendary pomegranates or lush apricots could fetch). I discussed the role of the late-1990s drought.*

But there were two slides I could not resist slipping into the back end of my presentation: the ones depicting the Afghan government as a vertically integrated criminal syndicate. My objective was really just to indicate that opium wasn't the whole story. Opium was a piece of a much larger problem.

I talked the audience through the slides, explaining how money was defying gravity to travel upward within the corrupt system, and pointing out the strength of the protection guarantee subordinate officials received in return for that money.

To my surprise, those two wonky slides electrified the group. Attendees crowded down afterward to talk.

"You just described my country," said one officer. He pronounced it something like "cohn-try." He was from Nigeria. Nigeria, I mused . . . didn't they have an insurgency too? Boko Haram? Others joined us: from neighboring African countries, from Colombia, from Central Asia, from the Balkans. The correlation was uncanny. Almost every officer who told me my diagram hit home came from a place that was also confronting an extremist insurgency.

A roaring sound began to fill my ears. The link between kleptocracy and violent religious extremism wasn't just an Afghanistan thing. It was a global phenomenon.

---

* Poppy's value—to the farmers—is lower than that of pomegranates or other fruit. Structural factors make it attractive to grow anyway: One of those is access to credit. Opium buyers provide loans, otherwise unavailable. And they require repayment in opium, not cash. If a farmer wants to marry his son off, for example, he will have to count about $10,000—in bride-price, in building an extra room for the new couple, in throwing a huge party. If he has already tapped out his relatives for loans over the past few years, the only person to whom he can turn is often the opium dealer. But then he has to plant poppy to pay the loan back. Another factor is speed of return. A fruit tree takes five years to mature and begin producing. There was a drought in the late 1990s, so many trees died. To replace them, a farmer would have to be able to withstand years of no income from that patch of land, before his first harvest. Opium, on the other hand, is harvested (and so brings in revenue) the year it is put in the ground. And if an opium crop is lost due to weather or other vagaries, only that year's investment is gone. Loss of fruit trees usually means the loss of decades of work.

CHAPTER SIX

Revolt Against Kleptocracy

The Arab Spring: Morocco,
Algeria, Tunisia, 2011

A year later, in mid-January 2011, I was returning to Washington from a trip to Afghanistan. By then I was working as a special assistant to Admiral Mike Mullen, the chairman of the Joint Chiefs of Staff, who two years before had confronted me in a Pentagon hallway, worried about having to call my mother with condolences. I stopped for a few days' layover in Paris, my home base since 1993. I treasured the moments to catch my breath there, as I shuttled between Kandahar and the Pentagon—alien worlds, both.

But Paris, that January, was hardly becalmed. The unimaginable was transpiring in former colonies across the Mediterranean—countries with which France has retained intense human and political ties. A wild-fire of protest was ripping through North Africa, against the rule of long-standing despots. The myth of Arab servility, some genetic proclivity to autocratic rule, was dissolving. Zine el-Abidine Ben Ali, who had run tiny Tunisia for nearly twenty-five years, had just come crashing down. France was reverberating with the shock. WHO'S NEXT? blared giant letters across the top of the newspaper I picked up as I boarded my flight to D.C. Mug shots of half a dozen Arab leaders, from King Muhammad VI of Morocco to Egypt's Hosni Mubarak, hung in a row across the page.

In Washington, I was still throbbing with the jolt. "What do you make of *Tunisia*?" I fired at colleagues. What I got back, largely, were shrugs. Not until Egyptians poured into Cairo's Tahrir Square a few days later, demanding Mubarak's head—forcing their urgent demands into the consciousness of U.S. officials who had long found him convenient—did Washington begin to grasp the significance of the hurtling events in the Middle East.

For me, it seemed the most important upheaval in the international political order since the collapse of the Soviet Union in 1989.

Within days I was begging Mullen to send me. I spoke Arabic. I had lived in Morocco as a Peace Corps volunteer, had reported on the grisly Algerian civil war in the 1990s. I could provide a perspective that differed from what his system was telling him—just as I did for Afghanistan. I asked to cross the continent, comparing countries whose regimes had fallen with those where they hung on. I promised him I'd skip Libya, already a hot war.

The contrast between my sense of the unfolding events and what Mullen was hearing from his Joint Staff was stark. By then, Moroccan demonstrators were in the streets, sometimes clashing with police in gritty Casablanca—not trying to unseat their king but, almost bookishly, requesting detailed constitutional changes. They wanted to vote for their prime minister; they wanted an independent judiciary, a reduction in the king's powers. They cited the English model as a constitutional monarchy that made sense.

Algeria, I knew, remained an asphyxiated place, run behind the scenes by decrepit generals, its population still too shattered by the 1990s carnage to contemplate change.

That was not how the uniform military was viewing these countries, as I discovered when I asked for a briefing from officers on the North Africa desk. We were, they informed me, "pleased with the relationship" with the Moroccan government. We only hoped its long-term defense planning would "focus on counterterrorism." In Algeria, too, our objective was to "improve counterterrorism relations"; our main worry was that "Al Qaeda in the Islamic Maghreb might find a haven" there.

Indeed it might, but no one seemed to be wondering why.

As for Tunisia—which had just made history by overthrowing an autocrat in a swift, broad-based, nonviolent upheaval, similar to the loudly applauded anti-Soviet revolutions in Eastern Europe two decades before—we had no intention of showing "favoritism" to its nascent democracy by providing any extra support.

Terrorism, breakfast, lunch, and dinner. It was as though nothing had just happened.

I thought the Arab revolutions changed everything. I thought they should upend U.S. strategic posture, which for so long had been framed in reaction to radical Islam. For decades, I wrote Mullen, extremism had been the only outlet for people to express their legitimate grievances. Autocratic governments liked it that way, because the extremist alternatives to their rule were frightening—to the United States and other international donors, but often to their own citizens as well. "We would prefer thieves to murderers," an Algerian shopkeeper later put it to me, when I asked her about corruption. There was evidence that several of these governments had deliberately targeted their repression against the most thoughtful, reasoned, and moderate leadership over the years, while covertly facilitating militant groups to serve as ogres to scare people.

But now, by way of the cascading revolutions, populations across the Arab world had opened a different outlet for their grievances. Instead of supporting Al Qaeda, or sneaking off to join the ranks of a violent local offshoot, they had rebuffed religious extremism and ignited a popular uprising, focusing on dignity, social justice, and the substance, not just the empty form, of democracy. That was a reaction Americans should admire, since it so resembled our own founding revolt against autocracy.

There was a chance, I argued in those early 2011 days, that radical Islam might be losing relevance in the wake of the Arab Spring. It was a fragile moment of opportunity. The United States should do whatever it could to promote that outcome.

AFTER ASKING FOR a memo detailing what might go wrong, Mullen authorized the trip.

I began it in familiar Morocco. I had lived there in the 1980s and spoke its peculiar dialect of Arabic. In the capital, Rabat, I found an old hotel with a terrace, opposite the tasteful yellow parliament building.

Knots of demonstrators clustered almost every day under the palm trees that lined the boulevard. They were often led by people who had obtained a Ph.D., yet found no job in the public sector. The "overqualified unemployed," they were called. An engineer I met the first day on the fringe of one animated group angrily accused the government of "pillaging public resources."

"It's not just that people are poor," interjected another man. "It's the shanty-towns in this country, while others live in palaces and drive cars costing millions."

I was visualizing the Sharpoor neighborhood in Kabul: dirt roads and million-dollar wedding-cake mansions, garish and lit with hundreds of light bulbs, while Kabul groped its way without electricity. I was thinking about the $80,000 SUV a kid who used to work for me drove around Kandahar. He had taken a job with a security company linked to Ahmed Wali Karzai.

The standard Western explanations for the Arab uprisings highlighted grand macroeconomic or demographic phenomena, such as a "youth bulge." But on the streets of Rabat, I was hearing something else. Moroccans told me that what was pushing people over the edge wasn't just poverty or misfortune in general—it was poverty in combination with acute injustice: the visible, daily contrast between ordinary people's privations and the ostentatious display of lavish wealth corruptly siphoned off by ruling cliques from what was broadly understood to be public resources.

In his *Education of a Christian Prince*, Machiavelli's Dutch contemporary Erasmus warned against just such elite extravagance in the midst of want:

When he is thinking of increasing his revenue, when he is anxious to make a brilliant marriage for his grand-daughter or sister, or to raise all his sons to his own status . . . or to display his substance to other countries while on foreign tours, then the conscientious ruler must continually remind himself how cruel it is that on these accounts so many thousands of men with their wives and children should be starving to death at home, getting into debt, and being driven to complete desperation.

Such yawning income gaps, Erasmus implied, are rarely fortuitous. They result from a deliberate twisting of laws and prerogatives to benefit the powerful. "To reduce poor people to hunger and servitude" this way "is both very cruel and very risky." At some point, "the last straw breaks the camel's back, and revolution eventually flares up when the people's patience is exhausted."[1]

That revolution had just flared up in North Africa.

One afternoon in Rabat, I sat in an outdoor café at one of those miniature tables, crowded next to a neighbor who proved to be a former finance ministry inspector. Here was a man whose very job should have been to ferret out the corruption the demonstrators were protesting.

"If I stopped every violation," he dodged, "everything would grind to a halt. Sometimes I had to look with half an eye." He winked. Candid, he admitted that few corruption cases ever made it to court. "If it's a case with just one party, the state against an accused offender, then it's easy to buy off the judge."

Early in the conversation, the former civil servant had criticized the "overqualified unemployed," in terms I had heard other Moroccans use. "They don't want to work in the private sector, because they don't get the same benefits as they do in a government job." But before long— emboldened, perhaps, by his years outside the system, unwilling to keep up the charade—he conceded that most of them would have a hard time finding a good private sector position if they tried. "People have to be from the big families to get those jobs. Those companies and the families that run them plan on breaking the law—participating in rigged tenders, handing out kickbacks. They can't have outsiders witnessing."

Nationwide demonstrations were set for March 19. In Rabat the marchers lined up in ranks beneath banners proclaiming their various grievances, policed by elected delegates in yellow armbands. Not a café table was knocked over the whole day.

My last taste of Morocco dated from the 1980s, under the harshly repressive regime of Muhammad VI's father, Hassan II—when the mere use of the word "king" in folktales I was transcribing violated a dangerous taboo, for some disrespect might be coded in the language of an age-old fable. In the context of that memory, the language and imagery on display were almost inconceivably shocking. Protesters weren't just calling for an independent judiciary in the abstract. Names of ministers from "big families" festooned banners next to demands that they be put on trial: Abbas el-Fassi, for example, the prime minister, or Interior Minister Chakib Benmoussa. I almost gasped to see the words spelled out.

Toward the back of the cortege, I saw a man holding one end of a rope that separated two delegations. WE WANT A DEFENSE MINISTRY, his sign proclaimed. That seemed an odd demand. I fell in beside him to ask what he meant. He was a soldier. Or he had been, until he and a dozen comrades had disobeyed an order to do a construction job on a general's house. They were promptly drummed out of the army, he told me. "A soldier's job is to defend this country's borders, or to help in times of natural disaster. Not to build mansions for generals." Now, with his dishonorable discharge, he said he was unemployable. "We want the generals to be subject to civilian accountability. We want a defense minister."

This was the army whose counterterrorism cooperation so pleased the U.S. Joint Staff.

MOROCCO and its neighbor, Algeria, maintain frigid relations. But at the cost of disapproving frowns from immigration officers at each airport, I was able to fly from one country to the other without incident.

Algeria grasped my heart and twisted it, just as it had in the 1990s. The capital city, tumbling down its steep hillside into the Mediterranean, is like a once-bright sapphire, its surface pocked and corroded by some sulfurous poison. The people seemed to thirst for contact, that tumultuous spring. You could strike up a conversation just by remarking that you were reading the same newspaper a passerby was carrying.

Overwhelmingly, even a decade or more after the last of the violence that had traumatized the nation in the 1990s, the sentiment people expressed was relief. "We've been through so much," one woman put it, when asked whether she wished for a revolution like Tunisia's. "We're happy just to be at peace."

"There is democracy here now," said a resident of Blida, an area that had suffered the rack—slaughter after slaughter—in 1997 and 1998. "If you want to drink alcohol, you can drink. If you want to pray, you can pray."

It was this still-welcome respite from a nightmare of violence that kept Algerians, mostly, off the streets during the Arab Spring.

But it rarely took long to penetrate this still surface and touch grievances that echoed Moroccans'. Public resources—which in Algeria's case include oil and gas—were being scooped up for the private benefit of a criminal elite. One man invited me inside his house in the historic old city, or kasbah, which had been far too dangerous to visit when I was last there. He was trying to keep the place from falling apart like neighboring buildings, whose crumbled walls were grass-tufted stumps. Homemade girders spanned a hole in a floor. From his balcony we could see the hazy shapes of oil tankers waiting to enter the port. "Look at the money they have." The man jutted his chin toward the water. But no public resources were set aside for restoring a disintegrating World Heritage Site.

The Algerian government was financing some construction. On the road to Blida, fat blocks of unfinished high-rises squatted ponderously: public housing projects, thrown up fast, as populist giveaways to keep Algerians from joining the Arab Spring protests. "The Chinese are building them," a journalist commented. "The government isn't even using these projects to reduce unemployment. All the laborers are Chinese; they live in special camps. And the work is shoddy. The materials are substandard, and officials get kickbacks on the difference."

In Blida, a woman who had lost thirty-two members of her family to the 1990s extremist violence (her sparky young daughter was sure the regime had colluded) confessed to being transfixed by news of the unfolding revolts in neighboring countries on the Al-Jazeera cable television network. "We didn't realize all these Arab rulers were thieves," the woman said.

At the port, fishermen pointed out the police watching us from a stone balustrade above our heads. "They're terrified of Tunisia happening here." Two brothers who imported consumer goods acknowledged paying bribes to get their cargo through customs. But, one of them noted, "it would take an earthquake and a tsunami for change to come to Algeria."

An earthquake, I thought, or maybe just time—till the young, whose minds were less seared by the violence of the past, came of age.

"THIS ISN'T about unemployment. It's about a mafia running this country." That was my introduction to Tunisia, courtesy of Hazem Ben Gacem, one of the dynamic young professionals who were flocking to the service of their country in the weeks after Ben Ali's fall. "It's about bullying, extortion, public sector bribery. Everyone knew about the corruption, the sick practices. It got to be too much."

Tunisia in March 2011 was still high on euphoria over what it had wrought. Avenue Bourguiba, the broad boulevard with its treelined median that leads from the port to the base of the Roman-era bazaar, was still serving as a kind of outdoor political forum. Knots of people stood in feverish discussion, under the rows of palms and the eyes of soldiers who manned a few tanks behind lazy loops of barbed wire.

Stunned, Tunisians were still discovering the extent of the robbery that the deposed Zine el-Abedine Ben Ali and the family of his wife, Leila, had perpetrated. "It was like Ali Baba's cave," recalled Imed Ennouri, one of several accountants appointed to inventory the ill-gotten gains. "The jewelry, mounds of it. The stacks and stacks of fine carpets."

The Sea of Precious Virtues, an anonymous twelfth-century mirror in Persian, describes how "a king who is envious ruins" his subjects, "desiring that everything belonging to the people should be in his treasury."[2] The acquisition of wealth becomes addictive, wrote its author.

"A tyrant," agreed Erasmus four hundred years later, "acts in such a way as to get the wealth of his subjects into the hands of a few. . . . For avarice is boundless, continually goading and putting pressure on what it has set afoot."[3]

Taxi drivers would swerve to point out the businesses, the luxurious BMW or Mercedes showrooms, built on public land, that belonged to Ben Ali's son-in-law.

And they represented only the fraction of Ben Ali's riches that Tunisians could see. One young activist criticized the loan already provided to postrevolutionary Tunisia by the government of Qatar. "They let Sakhr el-Materi in," he said, referring to Ben Ali's detested son-in-law. "His money is in their banks. They could just give that back to us and forget the loan."

Tunisia is a tiny chip of a country, its society as tightly knit by personal relationships as Afghanistan's. One contact, a Ben Gacem, for example, opened doors everywhere. Within two days, I was sitting in on the executive bureau meeting of a newly birthed political party, Afek Tounes. The heated conversation veered among topics as diverse as whether international observers should be invited to monitor upcoming elections, or what sort of people the party should accept money from.

"We want Tunisia to be a democracy," a woman explained to me. "We want to break with corruption. But we do not want political Islam. The Islamist party has always set itself up as the only alternative to corruption."

Militant political religion as the only alternative to corruption. That was just the nexus I had seen in the Taliban's appeal in Afghanistan, and in the frequent presence of extremist insurgencies in other acutely corrupt countries. Public integrity, the proposition seemed to be, could only emerge through the rigid purity of religious practice—imposed by law if need be, or savage violence.

I met with two members of the interim cabinet—a collection of brilliant technocrats, most of whom had been working abroad. How I wished we'd had talent like that in Afghanistan. They too were still reeling at the extent of the corruption, whose dimensions even they had never imagined.

"The development gap has grown unimaginable," remarked Interim Finance Minister Jalloul Ayed, recently of Citigroup—so no stranger to excess. "Ben Ali and his family went berserk. They went on a wild spending spree that offends the social mores of this country. We weren't raised like that." Interim Transportation Minister Yassine Brahim could not summon words to describe the scene he discovered at the port of Tunis. He just shook his head, wincing. A story making the rounds referred to a court photographer, whose job was to go to the high-society weddings and snap pictures of beautiful girls who would then be invited to Ben Ali family parties.

The behavior was lifted directly from Machiavelli's warning: "To be rapacious and usurp the goods and the women of his subjects, that is above all else what will make [the prince] hateful."[4]

While remarking on the evident fact that their revolution was not anti-American in character, these ministers and others did raise questions about the responsibility of international actors. "U.S. policy is not in line with its values," said an Afek Tounes member, echoing comments I had heard across North Africa. Another young activist questioned international lending practices, pointing out that International Monetary Fund and European Union loans had gone into the pockets of the regime. "If investigation confirms that the money never reached the people but was stolen," he wondered, "could that debt be forgiven?"

Queries like these raise important issues about the ethics, but also the advisability in international security terms, of active and passive collusion with kleptocracies. Governments and multinational institutions, private businesses as well, should weigh them with more consideration than they have in the past.

Finance Minister Ayed was even more direct than the young activist. "We have seen nothing from the United States," he remarked acidly. A congratulatory phone call, a few bracing words from Secretary of State Hillary Clinton, and that was it. "Something extraordinary is happening here, bigger than anything since Hannibal. It would cost a fraction of a fraction of what Washington spent on Iraq, for the same result that was desired there."

Tunisians called for a Marshall Plan, to demonstrate to an expectant population that peaceful revolution could deliver results: "Eight to ten billion would transform Tunisia within a decade," said Sami Zaoui, another former businessman, who had thrown himself into a nonprofit in the wake of the revolution. "And the knock-on effect across the region would be huge."

Beneath these Tunisians' urgency floated a growing fear, whose contours were already visible. If their revolution against kleptocracy did not deliver some palpable measure of improved social justice, the people, in their frustration, might radicalize after all. "Tunisia might become like Iran," said Zaoui.

THAT MONTH spent in the vortex of the Arab Spring in 2011, together with subsequent trips, reinforced beyond even my most expansive predictions a maturing hypothesis. The wave of protests, the toppling of four governments, and the rocking of three others amounted to a mass uprising against kleptocratic practices.

That spring millions of Arabs chose a constructive way to force change. They chose political revolution—a peaceful, civic, inclusive, and responsible form of revolt—directed squarely at their own leaderships, not at Western countries, not even those seen as regime allies. But it was revolt nonetheless. It sent shock waves across two continents and spun off several protracted, bloody conflicts. Its unfinished episodes, in Bahrain, Egypt, Libya, and Syria, at least, presage further violence.

Throughout, Al Qaeda and like-minded militants crouch at the ready. As they have in Iraq, radical groups will exploit grievances that go unredressed. They will enforce a rigorously puritanical code of behavior, holding it out as the only prospect for achieving conscientious government in the interests of the community instead of the self-indulgent few. They will prescribe a purification of religious practice as the recipe for morality in public affairs.

Beyond the Arab world as well as within it, a closer examination of a few emblematic countries reveals remarkable patterns. Residents of many kleptocracies describe a qualitative change at the turn of the millennium, give or take a few years. Something seems to have gone off the rails around the late 1990s, as governing cliques turned economic liberalization policies—together with a newly indulgent public morality—to their personal advantage.[5] The role of extended ruling families, especially women, in masterminding the heist has attracted popular outrage. And yet many of these cabals deliberately invited members of subordinate ethnic groups or religious sects into their networks, thus welding the top of the structure across the very divides that separate the sufferers.

While obeying the same basic kleptocratic principles, ruling networks may cannibalize different state functions, or lay hands on different sources of revenue, as a function of their countries' divergent histories, institutional structures, and assets. The results read like variations on a theme.

CHAPTER SEVEN

Variation 1: The (Overlooked) Military-Kleptocratic Complex

Egypt, ca. 2010

"The people . . . the army . . . one hand!!"

With this cry—part statement of a counterintuitive reality and part fervent prayer—masses of Egyptians in January 2011 threw themselves off the precipice of their predictable lives toward an incalculable destiny. The slogan rose from thousands of hoarse throats, was printed and painted on banners and posters and the walls of buildings across the electrified continent that is Cairo. Matrons put conscripts in headlocks to plant wet kisses on their cheeks. Young protesters leaped aboard tanks to clasp the hands of their age-mates in uniform.

This sentiment presented the world with a riddle. How was it that Egyptians, in throwing off a military dictatorship, were joining hands with the very same military?

Central to the demands of the Egyptian revolutionaries was a halt to the rampant corruption that disfigured the government of Hosni Mubarak. Mug shots of ministers on huge placards and banners were striped with jail-cell bars—an urgent appeal for punishment of the guilty and an end to systematic impunity. "I was in prison for nine years," one demonstrator shouted at me that spring, the pain of it still cracking his voice. "I ate off the floor. I want these people to suffer a single day like I had it in jail."

"If you care about democracy," challenged another, "then use Mubarak's assets to pay off our national debt, and send the leftover money back to Egypt!" Protesters were demanding the return of stolen or squandered funds and their reinvestment to benefit the general interest.

Ironically, the Egyptian military is hardly innocent of just the type of arrogation of public resources the protesters were denouncing.

"Our involvement in the economy began with the 1967 and 1973 wars," related General Muhammad el-Kishk during a quiet 2013 conversation at the Artillery House, one of the vast, manicured clubs, open only to military officers, that line the broad streets of Nasr City in eastern Cairo. "We needed to provide for ourselves. In such emergency situations, we did not want to be requisitioning food from the mouths of the population." The initiative started with commissary, which led to a large parallel economy, including farms and wholesale imports, for such necessities as flour, dried legumes, cooking oil, and natural gas. "What surpassed our needs," continued el-Kishk, "we sold on the market. And people bought it. Our products were better quality, at about the same price," he asserted.

To explain the Egyptian military's expansion into other economic activities, el-Kishk cited the example of communications equipment. "We started making two-way radios. But after a while the market just couldn't absorb our production. We had the factory and the workers. We didn't want to lay them off. So we launched a new line of products." Now, apart from excessive numbers of antiquated M1A1 tanks, the Egyptian military oversees the manufacture of items ranging from jeeps to spaghetti—while also running day care centers and building roads and bridges across Egypt.

Egyptian and Western scholars who have highlighted this military penetration of the economy (figures range from 5 to 40 percent of total output) acknowledge the difficulty of estimating its dimensions. "Not only are army holdings classified as state secrets—reporting on them can land a journalist in jail—but they are too vast and dispersed to estimate with any confidence," write Shana Marshall and Joshua Stacher.[1] Clearly, though, the activities "add up to a very large, unaccountable, nontransparent Military Inc."[2]

"Nontransparent" is the word.

A 2013 visit to one of the factories of the Arab Organization for Industrialization, a conglomerate established by the Egyptian military and several Gulf counterparts in 1975, felt like stepping through a time warp into some Soviet-era top-secret laboratory.

A lemon-edged brick wall enclosed tree-studded grounds, a conspicuous contrast to the dirt-brown, trash-choked dereliction that is much of downtown Cairo. Watchtowers manned by uniformed conscripts punctuated the wall's heights. Another conscript waved my taxi through the main gate. There were few signs of life. The entrance foyer was deserted, a silent television playing scenes of the pilgrimage to Mecca. I mounted the stairs. A surly employee ordered me into a conference room, where ranks of well-kept black vinyl chairs from the 1970s stood at attention before an empty podium.

Two female engineers from the research and development department appeared and commenced an interrogation. Who was I, where was I from, what was my purpose, what did I intend to do with the information? A frown of suspicion creased the chief intelligence officer's brow as she challenged each of my replies. At length she gathered her notes and bustled out of the room—to return with an archaic if glossy folder of brochures, which would answer all my questions, together with the CEO's refusal to let me see the production line, though the visit had been arranged days before.

As I tried to reschedule the tour over the next several hours, I was able to strike up conversation. The factory, it emerged, merely assembled low-grade Chinese components for electronics goods visibly below the standards of readily available Samsung or Sony alternatives—as a subsequent visit to one of the conglomerate's dusty showrooms made plain. Its line of computers, discontinued since the 2011 revolution, had been sold only to government ministries. The twelve-person research and development department was puzzling over circuitry for a prospective solar streetlight project, also aimed at government purchasers. Both engineers acknowledged the lack of innovation. Young graduates were hired right out of college or technical school and tended to cycle through on their way to higher-paying jobs in the private sector, at least till the mid-2000s. But "once they leave, they are not allowed to return." So the company is sealed off from the dynamism of today's information technology sector.

Military foodstuffs, considered of poor quality by consumers despite el-Kishk's claims, also fail to command much of a market. At best, the products enjoy preferential access to some public tenders, such as the ministry of youth and sports canteens. The army's construction companies corner a large share of public works projects, admittedly doing a creditable job at such tasks as road building.

Asked if there was any macroeconomic design in all this activity—if the military was tailoring its commercial undertakings so as to promote broader economic development—el-Kishk rebuffed such an idea. "We just run the companies to make profit on the open market."

Its core function, defense, hardly bears mentioning. The Egyptian military has not seen action since the first Gulf War. And apart from a successful foray into Libya in 1977, its track record in the conflicts of the 1960s and 1970s was abysmal. Its ongoing affection for outmoded tanks—and an associated emphasis on conventional warfare—reveals a resistance to adapting its security posture to rapidly evolving threats that matches its imperviousness to industrial innovation.

Yet this military—this Potemkin force—basks in material privilege. Almost all land not currently inhabited is considered government land, and most can be acquired by the military.[3] So military-run businesses and housing developments obtain the ground they are built on free of charge. Military factories and officers alike benefit from a mini–command economy, which imposes socialist-era prices on producers of sugarcane and other inputs.[4] They enjoy tax forgiveness and exemptions from labor laws, as well as immunity from public oversight, since all army activities—even commercial ones—are classified as national security secrets. High-quality food and such services as accompanied transport and child care are provided to officers and their families for free or at subsidized prices.

Most egregious to many—including some lower-ranking retirees—are the luxuries reserved for the top officers. Rooms in posh resorts on the Mediterranean and Red Sea coasts are set aside for them. Conscripts attend to their needs. And desirable jobs—within such key government authorities as the ministry for local development, the administrative monitoring board, the geological and mining services agency, strategic provincial governorates, and military-affiliated companies—are regularly filled by two- and three-star retirees, who thus enjoy salaries and opportunities for extracurricular money-making alongside their pensions.[5]

Such self-dealing distortion of the economy can only be considered corrupt. And yet that was not the corruption that sparked the 2011 revolution.

"People don't like critics of the military," one young activist told me that spring. A cameraman covering the events concurred: "The people don't hate the top military brass. They don't know them to hate them."

One explanation, in other words, for Egyptians' tolerance of military excesses is that military corruption has been largely hidden from view. Camera-shy officers have tended to stay out of the limelight; transactions are shielded by budget secrecy; much of the wealth has been inconspicuous—the chief luxury assets are located along isolated stretches of the north coast, on the Suez Canal, or in distant Upper Egypt. Many of these assets, moreover, are held by the institution, with officers enjoying only usufruct, not personal ownership, of the villas and lavish hotels.

Another root of the perplexing tolerance taps deep into Egyptian national identity. The military remains connected in people's minds to the Free Officers' Movement, the birth of the Egyptian Republic in the early 1950s, and nationalist hero Gamal Abdel Nasser, with his emphasis on social welfare. "No doubt there is corruption in the Egyptian military," remarks the Oberlin professor and military expert Zeinab Abul-Magd. "But ordinary Egyptians won't react against it because of the long nationalistic myth. Even if they suffer, they look up to the military."

The army has assiduously maintained that myth, by means of a barrage of media propaganda, including sonorous television commercials, or the huge billboards in 2013 Cairo depicting, in one case, a soldier graciously accepting the gift of a flower from an adolescent girl. "We are the backbone of this country," General el-Kishk assured me. "We are the glue that holds it together."

"The army," in the words of one young activist, whose chiseled features could have been lifted off a Luxor bas-relief, "is for the country." The Egyptian military remains a powerful symbol, and—especially in comparison to other institutions—is seen as adding some measure of value to the community.*

SO IT WASN'T Hosni Mubarak's army that enraged the revolutionaries of 2011. It was, instead, a small network of high-rolling capitalists centered around the dictator's son, Gamal. Beginning in the late-1990s, this group was seen to have hijacked Egyptian state institutions, rewriting the laws, awarding themselves privileged access to land and other public resources, and employing police repression—all for personal gain.

"Everything changed when Gamal came back to Egypt," following a stint at the Bank of America in London. A retired municipal employee, two teeth blackened from lack of access to good dental care, recalls the moment in 2013, in his small apartment on a working-class street in Alexandria. A pile of newspapers occupies one end of a cheap, mass-produced couch. "A huge gap existed between him and the ordinary people and their experiences of Egypt. He had no feeling for Egyptians. He knew there were poor people, but he didn't know what it was like to be poor in Egypt. And that ignorance was reflected in all his plans, all the strategies he devised on his path to inheriting his father's rule."

An experienced judge named Yussef Auf echoes the analysis: "Gamal worked for five years in London and came back in 1999, planning to succeed his father. And everything changed."[6]

"It was a clique of big businessmen, close to the Mubarak family and the ruling party," says Mohamed el-Shewy of the Egyptian Initiative for Personal Rights. "They used their influence in parliament to

---

* In this regard, as in others, the variation described here fits Pakistan as well as Egypt. There a formerly governing military, which has lost every war it fought against archrival India, controls a significant proportion of the economy. Pakistanis still largely view the military as the most "competent" national institution, turning their ire instead against the corruption of the civilian leadership. A notable difference between the two countries is that the Pakistani military actively cultivates violent religious radicalism, in order to advance national security priorities in India and Afghanistan. As a combined result of both phenomena, the country is grappling with one of the most expansive extremist insurgencies in the world and has harbored Al Qaeda leaders for years.

issue laws in their favor," especially regarding public tenders and land allocations.

El-Shewy's colleague Osama Diab, a dynamic thirty-year-old, whose English accent reveals a recent London residency, refers to the "replacement of one ruling class by another." The new class, he says, "ran the country—socially, economically, and in terms of the dominant discourse. Everything looked like them, modern, younger, Westernized." As a child in the early 1990s, he recalls, "it was rare to see a Benz or a BMW. The cars on the streets were Ladas or locally made Fiats. But suddenly, hundred-thousand-dollar cars started showing up. There are gated communities, hotels whose luxury is positively provocative. People know how much these things cost."

The owner of a small clothes-ironing business in the working-class neighborhood of Boulaq put it simply: "The people at the top were working for themselves, not for the people."

Randa el-Zoghbi and her colleagues at the Center for International Private Enterprise say this "new guard" surrounding Gamal Mubarak created "parallel structures" within key government ministries. "They didn't touch the positions or salaries of the old bureaucrats—they just created a new structure alongside them." This structure, including a bevy of "advisers" funded in part by the UN Development Program, answered only to the clique, according to many. Says el-Zoghbi: "Their decisions were subject to no accountability."[7]

Egyptians connected the runaway capitalism espoused by this clique—and the staggering fortunes its members amassed—with a wave of privatizations that reached its peak between 1995 and 2005, throwing hundreds of thousands of Egyptians out of work. Employees in every sector were hit, from a bank teller, whose speedy typing got her nominated to churn out protest leaflets during the layoffs, to workers in cement or textile factories, to the employee of a state-owned manufacturer of kitchen appliances, forced into early retirement. "Egyptians bought the factory without having to bid on it, and they sold it to a foreign company within a year," he recounted with a wry shrug. "They did it to make money off the sale, not to invest in modernizing anything."

"The buyers did not invest in the factories," agrees Kamal Abbas, coordinator of the Center for Trade Union and Workers' Services. "There was no technology transfer at all. Factories that haven't closed are still operating with the same old machinery and methods dating back six generations. Society did not gain anything, and the profits were sent overseas."

The retired Alexandria municipal government official with the damaged teeth recalls his old friend, Public Works Minister Mukhtar Khattab, telling him about the prime minister's orders to cede the businesses: "He complained to me: 'They're selling the country!' Of course, he may have taken bribes to do it, but he was only an accessory."

While the acute lack of transparency during the privatization process makes proof difficult, the perception of most Egyptians is that these sales of public enterprises—for prices below the value of the land they were built on, goes the refrain—unfairly benefited the crony-capitalist clique around Gamal Mubarak. "They kept it amongst themselves," says Wael El Zoghbi, the director of the Egyptian Business Development Association. "There was no access to information." Business reporter Mohammad Gad reckons that "most sales were to the inner circle."

The retired Alexandria official refers to this inner circle as "the moneygrubbers." "The people used to sing a wedding song," he recalls, beginning a quiet chant: "'Marriage, marriage! The state and capital, marriage, marriage!'"

"This," assesses Judge Auf, "was one of the major reasons for the revolution."

In other words, the high unemployment that many Western analysts blamed for the 2011 overthrow of the Mubarak regime was not seen by Egyptians as a structural, macroeconomic phenomenon resulting inexorably from rising population or incompetent economic policies. It was seen as the direct product of corrupt practices perpetrated by an upstart clique of crony capitalists who had captured key levers of the Egyptian state and were using them to advance their private agenda.[8]

This new crony-capitalist kleptocratic structure was emerging alongside and separate from the military-kleptocratic structure. It lacked the military's historic legitimacy, and the traditional restraints on conspicuous consumption, and it scorned even the military's pretense of serving a social role. But indications suggest it was beginning to encroach on the military's economic domains.

PART OF the difficulty of countering this new corruption, say many Egyptians, is that it was all done by the book—technically, anyway. "That's part of the brilliance of corruption in Egypt!" exclaims Wael El Zoghbi. "They make it legal!" According to the retired official, "Fathi Srour [the speaker of parliament] made laws for Gamal so he could circumvent the whole judicial system." Diab, of the Egyptian Initiative for Personal Rights, agrees. "The legal system was created by the people who were going to benefit."

Such self-dealing legislation was anathema to mirror writers. "In enacting laws," Erasmus instructed the future Holy Roman Emperor, "special care must be taken to ensure that they do not smell of profit for the privy purse or of special treatment for the nobility."[9]

The frenetic new moneygrubbing behavior was emulated on a local level. The retired official, who ran one of seven Alexandria municipal districts, explains how public tenders worked in his own department. The state of the man's teeth, and the modest allure of his apartment—no water during the day, a narrow galley kitchen—indicate a rare, frugal lifestyle for someone who held such a potentially lucrative position.

"We had an engineer named Gamal supervising our public works contracts. I used to call him 'Thief.' He would arrange tenders with contractors ahead of time. Between them, they could write up the public notice so only one company was suitable. He'd help the contractor make his paperwork perfect. Then, for ten thousand Egyptian pounds, say [about $1,500], he'd let them use cheap copper wire for electrical installations, or a shoddy Chinese water pump, instead of the more expensive Japanese one that was budgeted. The bigger the contract, the more likely this kind of collusion."

On a drive on Alexandria's famous waterfront roadway, the Corniche, I saw the remains of a multistory building, collapsed to its rubble-strewn knees, due to just such shoddy construction.

"Engineer Gamal could have gotten a higher salary in the private sector, but he stayed with us because he made much more money overall," continues the retired official. Asked why he couldn't put a stop to his subordinate's practices, he says he did report Gamal to the Central

Auditing Authority. "And they moved him to a different city. It's really hard to prove this type of crime well enough to be able to prosecute," he sighs. "There's no flaw in the paperwork. You'd have to dig up the whole building project to find hard evidence."

The bane of millions of Egyptians' existence was the Amn el-Shurta, or auxiliary police, which had fingers in almost every activity. At administrative departments they acted as gatekeepers. ("You will have to hold at bay these stewards," wrote John of Salisbury, "who always bite or bark at you.")[10] At the airport, they colluded with taxi drivers to rip off tourists. In the streets, they allowed vendors to clog the pavement in exchange for bribes. At the checkpoints they set up, they frisked passersby. The auxiliary police shook everyone down. They could be unspeakably brutal. The head of a German research institute recalls the shrieks he used to hear wafting up from the basement windows of police stations during the Mubarak era.

The Boulaq neighborhood clothes presser, his round face lit by an unaccountably beatific smile as he irons a cotton *galabiyya* on a counter fitted into the half-door of his small shop in his working-class area of Cairo, describes being arrested by these auxiliary police a few years back. "They accused me of carrying a concealed weapon," a ridiculous notion just on the face of it, in light of his cherubic air. "The public prosecutor dismissed the charges. The police arrest people like that for no reason, just to beef up their statistics." And to make money on bribes, he adds. For a suspect, the change of a single word on a criminal complaint can mean the difference between days and years in jail.

"These aren't just flimsy cases—they're false cases," declares Judge Auf when presented with this example. He shakes his head. "For six years, I dealt with this in criminal court every day. Once a crime is written up by the police, the public prosecutor doesn't have much discretion. He has to investigate it. Then, if evidence is found—called the 'tools of the crime'—the case is made. The judiciary has no legal way of stopping it."

Such evidence is easy to manufacture, he contends. "The auxiliary police have stocks of it in their office: weapons, drugs, you name it. Depending on what level of crime they want a person convicted of, they plant it on him." In other words, the police easily circumvent a judiciary that remains, in the view of many, more honorable than other branches of government.[11]

The picture painted is of a free-for-all at subnational levels of government, and a pervasive police presence functioning as an enforcement arm for a newly emerging corrupt elite at the top—while serving itself along the way. Largely rendered a formality and legitimist in culture, the judiciary did not have to be fully co-opted into the corrupt system (as it was in Afghanistan) for that system to operate.

"The state really stopped functioning as a state," Auf says of the period beginning in the late 1990s. "It stopped collecting taxes or making regulations or implementing and enforcing its laws. It left people without supervision, and opportunists filled the void. It allowed a gigantic shadow economy to flourish."

Galal Amin, professor of economics at the American University in Cairo, has dubbed this phenomenon the "soft state."

> A soft state is a state that passes laws but does not enforce them. The elites can afford to ignore the law because their power protects them from it, while others pay bribes to work round it. Everything is up for sale, be it building permits for illegal construction, licenses to import illicit goods, or underhanded tax rebates and deferrals. The rules are made to be broken and to enrich those who break them, and taxes are often evaded. People clamor for positions of influence so that they may turn them to personal gain. Favors are sold or dispensed to protégés, relatives, and sycophants.[12]

For Amin, as for Auf, such "weakness of the state encourages corruption."

But perhaps the truth is the opposite. Perhaps corruption was not the result of Egypt's "soft state" but rather its cause. Perhaps the primary objective of the Egyptian state shifted in the late 1990s from governing to the extraction of resources for personal gain, and the softening of the state resulted from that change in focus. The subsequent decade witnessed the transformation of the Egyptian government into a criminal organization—or more accurately, two organizations, controlling different levers of state power: the military (for which the people retained a degree of affection), and the clique of crony capitalists that had coalesced around Gamal Mubarak, and was rapidly expanding its reach.*

The budding competition between the two networks—and the military leadership's realization that if Gamal Mubarak succeeded his father, its privileges would no longer be sacrosanct—may help explain the relative military passivity in the face of the 2011 revolution.

IN JANUARY the indignant Egyptian population, pushed beyond the breaking point by the kleptocratic transformation, erupted in a nonviolent, nonsectarian revolt. Abusive corruption brought down the Egyptian "prince"—as Machiavelli and so many other mirror writers had warned that it would.

It was not a religiously inspired uprising. In fact, a majority of engaged Egyptians later recoiled at the Muslim Brotherhood's ability to use its entrenched local networks to capture the fruits of a revolt it had been slow to join. Still, many, at least initially, saw the Brotherhood as the only clean alternative to the old regime. That reputation contributed to its electoral victories.[13] Extremist Salafi movements, nearly unheard of under Mubarak's repression, burgeoned after his demise, winning more than a quarter of the votes in the 2011–12 parliamentary elections.

Some Egyptians have taken the demand for theocratic government to further extremes, rejecting politics altogether. In disproportionate numbers, they achieved leadership positions in armed groups such as Al Qaeda, which disputed the Brotherhood's long-standing decision to eschew violence. In 2009 the Egyptian Ayman al-Zawahiri, who would become Al Qaeda's leader after the death of Osama bin Laden, argued on an internally produced video that "there is no doubt that the Egyptian regime has reached a level of corruption, filth, and agency that is unbearable." But, he insisted, Mubarak and the rulers of most other Arab countries "cannot be changed except by force. . . . The attempt to

---

* For a diagram, along the lines of the one that depicts Afghanistan's kleptocratic system, please see Appendix.

change the regime internally and through its laws and constitution will only lead to more corruption and oppression and dependence."[14]

Subsequent events in Egypt, many supporters of the Muslim Brotherhood would argue, have confirmed al-Zawahiri's words. The Islamist movement's political party ran in national elections, squeaked out a victory, and rewrote the constitution in line with its ideology. Hardly a year later, on behalf of a new generation of military leaders, the old security services moved in and toppled the Muslim Brotherhood–linked administration. They were applauded by millions of Egyptians, who feared that a crony-capitalist kleptocracy had merely been exchanged for a religious one. The streets of Cairo became a war zone, as hundreds of Brotherhood supporters were shot down amid the wreckage of the tents and flimsy barricades they had erected.

Nursing their wounds, many Islamists—especially the young—are ruefully acknowledging Zawahiri's prescience. "When the Muslim Brotherhood was completely destroyed in the coup and disintegrated," says Anas Hassan, a former member of the Brotherhood's youth organization and founder of the online news site Rassd, "it was the kiss of life to the Al Qaeda ideology. Now it is as if Zawahiri speaks out every week, to say 'I told you so.' No Islamist doesn't have at least five friends who were killed in Raba'a Square. And the way we were killed was very violent. So the theory of working inside the state crumbled for us inside our minds. Now nothing prohibits us from using violence. The social contract has dissolved. Stealing the weapons of the state to take it down is acceptable."[15]

Indeed, the crackdown seemed designed to radicalize Muslim Brotherhood members. Just as Algeria's generals had done twenty years earlier, the Egyptian military erased any remaining distinctions between non-violent political Islam and radical extremism, by branding the Muslim Brotherhood a terrorist organization. "All Islamists will find themselves labeled as terrorist," says Anas. "This game was forced upon us. And so we have to play it to the end." And indeed, violent attacks on Egyptian government installations have intensified, as the terrorist label became a self-fulfilling prophecy.[16]

CHAPTER EIGHT

Variation 2: The Bureaucratic Kleptocracy

Tunisia, ca. 2010

Disembarking on Tunisian soil in the spring of 2011, hardly a month after an entrenched despot was toppled by a popular rebellion, I was astonished at how smoothly the formalities went. The line to clear immigration was orderly. An officer ran his computer checks, stamped a red oblong into my passport, and I was through. Somehow I had expected more drama. I was not yet accustomed to the Tunisian bureaucracy: efficient, unwavering, quietly executing the directives of the state—whoever might be running it.*

Tunisia is squeezed between the turbulent giants of Algeria and Libya on the North African coast. The capital, Tunis, tilts its chin up to the bright Mediterranean sun, the sea breeze ruffling red and white flags strung from balcony to balcony across the alleys of the old kasbah. It's a white city, edged in sky blue, round arches picked out in black and white marble, arabesques of decorative nails gracing ancient wooden doors. Thoughtful street art speaks louder than words. The passion and pride in what the tiny country had just wrought still charged the

---

* The use of the civil service in Tunisia as an instrument of kleptocratic rule, which seemed so dramatically novel to me from the perspective of Afghanistan, turns out to be common to kleptocracies with more developed institutional architectures. This pattern characterizes all the examples in these chapters, to a certain degree. Still, Tunisia stands out as one of the more comprehensive versions, and one of the better mannered.

air when I arrived, early enough to witness the first efforts to convert revolutionary fervor into political organization.

It came as a shock to observers when the spark that ignited the Arab Spring flared in this of all places. Of all Arab countries, Tunisia seemed the best in the class: stable, presentably secular, engaged in a steady process of "economic reform."[1] A week earlier most of my Pentagon colleagues would not have been able to place it on a map. No one would have pegged it to touch off one of the biggest international upheavals in decades.

Like the Egyptians who would soon emulate them, Tunisians were pushed over the edge by the ostentatious behavior of a clique of self-serving crony capitalists, centered on the family of their ruler.[2] In this case, it was the longtime dictator's second wife, Leila Trabelsi, who got the blame, and her brother and a nephew and the husband of the daughter she had had with Ben Ali before they wed.

That marriage, in 1992, marked the moment when "everything changed" for Tunisia, according to locals. "With no shred of scruple, they looked upon Tunisia as a vast personal enterprise that they could tap at any moment," writes Lotfi Ben Chrouda, who worked as a servant in the Ben Ali household for nearly two decades.[3] He describes orgiastic parties, foreign delicacies delivered to Tunis via diplomatic pouch and rushed from airport to palace by police convoy. That would be the palace whose storerooms resembled Ali Baba's cave.

In the early fourteenth century, Walter of Milmete, who wrote a mirror for the future English king Edward III, warned of certain courtiers' boundless hunger for wealth, a dangerous addiction untethered to real-world needs: "the covetous are always grasping and . . . are never sated, because the more they possess, the more they desire."[4]

Karim Ben Kahla, dean of one of the country's top business schools—the Institute for Accounting and Business Administration at Manouba University—recalls a 2010 awards ceremony for student athletes, featuring the kind of pomp Ben Ali family members presumed was their due. He was herded outside, along with other professors and official guests, to greet the young son-in-law as he drove up in his Porsche—like an honor guard bowing before some visiting potentate. "It was humiliating!" Ben Kahla exclaimed.

Ben Kahla—who studied other examples of acute corruption as an expert with the African Peer Review Mechanism[5]—dated the "mafiazation of the [Tunisian] state" to the late 1990s, the same period Egyptians identify as the time Gamal Mubarak's kleptocratic network emerged. And again, it was economic liberalization that provided the ruling clan its opportunity. "The telecom sector attracted them," says Ben Kahla, "well-known international companies like Danone, and of course the banks." Leila Trabelsi's clan placed favorites in senior management positions, even at foreign financial institutions launching operations in Tunisia.[6]

To pinpoint the shift in the family's fortunes, Ben Kahla points to its indebtedness. As late as 2002, according to a list that was leaked to the press that year, Trabelsi's brother Belhacen ranked quite low among indebted businessmen. "After that, though, it was a very fast rise," remarks Ben Kahla. His argument seems counterintuitive—being in debt can be a calamity for ordinary people. But not within Tunisia's budding kleptocratic system, where no one expected Belhacen to repay his ballooning loans. The banks were giving away free money to him and other insiders, with the assurance of recapitalization from state coffers. Tunisia was becoming what Ben Kahla dubs a "feeding-trough state."

In *La force de l'obéissance* (*The Force of Obedience*), one of the most careful and well-documented studies of corruption anywhere, the French scholar Béatrice Hibou details the role of the financial sector in enabling the elite capture of Tunisia's economy—essentially by serving as a piggy bank: "The system of nonreimbursed (or nonreimbursable) loans . . . is a massive reality which has a macroeconomic, macrosocial, and macropolitical significance."[7] Political connections were usually key to accessing the free money.

> The relationship can be direct, as in the case of the crony of the inner circle to whom a banker cannot refuse a loan—even if he knows in advance it will never be repaid. It can also be indirect, via cutouts. Numerous loans have been granted to perfectly insolvent individuals who are known to be the intermediaries of these same cronies. Many public enterprises have been ceded to them, directly or via straw men . . . the operation financed by a nonreimbursable loan granted by the banks.[8]

Imed Ennouri, the public accountant on the postrevolution commission charged with tallying the Ben Ali assets, confirmed Hibou's analysis: "Every year there was a list of loans that were written off. Accountants would sign off on the decisions to keep getting work."

Such practices were made publicly palatable by an emphasis on the businesses' contributions to job creation, or on the need to support critical sectors of the Tunisian economy[9]—arguments that were used again after the revolution to fend off calls for accountability.

Shaped as I was by my long Afghan immersion, I was struck by the prominent position the financial sector occupied within the Tunisian kleptocracy. Though Afghan ruling networks pillaged the Kabul or Azizi banks too, banking was almost a curiosity in Afghanistan. Most transactions were still made with worn and crumpled bills, taped or even sewn together when they ripped. Tunisia's modern economy featured branches of well-known European financial institutions and a widely respected central bank. That such a sophisticated banking sector should serve as a wholesale clearinghouse to transfer national revenue into the hands of elite networks shows how embedded the kleptocracy was in formal structures.

Many of the other revenue streams the Tunisian first family captured are typical targets of acute corruption. As in Egypt and Afghanistan, public land was especially alluring. The former Ben Ali servant Ben Chrouda describes the clan's vast construction projects on the choicest and most historic parcels of seafront real estate, to which army engineers and agriculture or health ministry specialists were required to contribute their expertise.[10]

In Afghanistan, access to water determines a piece of land's value. In Tunisia, the key factor is suitability for tourism. The town of Kelibia faces Sicily on a fertile peninsula reaching deep into the Mediterranean. Great chunks of Roman columns lie strewn behind fences; Punic sites can be found yards away. The silky, ash-white sand on the main public beach sings out underfoot. But the shoreline is scarred by huge hotel complexes, several of them investments by Ben Ali cronies. Giant cranes bar the skyline.

In the summer of 2012, protesters gathered outside a mustard-colored compound. Dumping truckloads of coarse, yellow sand on top of the fine local variety, its owners were encroaching on one of the last stretches of public beach. As is typical in the Tunisian tourist trade, this hotel functioned as a closed system, the protesters said. A partnership with Italian investors, it employed no Tunisians except for a few guards, and shipped in all its foodstuffs from Italy. Not even Tunisia's luscious olive oil reached its tables. And like other seaside resorts, its beach access was off-limits to locals.

According to Hibou, it was government policy to cordon off the tourist trade this way, to shield foreigners from Tunisian realities, and to reserve the sector for well-connected insiders.[11] The isolation also allowed for another dimension that added to public discomfort with the whole industry: the sanctioned use of some resorts for sex tourism.

At Kelibia's covered market, a fishmonger swabbing the floor in front of his glistening display had plenty to say about real estate. "Four or five families control most of the land in this town," he reckoned. "Then there's the new harbor development, paid for with European funds. They cemented over our old port with it. And half the money was stolen."

The fishmonger's complaint highlights the role that international loans and subsidies often play, in Tunisia as elsewhere, in actively feeding kleptocracy. Moroccans complain about an unnecessary high-speed rail line linking their capital to the commercial hub, Casablanca. Their criticisms, like that of the fishmonger, illustrate that it is not just humanitarian aid in crisis or postconflict environments that gets captured as a "rent" by kleptocratic networks. Infrastructure grants—or worse, loans—supposedly provided after unhurried deliberation, serve the same purpose in acutely corrupt countries.

Customs was another favored entry point into the Tunisian economy for the Trabelsi clique: the "juiciest spot," in the words of Amine Ghali, who reviewed thousands of citizen complaints as part of an anticorruption commission that began work after the 2011 revolution. Interim Transport Minister Yassine Brahim was speechless at the depth and breadth of the corruption at the Port of Tunis when he visited it upon taking up his duties in early 2011.

A former customs official confirmed the allegations of many Tunisian businessmen and observers: that brokers working for the Trabelsi clan had their cargoes systematically whisked through, free of dues. "I argued with my director general about it," he told me. "And I got moved to an out-of-the-way border post."

The anticorruption commission's Ghali described an altercation he witnessed at the customshouse in the port of Rades: "A new captain was trying to scan a container. The importer made a call on his cell phone, and a Trabelsi cousin arrived, strode up to the customs official, and slapped him in the face, right in front of me. Then he grabbed the scanner out of his hand, and threw it in his car and drove off."

The result, most Tunisians agree, was a market flooded with cheap imported consumer goods that undermined both local industry and importers not wired into the network. Such distortions fray an economy, exacerbate unemployment, and reduce the resilience of a country like Tunisia to demographic pressures or global downturns.

The aspect of Tunisia's kleptocracy that struck me the most was the way it made use of the finance ministry. "They would use audits to subjugate people," said Murad Louhichi, a tax collector who witnessed the goings-on for years. "There's a lot of complex paperwork and formalities, which can be swept aside—or not." Tunisians, that is, were openly requesting tax waivers and getting them. However, "assessors would rarely make someone's file go away completely. They would put it on the bottom of the pile. The permissiveness could always be revoked. Nonpayment of taxes was used as a kind of welfare program to secure obedience. Or to punish someone who was too independent." A sudden audit and a claim for payment in full could shutter any business whose owner resisted the whim of a Ben Ali relative.

I was floored to learn of this ploy. The Tunisian version of the IRS—the ultimate symbol of a government bureaucracy—had been transformed into a tool in the hands of the kleptocratic network, enforcing its hold over an entire population.

Entrepreneurs across Tunisia confirmed such practices. "Ben Ali was fine," observed a rug merchant in the historic desert citadel of Kairouane, "only he was addicted to money. All the big businesses had to pay kickbacks to operate. If you hesitated, the son-in-law was sent to attack. He'd demand a share, and if you balked, your business was ruined."

An agricultural worker from the southern oasis of Tozeur, who used to grow Tunisia's highly prized *deglet nour* dates, echoed with a grimace: "The Trabelsis would enter your business. If you refused, they would break you. Any way at all: they'd get your loans called in, cancel your authorization, audit your taxes."[12]

In the lush, silent, cathedrallike date plantations in Tozeur and other oases of Tunisia's deep south, the harvest results from an intimate and age-old symbiosis between men and trees. In early spring leather-skinned cultivators shimmy barefoot up the striated trunks to daub pollen onto the pistils of each flower; in the fall they ascend again to cut the laden branches of fruit. Here government pressure could be even more diabolical—the public water authority controls the flow of the precious liquid through great pipes that traverse the plots. A Trabelsi-linked exporter seeking to increase his margins by way of a discounted wholesale price could twist a grower's arm by cutting the water to his land.

As in Egypt, corruption was not confined to the top of the Tunisian government—it abounded at subnational levels too. Villagers complained about preferential distribution of government-financed microcredits or subsidized seed and fertilizer. "The local party boss decided who got them," explained one small farmer, whose sickly calf was being examined by a veterinarian in the northeastern district of Nabeul. "He would give it to people who did things for him: worked on his house, or brought him gifts of honey or eggs"—what John of Salisbury referred to as "services and works that were not otherwise owed."[13]

Such "petty corruption" was allowed to flourish on the local level. But in Tunisia, unlike Egypt or Afghanistan, it was no licensed free-for-all. The Ben Ali network kept a close eye on the practices, by way of a fretwork of local ruling party cells.[14] Infractions were observed and then held over people's heads—officials and citizens alike—to lock in the loyalty of those who indulged. "The government would turn a blind eye to the petty corruption," summed up Ghali, of the anticorruption commission, "to ensure that officials followed orders later."

In other words, state capture in Tunisia was not carried out through a parallel structure that operated alongside an increasingly marginalized bureaucracy, as in Egypt. Rather, the Tunisian bureaucracy itself was placed in the service of corruption.*

As in Egypt, the legalities added up marvelously on paper. "They made villainous laws to circumvent law by law," the anticorruption activist Taoufiq Chamari exclaimed to me in 2011. Or to put it the way the English churchman did more than 850 years earlier: "Who is more iniquitous than he [who] . . . destroys law by law and is beyond the law, even while he burdens others with the law."[15]

In Tunisia, the well-oiled, efficient, and obedient bureaucracy, manned by compliant tax collectors or customs agents, implemented those laws—or not—according to the requirements of the kleptocrats in power.

Police helped with enforcement, but according to most Tunisians they were not as consistently brutal as their Egyptian counterparts.[16] "Ben Ali was too afraid of damaging his international image," said tax collector Louhichi. "There were lots of other ways to harass people." The marginalized army played no part in this system at all.

Because the Tunisian dictatorship was able to extort submission with comparatively little recourse to such classic abuses as torture or arbitrary detentions, Tunisian activists have introduced a novel concept into human rights discourse. They favor expanding the understanding of "gross violations" of human rights to include structured economic crime. "The idea is gaining ground among experts from the International Court of Justice and the UN system we discuss it with," says one of its proponents, the anticorruption commission's Ghali, who is also deputy director of the Kawakibi Democracy Transition Center. In a global first, "violations of social and economic rights" are covered in the remit of the transitional justice law passed in late 2013.

The idea is catching on with Tunisia's neighbors too. Drafts of Libya's law also referred to the Qaddafi regime's economic crimes. Ehab el-Khattat, a member of Egypt's first postrevolution senate, was among several legislators who pushed to launch a transitional justice process there. "If there's no clear connection to political corruption within tran-

---

* For a version of the state capture diagram tailored to Tunisia, please see the Appendix.

sitional justice procedures, then a separate channel should be devoted just to that," he told me. "If we don't do anything about it, we stand accountable before the people—and maybe there will be another revolution, against us."

Even in famously secular Tunisia, however, some fear a growing radicalization if Ben Ali–era officials and business magnates are not held accountable, and corrupt practices are not reformed. As in Egypt, an Islamist party, Ennahda, won the first postrevolution elections. In the capital, Tunis, the divide between Ennahda and the secular opposition is cast in cultural terms. But farther south, it is an ongoing sense of political and economic exclusion that bolsters Ennahda, as well as resentment of residual Ben Ali–era networks in local government.

In the southern city of Mednine, in early 2014, a cross-section of engaged citizens, including an unemployed blind man, a pharmacist, and two twenty-something youth services department employees, all indicated a preference for Ennahda—not for religious reasons, but as the most credible alternative to the old system. "We don't trust them," said Intissar Souidi, a pharmacist at the public hospital, referring to former officials. "They stole, they abused, they imprisoned people. They had their turn at governing, and they failed. At least with Ennahda, we have people who didn't steal."

As in Egypt, moreover, a heretofore-invisible Salafi movement emerged after the 2011 revolution. Gloves for women who wear full *niqab*, or head-to-toe veiling—unheard of even in Afghanistan—could be seen hanging up for sale in the Tunis bazaar. The avowed Salafi acolyte Marwan Jedda explains his orientation this way: "People wanted to bring down corruption and repression [in 2011], but neither has fallen yet. Corruption has increased in Tunisia. People demanded work, freedom, and dignity. As an Islamist, I have a solution. The second revolution will be an Islamic revolution."[17]

One group that Jedda describes as a "rising power" and praises as unequivocally "opposed to this system"—a "competing force in the street and for youth"—is the violent Tunisian jihadi movement Ansar al-Sharia. Accused of orchestrating the assassination of an Afghan resistance leader two days before the 9/11 terrorist attacks in New York and Washington, it is led by a radical Tunisian preacher, Sayf Allah Ibn Hussein, or Abu Iyadh. On September 14, 2012—after the U.S. ambassador to Libya was killed in Benghazi by the group's Libyan affiliate—Abu Iyadh orchestrated an unprecedented attack on the U.S. embassy in Tunis. Police surrounded the mosque from which Abu Iyadh encouraged the crowds, but he somehow escaped—and continued to broadcast jihadi exhortations in local media long afterward.

Photojournalist Talel Nacer, who hails from the impoverished inland mining city of Gafsa, and whose own father is a mild-mannered Salafi imam, warns that mainstream politicians "keep ignoring the serious economic issues that matter: I mean social justice and punishment for the people who stole. There are already strains within the Islamists. If things go on this way, the youth will flock to the Salafis."

CHAPTER NINE

Variation 3: The Post-Soviet Kleptocratic Autocracy

Uzbekistan, ca. 2013

"The *first* violation of human rights is corruption!" Uzbek activist Elena Urlaeva nearly hugs me when I try out the "Tunisian novelty" on her: the notion that acute, structured state corruption might constitute a human rights issue.

Her hair a wispy blond, her skin gone soft, Urlaeva looks at least sixty. She is a mainstay of the Uzbek human rights community, a veteran of legal challenges to arbitrary detentions—and of a few stints behind bars herself—of solitary vigils, in front-and-back poster-board panels that spell out in urgent Magic Marker the details of the abuse she's protesting.

"We talk about child labor, and torture, and religious freedom. We talk about them separately from corruption. But corruption is the reason for everything, the means of existence of the whole system."

Urlaeva is among a handful of crusty human rights activists who are called upon periodically by the U.S. embassy in Tashkent to speak to visitors. That is where I meet her, in a clean, windowless conference room. Observers suggest that the dictatorship of Islam Karimov, who has ruled Uzbekistan since 1990, tolerates them grudgingly, perhaps because it is not afraid of them: they don't have much of a following.

"There are fewer and fewer activists," Urlaeva's colleague Surat

Ikramov, of the Initiative Group of Independent Human Rights Defenders, concedes bitterly. "We're all fifty-plus years old."

What the regime *is* afraid of, says Masha Lisitsyna, Central Asia program director at the Open Society Foundations, is anyone digging into corruption. "If you do general human rights work, you may suffer," she says. "But investigating economic abuses—you can get killed for that, because it touches the system."

The other activity the Karimov government fears is the open practice of Islam. Neighborhood mosques are fitted with video cameras. Imams are vetted by the ministry of religious affairs. "Eleven thousand believers are in prison today," estimates Ikramov, who monitors court cases. "There are more than seven hundred in jail on terrorism charges, but the prosecutor doesn't have any real evidence."

The region reputed for religious conservatism is the Ferghana Valley, separated from the Uzbek capital by steep ridges of flame-colored rock, the easternmost spur of the oddly zigzag-shaped, diagonal country. "The province of Ferghana is in the fifth clime, situated on the edge of the civilized world," wrote the sixteenth-century Timurid emperor Babur, who was crowned there and remained enamored of the valley for the rest of his life.[1] Watered by the Syr Darya River, it has been known in centuries since for its lush fruit and fragrant blossoms.

To me, it felt like paradise. Ferghana was the picture of what next-door Afghanistan might have been, without thirty years of war. Uzbeks' love of gardens matches that of their Afghan neighbors— their open-plan houses built around sprays of apricot and plum trees, breakfast tables set within reach of their branches. Grapevines shade neighborhood streets, growing thick across arbors that span the lanes. Flowing canals thread through the towns, cooling them. Dripping boys laugh and shove each other aside as they compete to jump in.

Compared to that of Kandahar or even secular Tunis, Ferghana's religiosity is just about invisible. Gold-toothed women in short-sleeved frocks of flowery cotton, their heads covered with matching kerchiefs, sell rounds of bread and vegetables in the lively outdoor markets. Women excel in university studies and serve as doctors or in the police. Only once in several days did I see a man leave a conversation to perform his sundown prayers in a dedicated room of his house. "People don't show they're religious," comments a journalist, "but they feel it."

ON MAY 13, 2005, as dusk was falling and with it the rain, soldiers lay prone behind sandbags that blocked the main street of Andijan, the Ferghana Valley's easternmost town. A crowd of panicked civilians lurched toward them, keening in fear. The soldiers opened fire. Women and children in the center of the melee, where they had thought they might be safer, crumpled to the blood-soaked pavement.

"We were just shocked," recounted one survivor. "It was like a bowling game, when the ball strikes the pins and everything falls down. . . . There were bodies everywhere. I don't think anyone in front of us survived."[2] The people came under fire from the roof of the nearby cinema and apartment buildings lining the road, from behind trees and a school. No accurate body count has ever been established for the events of that day, but the best estimates range near five hundred men, women, and children.

The night before, young men had broken into the jail to free a group of defendants who were incarcerated while they stood trial in a long-running, increasingly contentious case. Crossing town, gaining reinforcements on the way, the rebels had captured city hall from the lone night watchman.[3] In the morning, townspeople began flocking to the main square in front. A podium was set up; someone came with a sound system, and people took turns at the microphone to voice their complaints against the Uzbek government.

Armored personnel carriers appeared and sped down Navoi Prospect, the street that forms one side of the square, firing random shots into the crowd, killing at least one child. Asked later by human rights investigators why people had braved such violence, why the crowd kept growing all day, survivors recounted a rumor: "There was a TV where people allegedly saw on the news that the president would be coming to Andijan" to hear them out. "People were waiting for the president to come. They wanted to meet him and explain their problems."[4]

They wanted Karimov to *listen himself, without intermediary, to what his subjects had to say to him.* Specifically, they "wanted to know if the problems came from the local level, or if they came from the top."[5]

Such a notion—that government misconduct might be the fault not of the ruler but of subordinate officials gone rogue—is not necessarily baseless. A chorus of mirror writers across the cultures and centuries warned their royal readers to do whatever they could to prevent just that tendency.

"It is absolutely necessary," Jonas d'Orléans admonished Emperor Charlemagne's grandson in 831, "for [the king] to scrutinize with the greatest attention every one of the subordinates installed under him."[6]

Writing around 1090 for a sultan whose empire stretched almost to Andijan itself, Nizam al-Mulk repeated the instruction incessantly: "It is indispensable to know the conduct of every one of the judges in the kingdom." "Information must be gathered on the situation of the tax collector, that of the judge, the military commander, and the head of civil administration." "For . . . if the minister does ill . . . the kingdom is delivered to troubles and agitation."[7]

Andijan residents seemed almost to hope that their local officials were running amok. For in that case, they had a chance of obtaining recourse. Many had been convinced that Karimov was on his way to provide it: to listen to their side of the story and to discipline his offending subordinates.

Instead, his troops shot the townspeople down.[8]

At the root of the turmoil was the drawn-out trial of two dozen local businessmen who had formed a community emphasizing solidarity and business integrity. They are believed to have been inspired by a jailed religious thinker named Akram Yuldoshev. In his twenties, he had briefly been part of an Islamist group with a strong presence in Central Asia called Hizb-u Tahrir. But Yuldoshev broke away from it around 1990, to begin preaching his own interpretation of Islam, which, if his writings are any guide, emphasizes the quality of believers' faith rather than the details of their practice.[9]

The businessmen, referred to collectively as the Akromiyya, were branded as militant extremists.[10] Their arrests were based on such charges as "attacks against the constitutional order" and criminal conspiracy.[11]

"I declare that according to information we have," pronounced Karimov at a press conference the day after the massacre, "they are a branch of Hizb-u Tahrir.

> Their ideas and goals, in fact, do not differ from HT's goals. Their final goal is to unite Muslims and set up a so-called Muslim caliphate, with all shari'a laws, which they preach. The first task was to overthrow the existing constitutional order, bring down the local authorities and then to establish the order.[12]

And yet the demands and grievances the demonstrators took turns venting at their makeshift podium that May 13 never referred to religion. What they referred to was corruption. According to one report, "People spoke about social and economic problems (lack of transparency, corruption in the government, unfair trials, abuse by police . . .)."[13]

The protesters used the session to confront some of the local officials they blamed for the abuses. "They brought the head of the prosecutor's office and the head of the tax department . . . to the podium," one witness told Human Rights Watch. The officials pleaded that they were ordered to do what they did. "The prosecutor said . . . he knew [the defendants] are good [people], but 'we can't do anything, we were ordered to do it [convict them], we are like puppets in the hands of the power.' The head of the tax inspectors also said they were compelled to do what the government ordered."[14]

Researchers differ as to how religiously conservative the Andijan businessmen and their families were. But the group clearly did seek guidance in religious reflection for how to conduct their affairs differently—at least within the bounds of their community—from the corruption of the prevailing system.[15]

The main challenge the accused seem to have posed to the Karimov government was not so much ideological as economic—and ethical.

> The defendants' businesses—which included furniture factories, business supply companies, bakeries, tailoring firms, construction companies, and transportation firms—employed thousands of

people in impoverished Andijan. . . . They established a minimum wage that exceeded the meager government-mandated wage, paid employees' medical expenses and sick leave, and provided free meals to staff.[16]

After interviewing refugees from Andijan, Alina,* an oddly soft-spoken investigator who would later be forced into exile for her work, concluded that "they had an honest business attitude, there was no corruption or bribery, and they were prospering. New businesses were joining the network; they were hiring more people, and they worked under a code of ethics."

"They kept their distance from political parties," affirms Alisher Ilkhamov, of the Open Society Foundations. "But they had a social network; they were doing charity work, addressing social issues. They would tax themselves, about twenty percent of their income, and devote the money to charitable goals."

Expenditures from the fund included: "paying for members' prescriptions or doctor bills, or helping them out in a financial crunch, providing medical supplies to the local hospital, or organizing a kids' soccer tournament."[17]

Akromiyya "was an alternative to the corruption system," says Ilkhamov. "At least in terms of how they treated each other. To survive, they sometimes had to give gifts to local authorities, but still, they represented a challenge to the regime's moral authority."

Alina deems that "if you are honest in Uzbekistan, if you don't want to take bribes, you are a threat. The government hated them for that. This group was gaining respect and the trust of local people. It was

---

* "Alina" is a fictitious name. Her research was cut short when information she was unearthing about the Karimov family's corrupt activities led to her arrest. She cannot pursue or openly discuss her work, even from abroad. When she was released from prison and allowed to flee Uzbekistan, she was warned that if she were ever to publicize her findings, her family would pay the price. Such warnings are not empty. Dissident Uzbek religious leader Obid Kori Nazarav was shot in the head February 2012, in the small Swedish town of Strömsund, where he lived in exile. In the summer of 2013, the seventy-one-year old father of Bahodir Choriev, a dissident who writes extensively on economic issues, was arrested and charged with rape.

spreading throughout Ferghana. The government thought that if let alone, it would grow in stature and power, and it could make a big political movement."

Human Rights Watch puts it this way:

> Operating outside the government-controlled banking system, the businessmen were beyond the usual levers of state control. In many areas of commerce and industry, they successfully undercut the market share of pro-government monopolies. They enjoyed the loyalty of thousands of employees who were generally paid better and had better working conditions than most others in Andijan. The entrepreneurs' popularity on these grounds presented a challenge to Uzbek authorities.[18]

What the Akromiyya's practices were implicitly challenging was a post-Soviet, Central Asian version of Mubarak's or Ben Ali's kleptocracy.*

In Uzbekistan, the flashy moneygrubbers who had suddenly appeared at the top of the pyramid were symbolized not by the aging dictator's son or his wife and her clan but rather by his oldest daughter, Gulnora Karimova. "She's the most hated person in this country," affirms a professional interpreter. U.S. officials agree. "The fear and loathing that many alienated businessmen in Uzbekistan have for her suggests that her life in a post-Karimov Uzbekistan would be less than secure," reads a 2008 diplomatic cable.[19]

Alina recounts a conversation with a businessman, himself notorious for less-than-straight dealing. "He told me: 'I hate Gulnora because she is the most greedy person and she took most of my businesses. When Karimov dies, we will put her in a cage and drive her around.' She has attracted so much hatred of businesses for her greedy, greedy ways."

---

* Of the other independent states that emerged from the Soviet Union and its dependencies, Azerbaijan probably resembles Uzbekistan most closely. Ukraine under Yanukovych, as well as Romania, present similar characteristics, though both display a somewhat more equal competition between competing kleptocratic networks than Uzbekistan. None of these, however, has a resource flow that resembles Uzbekistan's cotton monoculture. See pages 113–15 of this book.

Like Egypt's Gamal Mubarak or the Trabelsis in Tunisia, Karimova established herself as an unavoidable intermediary for major private investment in Uzbekistan, with an emphasis on the telecommunications sector. "Telecom was always her hobby," says Alina. "She was running the licensing department. The ministers were not really deciding."

In one of the most spectacular scandals to result from Karimova's practices, the Swedish-Finnish firm TeliaSonera, the main cell phone provider in the two Nordic countries, was under scrutiny for allegedly paying up to $400 million in bribes to obtain a license for its Uzbekistan-based subsidiary. Related probes for money laundering were launched in Switzerland and France, with police combing through suspect bank accounts and luxury properties.[20]

John Davy, a former chief financial officer for TeliaSonera's Uzbek subsidiary, told a Swedish documentary team that authorities would regularly interrupt phone service to pressure the company for additional payments.

> What happens is . . . down goes the switch, and all of a sudden we lose a hundred base stations. We would have thousands of subscribers screaming about why they don't have their service. So after two-three days we have to make a $100,000 payment to a charitable organization, of the choice of the—whoever. . . . We would pay our donation and up goes the base station again. This would happen every month.[21]

Many such "charities" are operated by Karimova, who as early as 2005 had "established a network of three umbrella grant-making institutions to disburse a wide range of social, cultural, and educational programs."[22] One woman, herself an NGO administrator, told me in early 2013: "My mother wanted to start a small business, a shop with two employees. The tax authorities told her she had to contribute to Karimova's 'charity,' and then she obtained her authorization."

"The picture you get," says Swedish reporter Fredrik Lauren, who coproduced the TeliaSonera documentary series, "is that Gulnora owns the telecom sector. To save labor, she and her cronies established a kind of blueprint for all investors: Beeline, VimpelCom, MTS. Gulnora says,

'Yes you can get a ticket—for twenty-six percent of the company, and a compulsory sell-back for a fixed price.'"

TeliaSonera CEO Lars Nyberg, who resigned in the midst of the scandal, insisted that the payments the company made to Karimova were investments in local industry, not bribes. "Of course!" retorts Lauren. "That's why they structure it this way. So it all looks very businesslike. But the money doesn't deliver anything except the right to play."

Gulnora Karimova mastered the art of "circumventing law by law."

Along with telecoms, ritzy restaurants and bars were also her domain. Tashkent residents told me the best restaurants and nightclubs in the city were divided between Gulnora and her younger sister Lola, who also shares her sister's interest in fashion. With a guilty start, upon hearing this, I checked the label of an elegant if overpriced jacket sewn from a renowned local weave of yellow and burgundy silk, which I had bought in a shop inside the best traditional restaurant in Tashkent. Sure enough, the label read "Lola."[23]

When Alina was arrested and had to flee Uzbekistan, she was looking into Karimova's apparent involvement in another kind of nightlife: the trafficking of women for sex. "She became very close to a prince from the United Arab Emirates, who used to go to Uzbekistan to hunt. She would host him. Then she started a travel agency that would take charge of obtaining visas for tourists from the former USSR traveling to the Gulf. It was a cover for trafficking."

Alina recalls that one day when she was at the airport to meet her uncle, she was startled by the allure of passengers boarding a Dubai flight. She queried a friend in customs and border control. "I asked him, 'Is there a fashion show or something in Dubai?' Ninety-five percent of those passengers were beautiful women, younger than me."

Alina's friend shot back a "Don't you know?" and led her outside on the pretext of taking a cigarette break. "He told me that flight was part of Karimova's prostitution business." She began checking with tourist company managers and discovered that many had recently lost their licenses, as Karimova tightened her grip on the industry.

To be rapacious and usurp the goods and the women of his subjects, that is above all else what will make [the prince] hateful.

Part of what may have made Karimova's behavior especially hateful to Uzbeks was the shock it delivered to sensibilities still influenced by the vestiges of a communist ideal. That ideal, of shared resources and the subordination of personal ambitions to the needs of the many, may have been corroded with hypocrisy, but it had powerfully conditioned the outlook of millions of Soviet citizens for decades, including Uzbeks. And it had delivered a quite decent, and broadly comparable, standard of living across the far-flung USSR.

When the Open Society Foundations' Ilkhamov reflects on Uzbekistan's own moment when "everything changed," around the turn of the millennium, he describes the shift in those terms: "The elite was released from remaining checks left over from the culture of the Soviet period."

Gulnora Karimova was not alone at the summit of Uzbekistan's kleptocracy. As in other countries, rival networks seemed to respect an uneasy division of spoils. Gold, one of the country's main exports, belonged to President Karimov, according to numerous Uzbeks. Gulnora had telecoms. For its part, the powerful National Security Service (SNB) controlled exports and cross-border trafficking.[24] "The SNB takes a cut of every export," judges Marlene Laruelle, Central Asia expert at the Elliott School of International Affairs at George Washington University.

"I once watched an Uzbek officer get onto a truck on the Kyrgyz side of the border, ride across, then jump down," says Alina. "They have orders as to which trucks to check and which not to check. Not only do they not check them, they actively protect them." According to a U.S. Drug Enforcement Agency official working in the region, Uzbek authorities draw attention to drug trafficking into and through neighboring Tajikistan while facilitating trafficking themselves, especially via barge, across the Amu Darya River, which marks the border with Afghanistan.

As in Egypt, public tenders represent a significant revenue stream. "All the stadiums, all the sporting complexes they build are a government racket," asserts a local journalist, who insisted we meet in a nondescript chain restaurant, also citing security concerns. A short man, his hair graying at the temples, he spoke in a persistently humorous tone, despite the pressures. "Local businesses have to donate materials and sometimes labor," he explains. "Hospitals are required to perform renovations every ten years. The director will submit a million-dollar repair budget, say, and the health minister will demand two hundred thousand dollars."

Uzbek cities—especially those that attract visitors, such as Tashkent, the capital, or Bukhara and Samarqand, legendary way stations on the historic Silk Road—give the odd impression of being built in layers. Lining the clean, well-maintained avenues are freshly painted new buildings, often in a classical Russian style. But behind them stand rows of Soviet-era apartment blocks, each more squalid than the last. The expropriation of property to make way for the new buildings is a source of widespread consternation among city dwellers.

"I know of people who bought their apartments, but the buildings were torn down shortly afterward and the land was transferred to private developers close to Karimova," recounts one woman. "The government knew of the plans to destroy the buildings when it sold the apartments. Some people had heart attacks!" Compensation for seized property is widely agreed to be derisory.

Like their Afghan, Egyptian, or Tunisian counterparts, however, Uzbeks' most frequent contact with their kleptocracy is through everyday shakedowns, especially at the hands of the police. Doctors routinely require extra payment to provide service. And the education system had nearly everyone I met in fits. A driver told me he had to pay his children's teachers for grades; there was no way around it. A historian explained he had resigned his teaching position because he did not want to take bribes. And the journalist who asked to meet in the anonymous restaurant was wringing his hands that very day over whether to sell his car to secure a place for his son at a university.[25] Uzbeks have to pay bribes to get on the list to buy a new Chevrolet Spark or Cobalt—and sometimes just to receive their government salaries.

"No deed and no word is free of charge, no one keeps still except for a price."[26] John of Salisbury, as usual, nailed it.

As in other kleptocracies, those at the bottom of the Uzbek ladder are not committing such larcenies purely out of personal greed. They are locked into a system that requires them to pay off their superiors. It is the system that the whiteboard diagram at ISAF depicted: the money-flow arrow is pointed stubbornly upward.

Within this kleptocratic structure, the purchase of office is a key vehicle for the transfer of money from subordinate to superior. "Every government job is for sale," says George Washington University's Laruelle. "The prices are known. I have seen a neighborhood or village take up a collection to buy a young man's position in the police—so they would have one of their own 'inside.' Then the kid is doubly indebted: he owes a monthly kickback to his superior, and he has to reimburse his neighbors."

No general or judge, no commander or courtly official, not even a herald or huckster, is appointed except for a price.

"It's a very vertical system," confirms Alina. "Back in 2003, people were paying between two and three hundred dollars for a job in the traffic police—depending on where they were stationed. Checkpoints in neighborhoods with a lot of cars and wealthy people cost more than others. Then the precinct boss says, 'At the end of the month, pay me two hundred or three hundred or lose your job. I take your money because I'm under pressure from my boss.' So a certain proportion of the money they make every month they pay to their boss, and up and up all the way to the minister. And this is true in all sectors."

At General Motors, Alina asserts, which builds and sells the vast majority of the cars on Uzbek roads, bribes are paid to get on an expedited list to purchase a car and then are shared between local dealerships and the Agency of Automobile and River Transport, which sends a cut to the office of the first deputy prime minister in charge of economy and finance.

In Nizam al-Mulk's *Siyasat Nameh*, the Persian king Anushirvan wishes out loud that his father had rejected such corrupt gifts from underlings with some sizzling rejoinder like:

I have established for you, military commander or provincial governor, the sum that should suffice for your salary and that of your soldiers. I know you received that money. This surplus that you are presenting to me does not come, I'm sure, from your father's heritage. It comes from what you have illegally exacted from my subjects.[27]

Most Uzbeks believe the authorities also allow the taking and giving of bribes in order to collect violations—as in Tunisia—to hold over people's heads. Rustam,* a trade union representative in Tashkent, tells me, "There are so many taxes it is impossible to pay them all: payroll taxes, business income taxes, taxes for the equipment you maintain. . . . So people make a connection in the tax office to pay less. You employ ten people, but you say three. But then you've broken the law and they know it, and you are afraid of the government. The whole government is set up that way—to make you do wrong—so then they have you on a hook. And when they want"—Rustam leans back and jerks his hand upward, mimicking the gesture of a fisherman—"they yank you out of the water."

The doings of local officials—including their corruption—are carefully monitored from the top. The journalist in the chain restaurant describes regular nighttime video conferences between the prime minister and local officials, down to the district level: "They can use these sessions to dramatic effect. Sometimes they haul people off to jail, right on camera. They shout at people, insult them. It's a way to embarrass and intimidate them."

One feature that stands out in the Uzbek kleptocracy is its reliance on forced labor. The country's most important economic output, along with gas and gold, is cotton. Uzbekistan is among the world's top producers and exporters of the fiber, which, along with related industries, constitutes between 13 and 25 percent of GDP, according to estimates.[28] But oddly, the mechanization of the centrally controlled sector has *declined* since independence in 1991.

"In 2011 and 2012, they started calling more people up from the big cities" to work in the cotton fields, says trade union representative Rustam, "doctors and teachers—people from a level of society that is unsuitable to fieldwork." He himself was drafted. Asked what it was like, he emits a puff of disdain. "I paid someone to go."

"Parents understand they can pay to get their children out of it,"

---

* "Rustam" is also a fictitious name.

says Matt Fischer-Daly of the Cotton Campaign, a consortium of human rights groups advocating an end to forced labor in the Uzbek cotton industry. "They bring the money to the principal. They are told that it pays for someone else to go pick. But who knows?"

Millions are forced to work each year, for periods ranging from two to six weeks. Conditions are rudimentary—and the pretext for extracting more payments from the laborers. "If you don't want to stay in the dormitories or tents they provide," says Rustam, "you have to pay locals for a bed in their house and for transport to the fields. You're supposed to pick fifty kilograms of cotton per day, but no one can. You pay a fine, or you buy cotton from someone else."

"Businesses get a call from the mayor," confirms the reporter in the restaurant. "They're told to send five people to the cotton fields. Houses nearby have to make room for them to sleep. Restaurants have to send food."

Human rights advocate Elena Urlaeva observed the 2012 harvest. "Doctors, teachers, everyone who is paid by the state was sent to Jizzakh by train. The orders go down from the prime minister to the governors and mayors. One person out of six in a given office has to go. Sometimes they stop drivers on the road and make them pick for a few hours. In 2012 all high school students were called up, about one million kids."

A U.S. embassy official visited a military academy for noncommissioned officers in the fall of 2011. "There was no one there. They were all out picking cotton!"

As the angry William of Pagula put it to England's Edward III in the fourteenth century: "They made the servants of Christ work day and night in your service . . . if [the people] had another head, they would rise up against you."[29]

Urlaeva suggests that the recent increase in adult cotton harvesters may be a result of international human rights campaigns targeting child labor: "There were fewer cases of children in the fields last year. They've been replaced by adults, by teachers and doctors. It shows that international attention has some impact, anyway."[30]

And it is not just the conscripted laborers who suffer from the government control of the cotton sector. Farmers are squeezed almost as painfully, by means of some holdovers from the Soviet economy.

"All land in Uzbekistan belongs to the government," says the journalist. "Farmers only rent it. They get a quota for how much cotton they must produce. And instead of bank loans for agricultural inputs, the government deposits advances on the purchase price in a bank account in tranches. For fertilizer, for machinery, and for labor at the time of harvest. Then the farmer has to sell his cotton at the government rate. At the end of the year, he breaks even at best."

Many Uzbeks speak of farmers grown desperate, of suicides, or migration to Russia or Kazakhstan.[31]

Two consortia of gins buy raw cotton from farmers, says the Cotton Campaign's Fischer-Daly, and three majority state-owned organizations control exports: Uzprommashimpeks, Uzmarkazimpeks, and Uzinterimpeks. "No one knows who owns the 'private' shares of these companies. And the proceeds of the sales are not transparent."*[32]

Unlike Egyptians, with their patriotic tolerance for military abuses, few Uzbeks have kind words for any of the networks that make up their country's kleptocracy. And yet they are not actively protesting it. As human rights activist Surat Ikramov remarks, young people are staying away from groups like his.

Where they are going, he notices, is to the mosque. "I live right by the Hast Imam mosque, and I watch people going to prayer. Most of them are between sixteen and thirty years old. People are becoming devoted because they are more and more frustrated with the government. They are turning to God for recourse."

"Definitely," the journalist concurs. "People are radicalizing because they are angry at the system. A polarization is taking place in this country."

Laruelle agrees. "Democracy and human rights groups are discredited," she says, "because they are connected in people's minds with the economic shock therapy after the fall of the Soviet Union."

Under pressure from the International Monetary Fund and Western economists brandishing the triumphalist free-market ideology of the Reagan-Thatcher era, new countries emerging from the Soviet rubble in

---

* For a diagram of the Uzbek kleptocracy, please see Appendix.

the 1990s abruptly canceled price supports and subsidies and auctioned off state-owned enterprises at fire-sale prices. The result, for most, was a dizzying plunge into economic misery, while others made off with the spoils.

Now "people are looking for social justice, not abstract concepts of democracy or human rights," says Laruelle.

The place where Uzbeks discuss such concrete issues that preoccupy them, she maintains, is in their prayer circles. "The only people who talk politics and social justice these days are the Islamists. They have legitimacy because of their works of charity. The argument they are making is that the regime is corrupt and unjust *because* it's secular. Such reasoning did not have much resonance in the past. Now it does."

Hizb-u Tahrir, for example, the Islamist group with which Karimov conflated the Andijan businessmen after the 2005 massacre, lashed out in a Web posting at a highly publicized visit by Gulnora to Kokand, an ancient Silk Road city on the road from Tashkent to the Ferghana Valley, in mid-2013.

> G. Karimova is at a loss after her thoughtlessness, her self-interested and greedy initiatives, and her dark deeds have become public knowledge, and led to a search of her house in France and an investigation of her subordinates in Switzerland. . . . For decades, her father along with his subordinates has . . . shamelessly drunk the blood of ordinary people [and] plundered the country's wealth. . . . Such savage and selfish humans must never be allowed to govern, otherwise the lives of the Muslims of this land will be intolerable.[33]

Michigan State University visiting professor Martha Brill Olcott—who has spent much of the past thirty years in the region—says the sentiment she derives from discussions with religious leaders is that "it's not possible to get at the problem of economic corruption except through spiritual purity."

Here again, corruption—an ambiguous word in every language, implying moral as well as material depravity—seems to nourish a turn toward religion, seen as the most powerful means to combat it.

IN THE FERTILE, conservative Ferghana Valley, drivers line up for hours to buy natural gas to fuel their cars, and women who weave silk do without heat in the winter because of chronic shortages—in this gas-producing country. Nevertheless, peace reigns. People prefer to gather for prayers, not in mosques, but behind the closed doors of their homes, to avoid attracting attention. Restaurants are required by law to serve alcohol, and some have received government subsidies to convert their family-style dining rooms into vaulted clubs with music that pulses deep into the night. The aim, according to residents, is to lure the youth away from religion. The Karimov regime is quick to label devout Muslims, or people who refer to religious principles to guide their conduct—like the Akromiyya businessmen—as radicals.

It's a characterization that may become a self-fulfilling prophecy, especially if used as a foil to shift attention toward cultural issues and avoid addressing underlying grievances.

Such radicalization may in fact be the objective. It would represent yet a further example of symbiosis between authoritarian regimes and religious extremism, as was visible in Russia during its 1990s conflict with separatist Chechens, in Algeria, or most recently, in post–Muslim Brotherhood Egypt. Entrenched kleptocracies may find it simpler to face off against violent extremists, who terrify their populations and the international community alike, and who can be killed as enemies, than to confront political or economic movements calling for deep-seated government reform.

As for frustrated Uzbeks, a virulent, exiled, jihadi group, more radical even than Hizb-u Tahrir, does exist. It is called the Islamic Movement of Uzbekistan (IMU), and is active in Afghanistan and Pakistan and other parts of the region. U.S. intelligence sources say that evidence recovered from Osama bin Laden's compound in Pakistan records a spate of Uzbek recruits and contributions to the IMU and Hizb-u Tahrir, in the wake of the Andijan massacre.

CHAPTER TEN

Variation 4: The Resource Kleptocracy

Nigeria, ca. 2014

I n Africa's populous giant, Nigeria, conservative Muslims are found not in the lush southern valleys but in the dry and gradually desertifying north. Among the oldest cities in West Africa is Kano, on the fringes of this zone. Its dense, vibrant core once cinched together trade routes crossing the habitable lands on the southern edge of the Sahara with those leading north to the centers of thought and industry on the Mediterranean. Today, in that compact old-city hub, stalls at ground level and suspended overhead on a kind of open-air scaffolding overflow with bright-hued bolts of the region's famous fabrics. Men wear straight-sided caps and flowing robes of lightweight cotton, whose designs seem embossed on the glossy surface.

A remarkable religious diversity flourishes in this historic town. Christians and some animists make up a sizable minority of its population. As the night shift started in a small plastics factory on its outskirts, I sit with the owner, Ali Harisu Kadiri an-Nasiri, who is also the leader of one of the area's Sufi orders, as he describes his group's ritual veneration at the graves of holy men. We crane together over his cell phone to watch a video of members twirling in a characteristic Sufi dance.

Kano residents can distinguish among different Sufi orders by the configuration of their prayer beads; the practice of different groups emphasizes different sacred numbers. Most Kano Muslims are more conventional. According to an-Nasiri, it is only since about 2007 that fundamentalist Salafis have been a presence around town, taking over mosques and founding schools. After class, flocks of schoolgirls flutter home through the streets in their plumage of long uniform veils. Residents say parents patronize religious schools less out of ideological affinity than because they are cheaper and more professionally run than public schools.

Still, Kano residents, along with their neighbors in states across the Nigerian north, applauded the adoption of Islamic law, or shari'a, in 2000 for criminal as well as civil cases.

A dozen years later, on January 21, 2012, explosions tore through police stations, the state security service headquarters, and a few other administrative offices across the city. More than 150 people died. The group that claimed responsibility for the coordinated attacks is known as Boko Haram—roughly translated as "Western education is forbidden." Ritually forbidden, that is. Unclean.

This moniker categorizes Boko Haram in many Westerners' minds. Such violent Islamist extremists, many believe, are unlettered, backward, viscerally opposed to the intellectual achievements or cultural openness of Western society. About a year after the Kano attack, Boko Haram and a splinter faction known as Ansaru were designated as foreign terrorist organizations by the U.S. Department of State.[1] In 2014, the group horrified the world by sweeping down on a rural school, kidnapping nearly 300 girls, and melting away with them into the forest.

Boko Haram burst onto the international stage in the summer of 2009. Traveling to a funeral by motorcycle, the story goes, like a mechanized herd jostling down a dust-powdered road some three hundred miles east of Kano, members of a reclusive, puritanical community that openly admired the Afghan Taliban ran afoul of the state police. That was the day the police had chosen to enforce a law requiring motorcycle helmets. An altercation ensued. Shots were exchanged. And then came the carnage: more than a month of pitched battles across four Nigerian states, makeshift bombs, mass arrests, and summary executions. The deaths on both sides, and among passersby, numbered into the thousands.[2]

The CLEEN Foundation, which advocates for justice sector reform in Nigeria, has been researching the reasons for radicalization, especially among the youth, in the northeastern states. Its findings on the origins of Boko Haram suggest uncanny echoes of Uzbekistan. Boko Haram members, who followed the teachings of a charismatic preacher, taxed themselves, says CLEEN's Valkamiya Mary Ahmadu, much as the Akromiyya did in Andijan. But instead of using the money for social welfare purposes, "members could access the fund to found small businesses."

A common entry-level business endeavor in Nigeria is to set up as an *okada*, or motorcycle taxi. Buses that ply highways between cities leave riders off on the verge, where secondary roads join. A flock of motorcycles awaits to whisk passengers to their homes in nearby villages for a few cents a ride. Numerous members of the militant group took up this occupation. By forcing *okada*s to buy helmets for themselves and their passengers (or pay a bribe not to), the police were attacking the community's economic viability, CLEEN's research suggests.

Other experts say the group had been stockpiling arms for months, and the clash with the police was part of a deliberate move by local government to rein it in.

Still, even in a country whose very name has become synonymous at home and abroad with fraud and corruption, the Nigerian police are infamous for their excess. "They're worse here than in any other country I've worked in," says an experienced international rule of law practitioner.

"The police are like flies that settle on your arm," a civil servant in the Kano State government puts it. "You can't even see how many there are buzzing around, in the air, coming and going."

In a report entitled *"Everyone's in on the Game": Corruption and Human Rights Abuses by the Nigeria Police Force*, Human Rights Watch details the exactions. Ordinary Nigerians are "routinely subjected to police extortion," it concludes, as "an inevitable fact of everyday life." One trader is quoted as saying:

> When we put our goods on the ground to sell, the police say it's not allowed, that we have to pay them money to sell there. Other times they take our goods and ask us to pay to bail them out. This happens every day. . . . The police will chase you away until you pay them something. The police are not protecting us; they are fetching money for their own pockets.[3]

According to Kano residents, the police preside over the illicit trade in the town's bustling main market, extracting their cut from the sale of counterfeit medicine and other dangerous goods. They "frequently impound cars and motorcycles." They make victims of crimes pay for the write-up. "And even the pen," snorts Yunusa Zakari Ya'u, executive director of the Centre for Information Technology and Development. (*Neither work nor pen nor the various inks come without price.*)

"They arrest people, and don't take them to court. And they begin negotiating their release. Or there's a second way: the court orders your release, but the police bring you back to detention, and start negotiating." Or with a stubborn bargainer, they turn to torture to extract the money they're after.[4] They routinely board vehicles at improvised checkpoints on highways and city streets, to shake passengers down.[5]

In the eleventh-century Persian mirror *The Sea of Precious Virtues*, the tenth rule of kingship is to "restrain the hands of . . . mercenaries." The king must "protect the caravans on the highways," for "taking illegal imposts is just like brigandage and theft."[6]

Deputy Commissioner Muhammad Guri runs a specialized police bomb squad in Kano. It had not deployed in two years, he tells me, though the most recent suicide blast in the city dated back only three months. To reach his cramped office—where a young aide in civilian clothes reclined in an armchair, feet up on his boss's desk, shouting into a cell phone for some time before sauntering out—I had to get past a desk downstairs. The initial reaction of the two officers behind it, the ingrained reflex, was to delay. It reinforced their power, placed me in a position of need.

Guri helped lead a multiyear U.K.-financed community policing initiative, which included meetings with initially reluctant neighborhood leaders and a hotline for complaints. What was hardest, Guri acknowledges, was "to change the mentality of our men. They joined the police to make money." After a high point in 2007, the program flagged around 2009, he says, when the foreign funding ended. The Nigerian government never mainstreamed the training and procedures the program piloted.

This is the environment in which Boko Haram launched its campaign of attacks on the police. Even among Nigerians who disapprove of the group's aims, the violence elicits a degree of approval. "When they attacked police stations," says Ibrahim Aliyu Nassarawa, the chairman of the Kano State bar association, "people were happy. They didn't join, but they were happy."

VENALITY hardly stops at the police in Nigeria.

The first tipping point on the road to acute, systemic corruption, says former Global Fund for Peace president Pauline Baker, who lived there for decades, came in the 1980s. That was when the oil boom began. "There was military rule, meaning no accountability, and then free money from oil."

Nigeria is a case study in what has come to be called the "resource curse." Valuable raw materials are discovered in a country lacking robust institutional safeguards, and the "rents" these resources produce rupture any contract between rulers and ruled. Quality of life changes negligibly, or even negatively, for regular people, despite the bonanza. At roughly two and a half million barrels of crude per day, Nigeria is the world's thirteenth-largest oil producer and the largest in Africa. (The United States imports some 40 percent of the country's production.) But Nigerians' life expectancy, educational achievement, and average income, taken together, is about the same as that of their resource-poor neighbors.[7]

Official oil revenues are split between the federal government on the one hand, and the thirty-six state and more than seven hundred local government executives on the other.[8] This downward distribution of national revenue contrasts with Afghanistan's system, in which provincial governors receive almost no share of the national budget, but get carte blanche to extract resources at their own level however they want.

Not all of Nigeria's oil revenues make it into the official budget, though. On January 20, 2014, Nigerian finance minister Ngozi Okonjo-Iweala announced that nearly $11 billion earned from the sale of crude between January 2012 and July 2013 was missing from the federation account. "We must see the justification, with receipts where the money has been spent," declared the former World Bank managing director.[9] A month later her colleague, Central Bank governor Lamido Sanusi, was fired. In testimony before the Nigerian senate, he had estimated the missing funds at closer to $20 billion. And, he later told the *New York Times*, he was beginning to investigate the private banks that he suspected of laundering the money.[10]

This leakage of national wealth is typical, attests the MacArthur Foundation's Kole Shettima. "There are always shortfalls in the federation accounts. It's a permanent fight between the Finance Ministry and the Nigeria National Petroleum Corporation—where the real issue is. It's a big cartel feeding off the backs of the people."

In the view of a Western official in the capital, Abuja, Nigerian president Goodluck Jonathan "has not been as clever as his predecessors. He and his circle have been taking too much oil money before it gets into the budget." Another high-ranking Western diplomat remarks sardonically that the oil minister, Diezani Alison-Madueke, is "just doing her job—providing Jonathan with money." An official at a different embassy, who monitors the oil producing south, dubs her "Jonathan's ATM."

Nor is this off-budget money the only loss of Nigeria's oil revenues. Former members of government, according to several Nigerians, receive a block of oil rights upon retirement, to sell as they wish.[11] They often use the cash to sponsor others to run for political office—who are expected to pay back the favor with interest.

Then there's "bunkering." That's the wholesale theft of crude oil as it flows between the wells where it is extracted and the tankers waiting offshore to carry it to foreign buyers. In the romantic image, small-time local thieves tap into the tangle of oil pipes snaking through the swamplands of the Niger Delta and refine the pilfered crude in barrels deep in the tropical jungle.

But such small-scale Robin Hood theft is the least of the problem. "This is not a hammer-and-chisel job," says the Western embassy official who monitors the Nigerian south. "It's very sophisticated siphoning. This can only be the work of industry people. It's too technical. People get a slot. The security services allow it."[12]

"The state is part of the illicit siphoning," concurs an oil company official.

"This has moved so far beyond bunkering, you wouldn't believe," says one of the most distinguished American scholars of Nigeria, who knows many of the key players personally. "These are government enterprises. Everyone in a position of authority signs off. Oil is diverted by the barge-load." The military too, which by law protects the pipelines, "is up to the eyeballs in oil theft."[13]

Indeed, such majors as Shell and Italy's ENI began temporarily shutting down pipelines in 2013, wherever significant siphoning was detected. "The scale of these activities has reached unprecedented levels," wrote Shell Nigeria chairman Mutiu Sunmonu in a company report, calling the theft "a parallel industry."[14]

Nigeria does not convert its own crude into consumer products, moreover. The country's four refineries languish in disrepair. The government imports fuel from abroad and sells it at a subsidized rate—another opportunity for corrupt scams.

Given the unique opening that oil, like other types of mineral wealth, provides for centralizing production and capturing the resulting wealth, it is perhaps unsurprising that other segments of the Nigerian economy have been allowed to wither.[15]

In a country where rains lash much of the territory for half the year and seeds need merely to be scattered to grow—the envy of a parched place like Afghanistan—the diversity and productivity of Nigeria's agriculture have plummeted since the 1960s. At that time, it was an agricultural exporter; now it imports basic foodstuffs, its overall productivity barely higher than what it was a half century ago. And according to the Nigerian government's own figures, public investment has been "exceptionally low," even by African standards.[16] Underinvestment in transportation infrastructure and power generation has also damaged the food industry.

Innovators in a sector that still absorbs most of the country's manpower crave the least sign of official encouragement. The eyes of a taxi driver in the capital, Abuja, who had graduated college in agriculture, lit up as he described the business he dreamed of founding: a closed-system farm, where he would produce high-quality meat for Abuja's upscale hotels and restaurants, by planting soy for oil and feeding the nourishing stalks to the cattle. He had a plan all mapped out but could not obtain a loan at less than a crippling 26 percent interest rate.

Nigeria's manufacturing, like Egypt's, has also largely died out—

victim, say residents, of privatization to cronies under pressure from the IMF, and customs and tariff regimes designed for members of the kleptocratic networks to work around. The Kano State civil servant took me on a tour of shuttered factories and warehouses: Bata shoes, an electronics factory, despairingly empty.*

The result of this oil "monoculture" is a winner-take-all economy, in which unemployment and penury rise steadily, while political office guarantees a space at the Nigerian version of Tunisia's feeding-trough state. The *official* salary of a senator tops one million U.S. dollars per year. With such fabulous sums in play, Nigerian politics has become a blood sport.

For in the view of most Nigerians and country experts, the second tipping point on Nigeria's path to kleptocracy was—ironically—its conversion to civilian rule in 1999.

Competition can be gruesome. Just to be designated a political candidate costs money—some $10 million for a recent election for state governor, estimate local observers of Nigeria's political economy. "Godfathers," often former officials who amassed a corrupt fortune when in power, sponsor a client to run for office by covering the fee, on the expectation of rich dividends after a successful campaign.

Then come the expenses of the campaign itself—and of ensuring the results. Candidates, or their godfathers, arm and pay urban youth gangs to rough up opposition rallies. Or office seekers collude with extremist groups for this purpose—Christian or Muslim or animist or some combination.[17]

Or the police may be rented to serve as enforcers. "The governor pays the police commissioner to 'protect' him during the election," says the Abuja taxi-driver-cum-agricultural-engineer. "If he's not getting enough votes, the police kidnap the box and they print ballot papers."

If his candidate wins, "the godfather gets access to the state coffers.

---

* The country whose resource-based kleptocratic model may most closely parallel Nigeria's is Algeria, also an oil state, formerly a military dictatorship; minority Berbers provide some of the cultural diversity that is even more remarkable in Nigeria. Like Nigerian government officials, suspected of colluding with violent groups, including Christian rebels in the Delta as well as Muslims in the north, the Algerian government has long been thought to pay off or incite violent Islamists.

Often he is the one who appoints the directors of key departments," concludes the director of a local NGO working in the democracy-building and justice sector.[18]

Presidential voting in 2007 and in 2011 (especially the aftermath), was marred by paroxysms of violence, as youth "cults" or militias, often outlandishly garbed and paid and equipped by political bosses, attacked candidates, election officials, houses, schools, churches, and mosques. Hundreds died during and after both elections.[19]

In this context, it is no wonder that many Nigerians—who gained the right to vote so recently—are increasingly disgusted by the electoral process. "I don't vote," says Ruth, a determined young woman with the heart-shaped face and curved eyebrows of a Buddha, who cleans houses for a living.* "Why stand on line for people who are just enjoying themselves? Their perfume is fresh and their hair is wet, and they don't help with a better road or education for our children. I'd rather sit in my house and drink a glass of juice."

Still, while the disgust is palpable, and the dramatic political violence—often laced with sectarianism—grabs international headlines, Nigerians direct much of their ire not at elected officials but at the civil service.

"We call them 'evil servants.'" The CLEEN Foundation's executive director, Kemi Okenyodo slaps at a newspaper on her desk, where the latest scandal, the aviation ministry's $1.5 million purchase of armored BMWs that were never delivered, is plastered across the front page. "Politicians can't navigate the terrain without the civil servants."

"The civil service is more corrupt than the politicians," echoes Shettima.

"The worst," concurs the Kano bureaucrat, "is the civil service. Politicians can't do anything without the civil service."

For while billions in off-budget oil money may go directly to Jonathan and a few cronies at the top of Nigeria's kleptocratic system, vast oil revenues do make it into national coffers and, by way of the allocation system, down to the states. Once the money is thus integrated into offi-

---

* The name "Ruth" is fictitious.

cial budgets, the best way to siphon it off is through the complex public procurement process. Venal functionaries—cut from the same cloth as the Alexandria engineer, Gamal the Thief—draft fraudulent contracts for unnecessary projects. The documents are deftly designed to favor select contractors and to inflate costs. In this way, instead of contributing to economic development or education, public spending is hijacked for private gain.

"Let's say Kano State is going to build a health facility," explains Ya'u of the information technology NGO, which works on budget accountability. Funds for the project come from Kano's share of the oil money. "The minister suggests the design. He puts it out for tender. That's where the corruption takes place. The ministry draws up the bill of quantities—that's done by the technical people, the commissioner. The bill is padded. There's money for the permanent secretary, for members of his or her family, and for higher levels we don't see. A contractor is called. 'I'll give you this contract. The job will cost 50 million. But I've budgeted 150 million.' Often a bid is not necessary. In some cases the contracting companies that win the bid belong to the commissioner himself. The contractor is told: 'We will give you 50 million.' You, the contractor, sign for 150, and return the balance to the commissioner. Then, knowing the greater amount of money has gone to others, you want to maximize your profit. So you deviate from the plan. You do substandard work. You know nobody's checking."

"People leave people inside the bureaucracy when they retire, to help them get contracts." Ruth, the housekeeper, provides real-world detail. "Sometimes marriages are made for this purpose, to hide it at least a little. If the child's spouse who's in the civil service doesn't deliver, then there's a divorce."

Ruth's sister works in the defense ministry IT department, a good observation post. She walked me down a dilapidated ministry hallway, to a spare office. The plastic veneer on the cheap desks was cracked, the computers out of date. In a pained, low-pitched voice, she described a feeding frenzy.

"When it comes to a contract or a job that attracts money, only the director and the deputy director, and maybe one other person, have knowledge of the real terms of the deal. The electronic copy shows something different. No contract is awarded without someone inside. If someone unconnected brings a proposal, the insiders can rearrange it in their own way, make it sound like their idea. Then they call in a contractor they can get their share from. Every minister checks the money on a project first—not its usefulness. If it's 10 million, the director says, 'Make it 12 million.' Procurement will say, 'Make it 15 million.' And the permanent secretary says, 'Make it 25.' This is so common now that everyone is looking for an avenue to get something out of everything. You have to get your own portion."

Such an atmosphere prevails in almost every structure, large or small.

"There are supposed to be four students per dormitory room," says Muhammad Aliyu, who teaches economics at Bayero University in Kano. He and dozens of colleagues were on strike to protest conditions. "Right now they are packing them in, ten to sixteen per room. For each bed space, budgeted at four million *naira* [about $25,000], you can buy a small house! We are teaching four hundred to six hundred students per class, especially in sought-after subjects like economics, math, and chemistry. The wealthy don't even bother. They're all sending their children outside to study."

I watched a hospital charge Ruth more than ten dollars for the saline solution that an intern dabbed on the badly injured hand of her three-year-old son. Stitches would have ruined her. The official-looking receipt the receptionist provided did not match the sums demanded at check-in and listed the saline solution as "medicine."[20]

As for the banks, "they give money to their cat and dog," says Ya'u. "That's why there's so much scandal in the banking sector, why so many banks have collapsed." That's for the connected elite. Nigeria's official interest rate is 12 percent, and banks routinely double it for ordinary customers. Those ordinary customers are charged for every deposit, transfer, or withdrawal they make.

"Civil society" has structured itself just as assiduously to snap up development dollars. "Government Operated NGOs" (GONGOs)[21] capture a resource stream that includes oil-funded public welfare spending but also international development assistance. On my arrival in Abuja, a customs agent named Godsgift Nwoke Opusunju slipped me her card and a promise of help should I ever need any. One side recorded her position with the customs authority. The other advertised her NGO, Rescue and Counseling International. "State governors open up NGOs to get their hands on the money," says a Kano businessman who studied in the United States. "You're not supposed to have an NGO—you're the governor!"[22]

Jobs in such GONGOs—or the civil service—are not easy to get. The type of specialized position that provides scope for contract fraud requires a college degree.

It is in this context that many Nigerians say Boko Haram's vilification of "Western education" should be understood—at least in the early years. "The system of going to school and getting a job in the civil service and skimming off contracts—that's what they're angry at," says the Kano businessman. "We all feel that way. We're all frustrated. If they had taken a secular approach, all Nigeria would be with them."

CLEEN Foundation's Kemi Okenyodo agrees. "Boko Haram initially had the principle of kicking back against the corruption in the state. It wasn't against Western education per se. Western education was seen as a tool for corruption, for oppression."

Muhammed Tabiu, a Kano lawyer and deputy program manager for a Nigeria-wide access-to-justice project called J4A, sees the movement within the historical context of the region's desire for shari'a law. "We've had shari'a law here historically. But under colonial rule and even afterward, those courts were seen as the courts of the people in power. In 2000 the people wanted 'our' shari'a courts. The whole agitation for shari'a was a search for a solution to corruption. You can't get a fair deal. You have to bribe. The law itself is alien. You can't get justice. People felt that *boko*—Western education that traced back to the mechanics of colonial rule—was the way we got to this state of affairs."

Indeed, Western Africanists and residents of countries from Nigeria to South Africa alike deplore what they see as a pattern: that post-independence elites seem to have left much of the structure of colonial-era administration intact, just taking over as beneficiaries of the oppressive and extractive system in positions left vacant by the departed colonizers.

Kano bar association chairman Nassarawa agrees with Tabiu: "When they say shari'a, they aren't just talking about legal technicalities. They mean politics, economics, social justice."

Ya'u puts his analysis in almost identical terms: "It was political shari'a: people saw that the injustice was simply too much. Corruption was everywhere, and no development. People thought that if they implemented shari'a, corruption would be cleaned out. People will cut off their hands. But then they saw the criminals still had their two hands." The criminals in government, that is. "They said, 'We need more.' Then you switch to violence."

For Tabiu too, the disappointing results of the 1999–2000 shari'a movement contributed to the emergence of Boko Haram. "The shari'a that was implemented then was the same structure, just with a new name. It was the same personnel, the same judges, the same staff, the same culture. Some will search for a legitimate way to fight this outcome. They will work for reform. But some say, 'Whatever tweak you make to this system will not work. You have to overthrow it entirely, bring some pure, pristine system in its place.'"

IT'S NOT JUST Nigerian Muslims who look for relief to a "pure, pristine" moral system. On nearly every street corner, from the swankest neighborhoods of Abuja, to the slums on its outskirts, to outlying villages that peck and bathe their feathers in the savanna dust, an innumerable assortment of evangelical Christian churches advertise Bible readings and Sunday services. The animists that historically inhabited the southern half of the country have been converted in droves.

At the Mountain of Fire Miracles Ministries, on an early November Sunday in 2013, a well-dressed orderly stopped me at the gate and signaled me to remove my silver earrings before entering, as well as the small white-gold necklace I inherited from my grandmother. I knew not to wear trousers but did not realize such accoutrements were considered immodest—as many Muslims consider the display of women's hair to be immodest.

The cavernous, three-story cement building was packed with parishioners seated in rows of white plastic seats. Women wore long skirts and jackets in vivid batiks, with matching swaths of cloth wrapped in complex origami-like folds around their heads. Two video screens allowed those of us at the back of the second floor to watch the preacher as he strode the stage below us, flanked by a UN-style array of international flags, declaiming his message about "Breaking the Power of Satanic Delay." Like a call-and-response chant, his words were translated line by line from English to Hausa.

"The time for your advancement has come," he cried. "And no one can stop it." The men and women around me, crisp in their Sunday clothes, leaped to their feet, their teeth gritted, their heads swaying back and forth in emphatic negation. Elbows flexed, fists clenched, they beat the air in tight motions. "Your Father in heaven . . . He cannot be pocketed. He cannot be manipulated. Nobody can poison his mind against you."

Many of the preacher's analogies employed the everyday vocabulary of corruption. "Satanic delay is what I want to call demonic adjournment. The case is so straightforward. The case is so clear. A primary court could judge it. Then somebody look at the case: 'Okay, I adjourn this case for another three months.' And that is the end. What is satanic delay? A means put forward by the Enemy to hinder us."

Or satanic delay is "when the Enemy place a stop-work order on the building of life. Like a contractor who borrowed money from the bank to start the construction. Bank money is on interest. And somebody place a stop-work order on that project. Interest is growing daily. And we are running around: 'Please, please don't let me die!' Oh, Lord!!" The preacher was roaring now: "Let him that want to frustrate my efforts as I pursue my destiny be frustrated by fire!! . . . Enemy of my fulfillment! I am praying on this mountain today! Wherever you are! Be disgraced! Be disgraced. Be disgraced. Be disgraced. The Lord destroy you today! Scatter by fire!!"

Asked afterward why they had selected this particular church to join, parishioners described obstacles in their lives of the type that the sermon had highlighted. One young man said he had been the first in his family to apply to college, but for flimsy reasons, he was not admitted. "The church correctly identifies the problem," he said. "It tells the truth. The enemy camp kept me from getting admission." Another worshipper praised the church for making him "tarry in prayer." He was an ophthalmologist and had wanted to launch a free vision-screening program in his neighborhood. The project would have cost about $1,000. Though some department directors favored it, he said, the council chairman refused. "The Enemy created an obstacle for me," the man concluded.

Like Salafi Muslims, many Nigerian Pentecostal churches emphasize the puritanical lifestyle required of members: no smoking or alcohol; no trousers or bare shoulders or jewelry for women. Another parallel with militant Islamists is the pressure these churches place on their own faith communities. Contrary to its reputation, Boko Haram does not aim the bulk of its attacks against Christians. Rather (apart from the police), its primary targets have been members of the Muslim elite: state governors, traditional emirs, or men in the mold of an-Nasiri, the Sufi leader in Kano, whom the group sees as co-opted and insufficiently Muslim. Similarly, evangelical churches reserve their harshest censure for fellow evangelicals. Members of the Deeper Life Bible Church, says Ruth, cross the road rather than associate with a woman wearing earrings or trousers: "They see you as a sinner or an unbeliever. Even if they see you going to church, they say your church isn't good enough."

Such puritanical focus on personal behavior has increased in recent decades, as corruption metastasized beyond the confines of officialdom to infect nearly all Nigerians' behavior.[23] When a vegetable seller is off saying his afternoon prayer, the man covering for him jacks up the price of a basket of onions by 20 percent, admitting with a grin, "That's how I profit." If a restaurant employee finds her friend a job swabbing the kitchen, she expects a monthly kickback on the salary. "We poor are causing problems for the poor," laments Ruth's sister, who works in the defense ministry. "We can't challenge the rich, or steal from them. The rich can use the law and their power to intimidate us. They can call a policeman to beat us. But we can't use the law against them, because they have money and they can buy the law. So we have to steal from the poor."

"Corrupt and corrupting," Shettima sums up the atmosphere in Nigeria today.

Such generalized ethical collapse encourages militant groups on both sides of the religious divide to preach personal morality as a cure for society's ills. "You purify yourself, then everybody will, and then society will improve, and God will be happy with you," Ya'u in Kano explains the logic. A fervent member of the Mountain of Fire Miracles Ministries testifies: "Naturally, you change your way of behaving, of dressing. And if everyone changes their own way of dressing and behaving, there will be a change in the nation."

And yet many Nigerians have accused these churches, with their opulent pastors and well-dressed officers, of replicating the very corruption they were supposed to counter. "They are taking money from poor people and keeping it for themselves," says Ruth, explaining why she, the daughter of a pastor, no longer goes to church. "They are supposed to give that money to the poor. When you see the cars they have or the watches they wear . . ."

In the view of Ruth Marshall, an eminent U.S. scholar of Nigerian Pentecostalism, "one of the huge disappointments of the movement was the idea that you could change the nation by radically changing individuals. Changing the polity by changing individual morality failed." One consequence, she says, is an evolution in Pentecostal preaching. "Spiritual warfare is beginning to dominate. There is more and more violent language in prayer rallies, more imprecatory prayer."

That is precisely what I was hearing at the Mountain of Fire Miracles Ministries. The pastor, unlike his counterparts in Boko Haram, never specified what Enemy he was talking about. He stopped short of urging his congregants forth against any particular structure or system or institution—or against any ethnic or religious community.

But to me, he seemed only a breath away. As I stood, surrounded by several thousand foot-stamping, fist-shaking worshippers, a jolt of fear passed through me at the raw power of the violence in the air.

Many Nigerians believe the political elites are deliberately trying to give that violence a sectarian cast, as the country is increasingly described in north vs. south, Muslim vs. Christian terms. The elites, say ordinary Nigerians, are the only ones with anything to gain in such a contest. The poor suffer equally no matter who is in power.

"The impulse toward a radical response to the abusive political economy is being diverted by politicians and religious leaders" and directed toward members of the other religious community, says Kano bar chairman Nassarawa. "The people have a common enemy. They are all victims. But the politicians want to prevent them from finding their common interest. So they go to a mosque or a church or a political group and tell them to fight against the 'other.'"

"The anticorruption message is being misrepresented and sold to the south as a sectarian thing, as north versus south," agrees Muhammad Mustapha of Democratic Action for Good Governance, "so the south won't have solidarity with the north."

Nigeria, profuse with colorfully diverse communities, displays a curious consistency, beneath that mottled surface. Acute, systemic public corruption, an affliction suffered by all, is eliciting remarkably similar responses across different belief systems. But given the radical form these responses are taking; given the lack of restraint in manipulating them—by Nigerian elites as well as foreign terrorist groups; and given the atmosphere of increasing desperation that drives people to extremes, Nigeria is starting to resemble some poorly tended makeshift refinery deep in the Delta swamp. It is fixing to explode.

CHAPTER ELEVEN

Up a Level

Afghanistan and Washington,
June 2010–January 2011

The Arab uprisings and my explorations of other kleptocracies were still in the future on the night of June 23, 2010, when I was sitting in the plywood hooch of the RC-South commander, General Nick Carter, at Kandahar Airfield. Transfixed by the screen of his desktop computer, I was reading the news out loud.

A magazine article had detonated like a rocket-propelled grenade in Washington. It depicted the command climate in the headquarters of my former boss, General Stanley McChrystal. The very first page was strewn with juvenile behavior and remarks attributed to his cocky young aides, dissing a who's who of civilian dignitaries.

Events were cascading. McChrystal had tendered his resignation—a second four-star general to be shattered on the anvil of Afghanistan. Scanning the latest, I let out a shout. General David Petraeus was being asked to step down from his position running U.S. Central Command, which had authority over the Iraq and Afghanistan theaters and most of the Middle East and Central Asia. He was being sent to Kabul to run the war.

I knew Petraeus. I had been corresponding with him about corruption and the insurgency in Afghanistan for nearly two years. He had referred to the Karzai government as a "criminal syndicate" during the White House policy debate on Afghanistan the previous fall.

When I had left McChrystal's headquarters five months before, I had given up hope that the United States would seriously address Afghan governance. But maybe there was a chance for a change of policy after all. I could feel my engines start revving again. I had just been appointed special assistant to the chairman of the Joint Chiefs of Staff, Admiral Mullen. With his approval, I stayed on in Afghanistan to help Petraeus transition in. I fell in with a handful of civilians from Washington think tanks he invited to join him in Kabul.

I remembered a couple of them from the swarm that had descended on the McChrystal headquarters a year earlier to conduct his strategic review. Upon their arrival, they had immediately been struck by the lack of progress addressing the "crisis in confidence" in the Afghan government they had identified then.

Petraeus dubbed us his "Directed Telescopes." The group included the rotund and amicable Fred Kagan, of the American Enterprise Institute, a powerful framer of arguments, and his tiny, bespectacled, secrecy-obsessed wife Kim, who ran her own think tank called the Institute for the Study of War. There was intense Catherine Dale, with her riot of red hair, who had worked as special adviser to McChrystal's long-limbed, Afghanistan-savvy operational commander. And for the first couple of weeks, the Brookings Institution's Steve Biddle, and Max Boot of the Council on Foreign Relations, were there too. Four "Junior 'Scopes," as we called them, were brought in later, research assistants in their twenties—perhaps the most productive members of the team.

The gaggle of us set up newsroom style in one of those tin-can buildings and, in an atmosphere of ebullient intellectual energy, plunged in to designing a comprehensive governance strategy. Much of our work built on the foundations that had been laid by the Anti-Corruption Task Force. But the improved understanding of the real nature of the problem that had developed since then prompted some changes.

If corruption in Afghanistan was the work not of individual bad apples, for example, but of structured networks, then they had to be studied as such. "Malign Actor Networks," we called them at first, so we could have fun dreaming up slide titles like "How to Fight the MAN." The same tools that ISAF used to map and understand insurgent networks, or that police investigators had perfected in the battle against organized crime, must be applied to corruption. Who had what roles and responsibilities? What were the criteria for membership? How did a given network intersect with others? How did it overlay with other social groupings, such as tribes? What was the preferred revenue stream? Did the network go after customs and tariffs? Smuggle natural resources? Monopolize logistics or security contracts? Construction? Land? How did the network transfer money? What logistics did it require? What means of coercion did it use? How did the leadership cover its tracks? What were key members' "patterns of life"—daily habits that might be exploited? What were the network's vulnerabilities? How did it adapt to pressure?

The Junior 'Scopes were assigned to compile a detailed list of intelligence collection and assessment requirements on the basis of questions like these.

We made clear that painful trade-offs would be necessary to gain the required knowledge. We called, explicitly, for the transfer of intelligence resources away from the task of tracking insurgents—such as the emplacers of roadside bombs that killed soldiers—and their assignment to the effort to understand the MAN.

We rearticulated many of the ideas for countering corrupt practices that had first been developed by the Anti-Corruption Task Force. Where the strategy broke new ground, however, was in its prescription for how best to prioritize targets. Rather than the bottom-up process the Anti-Corruption Task Force had initiated, with regional commands nominating and arguing for individual corrupt leaders against whom action should be taken, our group advocated a top-down, knowledge-based approach. A detailed understanding of the major corrupt networks and the interplay among them would permit a strategized, carefully sequenced plan of attack.

If a command decision were made to go after the Ahmed Wali Karzai network, for example, then potential repercussions throughout the system had to be thought through in advance. How would the rival Shirzai network react? Would it simply move in on the vacated territory? How could Gul Agha Shirzai be persuaded not to do that? Would it be politically useful to move against a different ethnic group's network at the same time as Ahmad Wali's, to fend off accusations of discrimination?

Actions to identify, reinforce, and physically protect constructive leaders, and to help empower truly independent local representative bodies, were also part of the plan. There had to be ways to help decent, upstanding, patriotic Afghans gain a foothold and thrive within institutions once they were cleared of the most corrupt operators.

We did not expect the MAN to take the assault we prescribed lying down. We predicted backlash ranging from withholding intelligence about Taliban to retaliation in kind against ISAF officials, including visa hassles or legal proceedings, or deft use of local and international media. Doubtless, Karzai would throw some of his famous tantrums. We warned of nastier reactions too, such as blockades of ISAF convoys at the border, or physical attacks on constructive Afghan officials or ISAF personnel.

Not every such blow could be parried. Still, we suggested some ways to mitigate the risks, such as preceding each move with a public information campaign, to prepare Afghans and Western voters alike and to undermine Karzai's ability to play on their sensitivities. Or deploying ISAF's own personnel to protect its flanks, instead of relying on local private security companies that belonged to corrupt officials. Or reducing the international troops' consumption of heavy luxury goods that had to be trucked in via long, vulnerable convoys.

By mid-July we had compiled our thinking into an enormous PowerPoint presentation—fully forty-eight slides. We put in for a meeting with Petraeus and started whittling it down. We were expecting an office call: the four remaining Directed Telescopes clustered around the stout wooden table that abutted his desk. We selected about a dozen slides we thought he truly needed to see.

To our surprise, Petraeus scheduled the briefing for the main conference room in the headquarters' stately Yellow Building. And he required the entire command group to attend. Petraeus himself walked the assembled brass through every slide in our deck, marking a check on each page with a flourish. In the pantomime of command, it was the highest form of official endorsement. We were elated.

As we discussed some minor revisions in his office a few days later, I heard Petraeus murmur something under his breath: "*This* is the revision of the Field Manual."

He was referring to an exposition of military doctrine that was selling in bookstores across the United States like a mass-market paperback: Field Manual 3-24, which laid out the tenets of counterinsurgency doctrine. Written in 2006 under the guidance of Petraeus and Marine General James Mattis, it had served as the theoretical underpinning for the troop surge into Iraq in 2007 and the altered approach that turned an impending debacle into what then, anyway, was viewed as a victory. Petraeus had led the turnaround and was a national hero.

FM 3-24 had seemed revolutionary when it first appeared, in the context of an Iraq conflagration that U.S. leadership was still stubbornly refusing even to call an "insurgency." But as students of asymmetric warfare soon began pointing out, Field Manual 3-24 only got U.S. military thinking back to where it had been at the end of the Vietnam War.

In the early 1970s the Marines were dispersing small "combined action platoons" into the Vietnamese countryside, embedding them in villages, in tandem with daring young aid workers, who were implementing small projects side by side with locals. It was a sharp contrast with the massive bombing campaigns against North Vietnam in the 1960s and Cambodia into the early 1970s. The U.S. military, by the end of the war, had more or less mastered the art of tactical-level counterinsurgency.

But that counterinsurgency approach remained close to the ground. It never addressed the South Vietnamese disgust with the elitist and corrupt government the United States had been backing. And that failure explains, in part, the loss of the war. Three decades later Field Manual 3-24 repeated the same error. As its title suggests, it was focused almost exclusively on how maneuver elements of U.S. forces should interact with residents and community leaders in the field.

But as long as U.S. military interventions and stabilization campaigns ignore the broader framework within which soldiers and aid workers are operating—or worse, as long as those interventions inadvertently enable host government abuses—then all the efforts by all the brave soldiers on a tactical level will add up to nothing. The unravelling of Iraq in 2014 is just the latest demonstration. It was time, Petraeus's musing implied, to take this reality into account. Soldiers, and not just those in Afghanistan, would have to begin considering governance. U.S. military doctrine had to embrace the issue.

That quiet remark rang like an oratorio in my ears.

The "Directed Telescopes" set off on a round of helicopter rides to brief subordinate commands on the new governance strategy. We'd arrive in a wash of dust thrown up by the chopper blades, weighted down by our regulation bulletproof vests. We'd dump our kit on bunk beds made of two-by-fours and troop off—round and short and flame-haired and mossy-eyed, trailed by our Junior 'Scopes—to some plywood conference room. Suspicious perplexity greeted us. Who were we anyway? On whose authority were we telling division commanders they'd have to upend their campaigns—reassign intelligence officers, overhaul procedures for partnering with Afghan military and police officers, expose their men to the risk of retaliation, wade into *politics*?

Fortified by that flourish that Petraeus had applied to his check marks, we stuck our chins in the air, imperious.

MEANWHILE an anticorruption operation was under way in Kabul. Just before dawn on July 25, 2010, an administrative assistant at the Afghan national security council named Muhammad Zia Salehi was led out of his home under arrest, on charges of selling his influence for the gift of a car valued around $20,000. Like income taxes in the Al Capone case, the bribery was just the crime that investigators could prove. In fact, Salehi appeared to be the bagman for a vast palace slush fund that President Karzai's closest intimates controlled and used to buy alliances, votes, or silence.

These discoveries had come to light as part of a sprawling investigation led by an old friend from Anti-Corruption Task Force days: sleepless, theatrically grumpy, meticulous Kirk Meyer of the DEA, one of the most talented officers in the U.S. law enforcement arsenal. He had told us corruption was only the third priority of his Threat Finance Cell and the special Afghan police unit it mentored, the Sensitive Investigations Unit (SIU), below terrorist funding and drug money.

True to its mandate, the SIU had dug into the workings of a major Kabul-based *hawala*, a traditional money-transfer operation, often used by extremists. Single threads soon lead to dense tangles. An unprecedented raid on the *hawala*'s offices in downtown Kabul reaped a huge trove of data. And the team struck a torrent of cash pumping out of Afghanistan's top private financial institution, the Kabul Bank. The resulting sinkhole was nearly a billion dollars deep—the result of $100,000 MasterCards handed out to select officials, directors' fat expense accounts, bribes for government tenders, and the kind of "nonreimbursable loans" that were then so common in Tunisia.[1]

Salehi's extortion of a set of flashy wheels was tangential to the Kabul Bank investigation. But the McChrystal headquarters and officials in Washington had asked Meyer to generate an anticorruption test case, so his team had compiled watertight evidence. The arrest was a coup. Watching from the sidelines, the Directed Telescopes crowed.

But before the sun set on that arrest, President Karzai had ordered Salehi's release. The boss had protected his underling. The implicit promise that structured the kleptocratic system had held.

Karzai was not bashful about his interference in the judicial process. "Absolutely I intervened. . . . I intervened very, very strongly," he boasted to ABC's *This Week* a month later. He was broadcasting the fact to members of his network—just as he had broadcast his promise not to remove any corrupt officials at that press conference after the arrest of the minor border police official the previous year. Karzai was advertising the strength of his protection guarantee.

He cited the conditions of the operation against Salehi:

> This man was taken out of his house in the middle of the night by thirty Kalashnikov-toting masked men in the name of Afghan law enforcement. This is exactly reminiscent of the days of the Soviet Union, where people were taken away from their homes by armed people in the name of the state and thrown into obscure prisons and in some kind of kangaroo courts.[2]

Nothing of the sort had happened. What Karzai neglected to share with *This Week* was that he had authorized the arrest himself. I went over the sequence of events several times with Meyer, with the embassy legal attaché who had participated in meetings with Afghan officials, and with the FBI officer who was now mentoring Steve Foster's Major Crimes Task Force (MCTF). Officers from that unit, which had developed the 2009 case against Border Police Chief Sayfullah, had carried out Salehi's arrest.

According to all those participants in the events, what had happened was this. Karzai, informed of his aide's corruption, had demanded to see the evidence. Deputy U.S. Ambassador Anthony Wayne had played the tape of a judicially authorized wiretap for Afghan national security adviser Rangin Spanta. Salehi could be heard demanding the payoff. Meyer told me Spanta began to cry, exclaiming he would tell Karzai that not only should Salehi be dismissed, he should be arrested and prosecuted. With Karzai's approval, the attorney general signed out an arrest warrant, and Atmar's successor as interior minister—after double-checking with the palace—directed the MCTF to carry out the arrest.

When the officers arrived at Salehi's house, they did not storm it or break down his door. They called his cell phone number, identified themselves, and asked him to come out. Irate, Salehi phoned a different security agency, whose men rushed to the scene and exchanged shots with the MCTF but eventually retreated. Next, Salehi dialed up the interior minister, who explained to him that Karzai in person had approved the arrest, and that he had better surrender.

But U.S. officials ignored these facts. As a way to allow President Karzai to "save face," one of them later explained to me, they volunteered that the arrest had perhaps been a bit heavy-handed. U.S. law enforcement personnel who had been working the case, not to mention their Afghan protégés, were stung by the betrayal. "I have seen many a U.S. arrest that was far less polite than this one," commented the FBI officer. Karzai began moving to shut down the two investigation units.

Petraeus swung into action, mobilizing a broad-based international coalition in support of the police units, their funding, and independence. It was masterful. Karzai backed off.

And whirled around to attack the judicial branch instead. On "sovereignty" grounds, Britain was forbidden to provide top-up salaries to the vetted prosecutors who made up the attorney general's anticorruption unit, cutting their take-home pay from $800 a month to $200. The two prosecutors on the Salehi case—one of them a woman standing about five foot four—were demoted and reassigned, amid insulting rumors. "When we really needed help," she told me later, "no one came. We were treated as if we were dispensable." The deputy attorney general, who had bravely signed several anticorruption search and arrest warrants, was fired, accused of espionage, and had to flee briefly to Iran.

In the face of this onslaught, the U.S. government took no meaningful action. Federal prosecutors assigned to mentor Afghan counterparts lodged protests and maintained hesitant contacts with their anticorruption protégés, but they had no top-cover. No American official with clout stepped in to protect the exposed Afghan professionals the U.S. government had coaxed to the dangerous forefront of the battle against corruption. Members of the U.S. National Security Staff in charge of the Afghanistan file "were the worst of the cockroaches," Meyer growled later. "They just scuttled for the dark corners."

Mirror writers like William of Pagula foresaw whom Afghans would blame in such an event. "To neglect to act," he wrote in his diatribe to King Edward III, "when one can deflect perverse people is nothing else than to favor them. The king would seem to agree to the wrongdoers [when] he does not hasten to correct what ought to be corrected."[3]

For many Afghans, the passivity of U.S. officials could only add up to complicity. "People think you want the corruption," a Kandahar friend remarked.

In the following months, the Salehi case file was seized by palace officials, and the charges were dropped. Anticorruption prosecutors were deluged with inconsequential cases, while significant prosecutions stalled. "What Karzai can do to me is ten times worse than anything the United States can do," the U.S. legal attaché recalled the chief of the Anti-Corruption Unit telling him. "If I go against Karzai, what can you do to support me?" The Afghan interior ministry refused to authorize further SIU or MCTF investigations. "The investigators are trying to lower the bar, but it's hard to get it low enough," the MCTF's FBI mentor told Admiral Mullen later that year. "We can't find a fish little enough to go after."

EVENTS MOVED so quickly in the first weeks after Salehi's arrest, there was no way to put all the pieces together. Looking back, I recognize that wishful thinking must have bleared my eyes to the obvious—

to the fundamental weakness of U.S. resolve. Decision makers, including civilians, still saw corruption as secondary to the immediate task of fighting insurgents. The basic equation had not penetrated: that corruption was in fact driving the insecurity we were struggling to quell.

The Directed Telescopes were preparing for a major event we had advised Petraeus to host, what was called a "commander's conference." It would be his first chance since assuming command to meet his key subordinates and share with them his vision for the campaign. It was the moment, we believed, for him to spell out his revolutionary new governance strategy. All the division commanders and their relevant senior staff were summoned to Kabul on August 14. The Directed Telescopes were hard at work designing slides for Petraeus's presentation.

As the helicopters began to touch down on the eve of the meeting, grumbling about the governance strategy grew audible. We heard of conversations at the operational command headquarters lasting late into the night. The division commanders needed some clarity, confirmation from Petraeus that his odd-looking collection of civilian advisers had indeed been speaking for him.

They got the opposite. To our appalled shock, as Petraeus worked through his presentation the next day, he dwelled not on our slides—which signaled a new approach that was countercultural in the military and would require patient explanation—but rather on slides telling the officers to do what they already knew how to do best: kill the enemy. Pausing to expand on the contents, Petraeus even argued *against* some of our slides.

We had no idea what had happened.[4]

BY LATE AUGUST, I had the growing sense that nothing significant could be accomplished from Kabul anyway. The corruption networks were just too vertically integrated: any move against any official, no matter how lowly, would reverberate all the way up the chain to Karzai. And direct involvement by a chief of state catapults foreign policy problems beyond the purview of locally based U.S. officials—even officials as powerful as an ISAF commander—to the level of the U.S. secretary of state or even the president. Anticorruption policy would have to be decided in Washington. I left Kabul on September 3, sure I could serve Mullen better now in his office than on informal loan to Petraeus.

Within days of taking up quarters in the Pentagon, and receiving my badges and the combination to the barrel lock on my office door, I was summoned to join a febrile conversation in Mullen's light-filled office. The cabinet was at last taking up the issue of corruption in Afghanistan. Secretary of State Hillary Clinton had submitted a memo at that day's Principals' Committee meeting. These periodic gatherings of the secretaries of defense and state, the national security adviser, the chairman of the Joint Chiefs of Staff, the head of the CIA, and a few other top officials were where all the final national security decisions were made. Briefing a half-dozen members of his personal staff on what had transpired, Mullen praised Clinton's memo as first time the U.S. government, at his level, had even attempted an analysis of the corruption problem.

As the conversation swirled around, my voice emerged as—unbelievably—one of the more moderate in the room. I had been struggling over the years to tone down my off-putting stridency. It was electrifying to hear raw common sense in such a high-level setting. One of Mullen's eclectic and irreverent special assistants wondered whether success in Afghanistan was even possible so long as Hamid Karzai remained in office.

If this conversation was happening in this room, I thought, maybe there was still a chance to influence U.S. policy.

Like my colleagues, I disagreed with my boss as to the quality of the memo Clinton had presented to her peers. Where his innate optimism perceived a great first step, I saw an attempted end run around the whole issue.

The memo developed the argument I had first heard the previous year in those early anticorruption meetings at the U.S. embassy in Kabul. There were three different types of corruption, went the reasoning, of differing gravity. "Functional corruption," or small-scale palm greasing, was of no great concern, since it did not jeopardize near-term efforts to fight the insurgency. High-level corruption was worrisome but largely because of its impact on U.S.—not Afghan—public opinion. Such criminality at the top of government was typical of that part of the world, the analysis judged, and could only be addressed carefully, by appealing to Karzai to take appropriate steps.

"We have come to conclude that unless Afghans take the lead in combating corruption, efforts are doomed," State Department officials insisted. The memo, in fact, called for *avoiding* large-scale reforms. What really mattered, it opined, was what bothered ordinary Afghans the most: "predatory corruption" on the local level—in particular, shakedowns at the hands of the police.

I saw in this analysis an effort to define the matter down to relative inconsequence, to dodge the glaring reality that the Afghan government at its highest level was the source of the corruption that was plaguing the people and would never voluntarily reform. "A fish rots from the head," my Afghan friends' voices echoed in my ears. "A stream is muddied from the source."

Most significantly, the memo entirely ignored the structured, vertically integrated nature of the corruption networks that had taken over the Afghan government. Predatory local officials enjoyed Kabul-based protection, I argued to Mullen, so efforts to address their behavior would inevitably lead to confrontations with Karzai. There was no way to isolate measures to confront "predatory corruption" from Kabul politics.

Any plan based on such a faulty analysis would never work.

Ironically, the memo placed most of the anticorruption burden on the military—through such initiatives as contracting reform and improvements in police mentoring. At a time when I had heard countless diplomats complain of being bulldozed by an overweening military, when the trope of military hubris dominated the pages of best-selling books about the war,[5] it was odd to see the State Department hand off to the military a problem that so obviously fell in its own lane. The U.S. civilian leadership was shirking its responsibility to develop a high-level strategic approach to the most significant political and diplomatic challenge of this conflict. It was yet another example of America's almost instinctive reflex to lead with the military in moments of international crisis. Civilian officials, as much as they may mistrust the Pentagon, are often the first to succumb. They seem remarkably adverse to exploring the panoply of tools they could bring to bear—let alone to putting in the work to develop a comprehensive strategic framework within which military action would be *a* component, interlocking with others.

What is it, I found myself wondering, that keeps a country as powerful as the United States from employing the vast and varied nonmilitary leverage at its disposal? Why is it so easily cowed by the tantrums of weaker and often dependent allies? Why won't it ever posture effectively itself? Bluff? Deny visas? Slow down deliveries of spare parts? Choose *not* to build a bridge or a hospital? Why is nuance so irretrievably beyond American officials' grasp, leaving them a binary choice between all and nothing—between writing officials a blank check and breaking off relations?

If the obstacle preventing more meaningful action against abusive corruption *wasn't* active U.S. complicity, it sure looked like it.

The U.S. approach to a complex world had been voluntarily constrained this way for decades. Robert W. Komer dissected it brilliantly in a 1972 analysis of U.S. failings in Vietnam, titled *Bureaucracy Does Its Thing.* The monograph spells out how the weak and discredited and not independently viable government of South Vietnam had deftly brought superior leverage to bear over its U.S. patron.

> For many reasons, we did not use vigorously the leverage over the Vietnamese leaders that our contributions gave us. We became their prisoners rather than they ours; the GVN used its weakness far more effectively as leverage on us than we used our strength to lever it.[6]

Substitute the Afghan government's acronym, GIRoA, for GVN, and Komer could have been describing the relationship between Washington and Kabul.

This almost instinctive reluctance to apply U.S. government leverage may be due in part to a "realist"—or legitimist—reflex, or else to a reasonable concern about the United States acting with the arrogance of past colonizers, or appearing to give lessons in domains where its own behavior may be far from perfect.

But tactics aside, a deeper aversion seems to be conjured by the specific question of corruption. I long thought the topic just wasn't sufficiently sexy to grasp people's attention. Yet over the years that I have worked on the issue—in Afghanistan, where the equation seemed so obvious and the stakes so high, and as corruption-related revolts spread across the world—I have watched decision makers and implementers, expert analysts, and even newspaper or magazine editors recoil from the subject, often aggressively. They have been unwilling even to ask the questions that might reveal an important driver of conflict worldwide.[7]

So powerful and so consistent has the hostility been that it has prompted me to reconsider. Perhaps corruption is not, in fact, a boring topic to think about, but rather a threatening one. Perhaps this issue, in some profound way, challenges people's worldviews.

Turning the problem over in my mind, I have discerned the contours of a hypothesis.

In light of their views on the organization of society and political economy, Westerners, especially Americans, can be separated into two basic groups. One camp believes in the necessity, and the virtue, of government. People in this category tend to see governments, in whatever country, as essentially devoted to the common good—staffed by public servants, in the full sense of the term. Of course there are lapses; of course some officials are venal; but such cases are seen as exceptions. For this group of Westerners, the notion that an entire government might be transformed into what amounts to a criminal organization, that it might have entirely repurposed the mechanisms of state to serve its ends, is almost too conceptually challenging to contemplate.

The other camp is characterized by suspicion of government. For people in this category, many of society's problems can be blamed on an excess of government interference and regulation. Lack of development overseas is the inevitable result of a collectivist approach, including planned economies and state-run enterprises. Privatization and deregulation, in the view of this group, are key elements of the cure. For if left alone, freedom and the market will function to the greater good of all. The overwhelming evidence that the market liberalization, privatization, and structural adjustment programs the West imposed on developing countries in the 1990s have often helped catalyze kleptocratic networks—and may have actually exacerbated corruption, not reduced it—conflicts with this group's orthodoxy, and so is hard to process.

For most Westerners, in other words, seriously examining the nature and implications of acute corruption would imply a profound overhaul of their own founding mythologies.

AT THE END of that September Principals' Committee meeting, the State Department was tasked to draw up an anticorruption plan based on the analysis contained in its memo. But Mullen argued for a second, tougher approach to the Karzai kleptocracy, to be rolled out when the State Department's prescriptions (inevitably) failed. Mullen discussed the idea with the politically cautious secretary of defense Robert Gates.

"It's not because we've pushed on corruption that our ties with Karzai are strained," Mullen pointed out to his personal staff. "Because we haven't pushed on corruption. I'm looking for a way to get serious."

The principals ultimately agreed on the need for some sort of tougher backup plan. The National Security Staff was tasked with drafting it. Mullen suggested we work on our own version in parallel.

So a few of us set about imagining what a more robust approach to Karzai might look like. The effort amounted to translating the work of Petraeus's Directed Telescopes up a level, to match the scope and the levers available to the U.S. government as a whole.

We arranged meetings with sometimes-bemused kindred spirits at the Departments of Treasury and Justice, and we called on a few top private-sector anticorruption specialists to review our ideas. A veteran of Foreign Corrupt Practices Act litigations pointed out that U.S. anti-corruption efforts traditionally punished the bribe payer, not the official extorting the money. "Every time I tried to prosecute officials, I got pushback from State," he said.

One tack was to place more conditions on the financial assistance the United States provides to Afghanistan. Or, to personalize the pain, why not take a leaf out of Karzai's book and cancel the top-up salaries of select members of his personal staff? Tourist or student visas could be denied. Members of corrupt Afghan networks who were dual nationals could be pursued under U.S. law—for example, for business dealings with Iran.

One sophisticated legal device we discovered was *in rem* forfeiture. Under that provision of U.S. law, no convicted criminal is needed, not even a suspect, to target the proceeds of a crime. If a link can be demonstrated between assets residing in the United States and a crime committed anywhere, then those assets can be seized. Afghan corruption booty—kickbacks from development contracts or fraudulent Kabul Bank loans—that was held in dollars or had been converted to property in the United States was fair game.

Another possibility we explored, though Treasury officials thought it politically difficult to achieve, was to develop a new sanctions regime—like the Narcotics Kingpin designation, or the Terrorism Sanctions Regulations—aimed at high-level corruption. Such designations prevent any U.S. citizen or entity from conducting financial transactions with certain individuals, organizations, or governments that fit the criteria. We played with potential language for a new "Egregious Corruption" designation and recommended some such regime be promulgated.

Expanding on the first conversation in Mullen's office, my colleagues and I sketched out several different courses of action, keyed to upcoming events on the calendar of U.S.-Afghan relations, that would make use of specific elements on our long list of tools, applied to the Afghan context in a strategized way. Although none of these courses of action was ultimately implemented, the effort serves as a model for how the leverage at the disposal of the U.S. government can be combined in precise ways to fit the real-world situation of a country at a specific point in time—and the careful planning that should go into the design of such a campaign.

One course of action, for example, was to assign a single administration "case-officer" to Karzai, to reduce the number of mixed messages he was receiving and his ability to play one U.S. official off against another.

Another, which might incorporate the first, was to deliberately push Karzai toward a binary junction at which his actions would irrefutably identify him as either part of the solution or part of the problem—in which case, a dramatic U.S. response might ensue. We suggested a two-month evaluation period and a list of concrete steps Karzai could take that would indicate he was truly intent on improving governance. He might authorize an independent audit of Kabul Bank, for example, or cease directly interfering in judicial affairs, or sign a memorandum of understanding requiring the removal of senior army or police officers known to engage in predatory corruption.

During the evaluation period, under this proposed course of action,

U.S. anticorruption activities would be redoubled as part of the test, with new investigations, and case-by-case U.S. interagency justifications, before continuing to pay abusively corrupt officials as intelligence assets. Karzai's reactions to these steps would be noted.

We examined his likely countermoves, such as scapegoating constructive Afghans, or denying visas to relevant U.S. officials. To parry such blows, the United States could reduce financial support to the ministries that those banned U.S. officials were scheduled to work with, or protect constructive Afghan officials by hiring them into international positions.

For each course of action, we considered the likely outcomes. Karzai might, after a brief struggle, improve governance, thus reducing the insurgency's draw and helping end the conflict. Or he might put up sustained resistance, employing the countermoves we predicted (or others). Or the Afghan government might implode altogether, as corrupt ministers, their impunity evaporating, fled the country. The plan suggested policy responses for each of these potential consequences.

Finally, we listed arguments for and against each course of action. We developed a total of five such scenarios, accompanied by similarly tailored contextual analyses.

Communicating with colleagues at ISAF, I also started culling through names of the worst offenders, men whose activities had placed them at the top of one or more prioritization lists for "nonkinetic targeting," according to the procedures currently being followed in different headquarters. My guidance was to come up with a top-twenty list.

The objective of that maneuver, I gathered, was to use it to confront the CIA on its approach to Afghan officials. By now it was a matter of public record that Karzai's land-grabbing, vote-stealing, drug-dealing younger brother, among others, was on the Agency payroll.[8] President Barack Obama had reportedly not appreciated learning about that in the pages of the *New York Times*. The "top twenty" list was designed for Obama and the principals to compare with the CIA's personnel records, to see how many of the most corrupt Afghan officials were also paid retainers of the U.S. government.

Mullen was simultaneously pushing the intelligence community to think through the interaction between corruption and violent insurgency more broadly—to see what evidence existed to support the equation that he was finding increasingly convincing: that outrage at a government's corrupt practices often provided fuel for insurgencies.

By then, data was piling up—for the Afghanistan case, at least. Officers who interviewed Taliban detainees were corroborating what I had been hearing from my neighbors in Kandahar for years. At the top of the list of reasons cited by prisoners for joining the Taliban was not ethnic bias, or disrespect of Islam, or concern that U.S. forces might stay in their country forever, or even civilian casualties. At the top of the list was the perception that the Afghan government was "irrevocably" corrupt. Taliban detainees reportedly judged that the corruption had grown institutionalized and was therefore unchangeable. They were running out of nonviolent options for altering what they saw as a fundamental flaw in their government.

Yet that autumn of 2010, I caught members of Mullen's own AfPak intelligence task force manipulating information like this to support conclusions *downplaying* the role of corruption in the Afghan conflict. The CIA put out a product purporting to examine the role of corruption in the outcomes of ten different insurgencies. The conclusion was that it had mattered in the success of only one. I pounced on the pages dealing with Vietnam, wondering how the authors were going to get around that example. Vietnam, they professed, was excluded because the insurgency had not succeeded; the war had ended in a national unity government.

One morning toward the end of September, I was stunned to discover details of the ongoing interagency debate on the anticorruption plan the State Department was still drafting plastered across the pages of several national newspapers.

"The U.S. is planning a concerted campaign against lower-level corruption in Afghanistan thought to be directly feeding the insurgency, and ceding more control to Afghans of the higher-level investigations that soured relations with President Hamid Karzai," read the *Wall Street Journal*, referring to a "shift" in policy.[9]

But no such decision had been made. The most recent version of the State Department's classified effort was sitting on my desk, the word DRAFT printed across the top. I was in the process of entering tracked changes. The plan had not yet been raised to the level of the Principals Committee for discussion, let alone been seen or approved by the president.

And it never would be.

What was playing out across the front pages of leading newspapers was a classic example of a patented Washington tactic: offensive leaking—providing confidential information to the press as a way to gain leverage in an interagency struggle.

The National Security Staff never would draft that robust plan for addressing the Afghan kleptocracy, which Mullen and Gates had convinced the principals to request. The Joint Staff's list of leverage and potential courses of action was ignored. The task was simply left to languish. Apparently, in government, you can fail to turn in your homework but still get a passing grade.

The question of pursuing a serious anticorruption policy was finally put to rest in January 2011. The battle was waged in the margins of an interagency document called "Objective 2015." It had occurred to someone that the U.S. government really ought to have a picture of what it was trying to achieve in Afghanistan—what that country would need to look like by the end of 2014 if it were to weather the withdrawal of international troops without imploding.

The document was an embarrassment. Just the grammatical errors in the first paragraph made me flinch. Rather than identify true minimal requirements for Afghanistan to survive without international troops, it cut down ambitions to fit what was deemed "achievable"—whether or not such goals were sufficient to ensure Afghanistan could continue to exist.

It seemed to me, for example, that for the Afghan government to last, motivations for joining the insurgency had to diminish. Afghans had better think more highly of their government by 2015 than they did in 2011. Yet in the document, the very modest goal of an upward trend in Afghans' confidence in their government was not listed as essential to mission success. It was considered only a "nice-to-have."

The real anticorruption fight, however, was not over such fundamentals. It played out in the fine print of the document's "implementation guidelines." Over the furious dissent of mid-level Justice Department (DoJ) officials, seconded by the Joint Staff—but not by their own chief,

Attorney General Eric Holder—the document barred DoJ attorneys from mentoring anticorruption cases. They could do generalized capacity building, but they could not help shepherd specific cases against specific Afghan government officials. The investigations units, even if they were able to continue functioning, would never be able to bring a case to court. The courageous anticorruption prosecutors could never hope for backup from U.S. officials if they were intimidated, harassed, or demoted.

The gavel had come down. By way of an apparently insignificant detail buried deep in an interagency document—a few words of guidance to DoJ attorneys—the U.S. decision to turn a blind eye to Afghan corruption was finally spelled out.

NOT TILL the spring of 2013 did the penny drop as to what had prompted Petraeus's sudden change of heart in the summer of 2010—and ultimately, what made the U.S. government shrink from addressing corruption in Afghanistan. On April 28, Matthew Rosenberg of the *New York Times* reported that the CIA had been paying millions of dollars per year, in cash, to President Karzai.[10] Toward the end of his article was the nugget of information that told the whole story.

The CIA's bagman was Muhammad Zia Salehi—that aide to Karzai who had been arrested, and then quickly released, in the summer of 2010. U.S. officials had walked into a circular firing squad. Salehi, the subject of the U.S. government's corruption test case, was also the U.S. government's intermediary for cash payments to Karzai. The choice of this target many have been deliberate—an effort to flush out into the open the profound contradiction at the heart of U.S. policy.

Two senior U.S. officials told me later that throughout the investigation of Salehi, the planning for the arrest, and his liberation within a few hours, CIA personnel had remained silent about their relationship with him. Even afterward, despite strong words at Principals' Committee meetings and that Joint Staff "top twenty" list, the CIA never provided the U.S. ambassador or the key cabinet secretaries with the names of the Afghans it was paying. The station chief in Kabul continued to hold private meetings with Karzai, with no other U.S. officials present.

In other words, a secret CIA agenda—which involved enabling the very summit of Afghanistan's kleptocracy—was in direct conflict with the anticorruption agenda. And with no one explicitly arbitrating this contradiction, the CIA's agenda won out.

After those first few weeks in command, Petraeus veered hard away from governance efforts and devoted himself to targeted killing, which he intensified considerably. Targeted killing of individual terrorist suspects is the special domain of the CIA, which Petraeus left Kabul to run—until his tenure there was cut short by an extramarital affair that had germinated in the Yellow Building at ISAF headquarters.

The Obama administration, sickened by the cost in lives and resources that the counterinsurgency approach was exacting, and perhaps uncomfortable with the power and discretion that large-scale military operations place in the hands of the brass, turned increasingly toward special operations and drone warfare to counter security threats. Targeted, technologically advanced, secretive killing, over which the president had direct control, increased after 2010, spreading to Yemen and other theaters.

But the point officials missed in making this shift—and in letting the priorities generated by this strategy trump governance objectives—is that targeted killings still represent a military response to a problem that is fundamentally political and economic in nature: a problem that is rooted in the conduct of government. The current U.S. approach sends a message, wittingly or not, to people who are often driven to violence by the abusively corrupt practices of their ruling cliques, and by frustration at seeing their legitimate grievances systematically ignored. The message seems to be: your grievances are, in fact, of no account. They will not be heard.

That message holds out no recourse, no means of appeal.

CHAPTER TWELVE

Forging an Appeal on Earth

The Netherlands, England, America, ca. 1560–1787

A n absence of appeal this absolute can drive men and women
to extremes—especially when they suffer treatment they feel
is acutely unfair. They will incur great risk, sustain material
loss, and take steps that might once have been unimaginable to them, to
try to redress the balance. Corroborating experiments like the "ultimatum game," or observations of the way some primates behave,[1] historical
examples demonstrate this tendency.

Take the sixteenth century, when Europeans were confronting just
such an implacable lack of recourse. Time had revealed, by then, the
fundamental deficiency in all those pious books of advice written for
rulers over the years. Princes were ignoring them. Fear of divine judgment had failed to persuade them to take their subjects' interests to
heart, treat them equitably, or abstain from thieving their property.

So some of those subjects set about fashioning a more reliable means
of redress. The project would prove revolutionary.

A 1573 complaint, for example, that the Dutch nobleman William of
Orange addressed to his overlord, seems to refer directly to the familiar
terms of mirror literature. What a contrast with recommended behavior
it was, William wrote, when "instead of doing justice to his faithful subjects and giving audience to them, listening graciously to their pitiful
complaints, [the prince] should send a tyrant to them who would cruelly
slaughter and ruin them all."

William was writing to King Philip II of Spain, beseeching him, "in all humility, to lend an ear to us and to weigh our cause on the scales of justice."[2] In other words: *to listen, without intermediary, to what his subjects have to say to him.*

But Phillip was in no mind to do any such thing. In fact, for decades, instead of becoming more accessible to their subjects, royal houses in Europe had been erecting more barriers. They had been consolidating their power and laying down the theoretical basis for an increasingly centralized and absolutist form of government. For justification, they were turning to a religious rationale: the divine right of kingship.[3]

In William of Orange's native Netherlands, this consolidation can be dated to the late 1400s, under Duke Charles the Bold of Burgundy. Ruling territory that stretched from the heart of modern France to the North Sea islands that trail off from Holland, he professed to have "received his power directly from God and from God alone."[4]

Half a century later the Habsburg dynasty was solidifying its control over most of Europe—including the Burgundian domains in the Netherlands. In a 1529 mirror for the Habsburg Holy Roman Emperor Charles V (for whom the humanist Erasmus had also written his), a Spanish Franciscan, Antonio de Guevara, argued stridently in favor of sole rule by a monarch, whose authority derives strictly from God, brooking no advice or dissent: "Princes are created by God's hand to rule. It is our obligation, therefore, to obey them in everything. . . . God wishes that one Emperor alone be . . . lord of the world."[5]

In 1548 Charles V himself wrote a book of advice for his son, the future Philip II, expanding the theory. Gone from Charles's text are the timeworn exhortations to mercy and justice and care for the people. This mirror's axiom is that kings rule through God, and that Philip should require "obedience and subordination" of all beneath him.[6]

Spanish by culture and personally secretive—in contrast to his broad-minded Dutch father—Philip II took careful note of this absolutist instruction.[7] As the biographer John Lynch puts it, "Philip's own sense of prerogative was highly developed."[8] He administered his far-flung realm "through officials whose actions he controlled down to the minutest details."[9] Both Philip's private devotion and his public royal display communicated the religious rationale he claimed for this type of rule. Philip was "well aware that Catholic sacred imagery and symbols were essential to his public presentation," to signify that his absolutism was divinely inspired.[10]

Indeed, one of the ways Phillip II tried to impose his imperious will on his Dutch domains was to try to extirpate the new Protestant heresy, by means of the brutal practices of the Spanish Inquisition, a campaign that had been launched in the previous century to root out Jews and Muslims from Spain.

Such an approach was guaranteed to hit rough waters in the Netherlands. Apart from their passionate interest in the Protestant ideas that were electrifying northern Europe, the disparate, stubborn, industrious, creative Dutch provinces had spent decades struggling to impose local restraints on their overlords' powers. They had already gone beyond the Mirrors for Princes' hand-wringing and nebulous threats of divine judgment or government collapse. They were beginning to construct practical mechanisms of appeal.

By the mid-1500s, the Dutch were in full, bloody revolt. Their resistance to Philip often referred to these nascent curbs on royal prerogative and instruments of redress—and to the corruption of the king's envoys. Burghers of towns around Ypres, for example, insisted that people accused of heresy be informed of the evidence against them. Those leveling charges should not to be able to "derive personal profit from their accusation," the burghers stipulated, outraged at the use of legal proceedings as a pretext for confiscation of property.[11] Flemish representatives rejected the plenary authority of the special envoys Philip dispatched from Spain, recognizing only "his majesty's ordinary [local] officers, each within his district and the limits of his jurisdiction."[12]

Beyond such specifics, the Dutch challenged the very substance of divine right monarchy, by demanding a say in how they would be governed. "The King," noted an argument submitted to a representative body called the States General in 1576,

> has promised [not] to . . . reduce or change the laws of the country, without the common and well-considered consent . . . of the countries and the States; also that he will not impose any tax, tribute, or excise-duty upon the people without their free consent, which

they will render him not as his right but by their grace. . . . He also . . . swears to treat each individual not at will but by right and justice . . . and like the lowest of his subjects he himself will be judged in all disputes without being allowed to breach or reduce another's right.[13]

Declaring that kings have no *right* to collect taxes, that the people "by their grace" offer him their money voluntarily, the Dutch rebels were negating the very idea of a divinely ordained king in whom all prerogatives are vested.

In the midst of the chaos engulfing them—indeed, propelled by it into uncharted seas—Dutch writers explored broader notions about the source of government legitimacy.

The principal end for which God ordained government to men was not to convert the good, won and gathered through great labour and industry, into its own property [aka kleptocracy], neither to misuse the power which is rendered to it for intemperate and unreasonable desires . . . nor to . . . govern at will. . . . Kings have been ordained by God for the welfare and benefit of the subjects.[14]

According to the pamphlet submitted to the States General, a lord should govern the Netherlands

following their rights, freedoms, privileges, and old customs, by which he swore most faithfully upon his arrival, and by which he was inaugurated and accepted, committing himself with a grave oath not to deviate from them in any point.[15]

Some writers went so far as to maintain that the principle of hereditary rule "has never been considered to be fully binding." Before rulers of the Dutch provinces could take up their functions, they had to be formally accepted by the representative assemblies. And they had to swear those "grave oaths" to uphold the people's rights—"on the legal condition that if they failed to maintain our ancestors' privileges, and the freedoms and rights of the country, we would not acknowledge them as lord."[16]

In other words, the Dutch were concluding that the ruler did *not* owe his power to divine ordination, as Philip's every word and deed proclaimed, but that he exercised power only as defined by a contract he entered into with his subjects.

Centuries of royalist claims about how God ordered political affairs were under attack.

Like the Uzbeks during the 2005 Andijan crisis, the restive Dutch hoped that their suffering was the work not of Philip himself but of subordinates gone rogue. They spent years trying to appeal directly to their monarch, over the heads of the Spanish envoys. But at length, and almost in spite of themselves, after repeated royal rebuffs, after years of barbarous torture inflicted on accused heretics, and executions and seizures of property, of land battles and naval forays, mass exodus, and the writing and printing of tracts by the thousands, the Dutch took the momentous step of withdrawing their allegiance from Philip II. In 1581 they formally abjured the Spanish monarchy.

The edict—the equivalent of a Dutch Declaration of Independence—spelled out a new view of the relative value of people and prince. "The subjects are not created by God for the benefit of the prince. On the contrary, the prince is created for the subjects . . . to govern them according to right and reason."

Right and reason. So did the Dutch begin the process of extracting God—or some people's interpretation of God—from the direct conduct of human affairs. They had inaugurated a new principle for organizing the government of a nation.

Under the new order, Dutch subjects would no longer have to stand by and hope that their ruler might listen to good advice or tremble at the prospect of divine retribution. For according to the Edict of Abjuration, the people had only "accepted their prince conditionally, by contracts and agreements, and if the prince breaks them, he legally forfeits his sovereignty."[17] The new reason-based construct of government included built-in means of redress. Rulers in the Netherlands would henceforth be subject to accountability, not just in the afterlife but here on earth, under the law of the land.

Though Philip reconquered the southern portion of the Low Countries, which eventually became Belgium and part of France, the independent northern provinces chose for the next two centuries to be governed by the people's elected representatives, whose role was not merely to check the abuses of a prince but to exercise sovereign power. A historic shift in human political history had taken place. The new disposition ushered in an unprecedented age of prosperity and creativity.[18]

Throughout this protracted struggle, petitions and pamphlets kept citing a collection of "freedoms, rights, customs, traditions, and privileges" as a basis for the new contractual form of government.[19] Those rights were enumerated in charters that Low Country notables had in fact made their rulers sign upon accession. Usually the princes put their seal to these papers during a public ceremony splendid with fanfare and pageantry: the lord's ritual "Entry" into town. The contractual nature of the documents, which stipulated that subjects could refuse obedience in case of infraction, laid the foundations for the remarkable constitutionalism of the Dutch Revolt.[20]

The texts themselves are detailed. Clauses prohibit the purchase of government office, require functionaries to "be content [with] a reasonable salary" and not extort more from the people. They prohibit arbitrary arrest and ad hoc tolls on the rivers and roads. They spell out the duties of judicial officers and require that locals, sensitive to the opinion of their neighbors, be chosen for government positions.[21]

The charters—the foundations and origin of modern democracy—were aimed largely at curbing corruption.

DURING THE blood-soaked years of their never-ending revolt, thousands of Dutch refugees flung themselves into their boats and crossed the North Sea to England. Some eight thousand parishioners crowded the Dutch Protestant church in London by late in the century.[22] English translations of tracts and pamphlets arguing the rebels' cause hit the streets within weeks of their writing, no doubt influencing the thought of a generation of Englishmen. Queen Elizabeth even provided some military support to the nascent Dutch republic. (She provided more helpful assistance by crushing the Spanish Armada that Philip sent against her realm. The ships carried an invasion force drawn from troops stationed in the Netherlands.)

But upon Elizabeth's childless death, the son of her Catholic cousin, Mary Queen of Scots, succeeded, as James I. He lacked Elizabeth's sympathies for the Dutch Republic. And James, just like Philip II before him, was a fervent exponent of divine right absolutism.

"God gives not kings the style of gods in vain," reads the opening sonnet of the mirror James I wrote for his son, Prince Harry. "For on His throne His scepter do they sway/And . . . their subjects ought them to obey."[23] Emphasizing in his first speech to the Star Chamber "what a near connection there is between God and the King," James insisted kings have no one to answer to but God alone.[24]

Even if subjects suffer tyranny, he told Harry, rebellion is "ever unlawful on their part."[25] Indeed, he advised his son not to suffer the least questioning of royal prerogative: "That which concerns the mystery of the King's power is not lawful to be disputed, for that is to . . . take away the mystical reverence that belongs unto them that sit in the throne of God."[26]

James I was succeeded not by this beloved first son Harry, who died young, but by a sickly and cosseted younger brother, Charles, who fully espoused his father's doctrine of divine right rule.[27]

Like their Dutch neighbors, however, the English were loath to live under a government that offered no avenue of appeal.

Upon his coronation in 1626, Charles I quickly began clashing with Parliament, whose powers he begrudged. Parliament took advantage of his need for money to entrench those powers—for only Parliament could raise taxes, and it refused to do so without concessions. The king dissolved Parliament and decreed a levy without its approval. When some MPs refused to pay, he threw them in jail, thus embittering the quarrel.

At stake was the ability of England's representative assembly to provide recourse for subjects and exercise real checks on a king who ignored their interests.

In 1628, for example, Parliament promulgated a "Petition of Right" in exchange for an appropriation for Charles. The text invoked the protections set forth in England's own historical charter—the Magna Carta—against arrest, imprisonment, exile, or seizure of property, except "by the lawful judgment of [a citizen's] peers, or by the law of the land." No one should be compelled to "yield any gift, loan, benevolence, tax, or such like charge, without common consent by Act of Parliament."[28] Charles approved the petition, but with no intention of abiding by it.

In 1629 he embarked on more than a decade of autocratic "personal rule." But in 1639 he decided to make war on Scotland and had no choice but to call the Lords and Commons into session again to grant funds to pay for it.

The MPs seized this chance to expand their powers. Their ensuing fight with Charles was full of drama—MPs rushing to bar their doors and vote on a measure while the king's soldiers pounded on the stout wood; bells and bonfires, posters plastered on London walls, songs and poems shouted in boozy choruses, and in 1642, Charles himself at the head of hundreds of men-at-arms, marching to Westminster to arrest five MPs.

Failing, he fled London. Parliament raised an army.

What the Lords and Commons were after by now was a true constitutional monarchy. A Grand Remonstrance and accompanying petition spelled out new conditions for a grant. Their terms enshrined no less than a coequal role for Parliament in exercising sovereign authority. "No public act . . . may be esteemed of any validity as proceeding from the royal authority unless it be done by the advice and consent of" a majority of the Privy Council. Top government appointments were to be approved by both houses, and appointees must swear to uphold the Petition of Right. Parliament was to be consulted even about the education and marriage of the king's children since, as future officials, their personal affairs affected the public interest.[29]

Charles instantly grasped the revolutionary novelty of such demands. To grant them, he wrote,

were in effect . . . to depose both Our Self and Our posterity. . . . We may have swords and maces carried before Us, and please Our Self with the sight of a crown and scepter . . . but as to true and real power, We should remain but the outside, but the picture, but the sign of a king.[30]

The ensuing civil war would rage, with a brief hiatus, for seven years. Charles planned and commanded battles both from the field and from the bowels of castles where Parliament imprisoned him. English soldiers raped and pillaged their English neighbors.[31] The Parliamentary army and the London mob grew more radically egalitarian as time went on, frightening even the House of Commons that had initiated the conflict. Eventually, the army purged Parliament and assumed decision-making power itself.

It took all that—as in the Netherlands, it took such an anguish of destruction and carnage and repeated betrayals—to drive the English to envisage severing their allegiance to Charles.

In *The Tyrannicide Brief,* a remarkable and penetrating analysis of the English Civil War, the human rights lawyer Geoffrey Robertson highlights the significance of the approach the rebels chose. Rather than commit tyrannicide (which even John of Salisbury had condoned)[32]— rather than take the easy tack, in other words, of poisoning Charles, or shooting him during some "attempted escape"—the rebels put him on trial. A public trial, following standard English adversary procedure.[33]

> The decision . . . to put Charles before a tribunal tasked to apply the common law, permitting him to justify his cause in public and requiring the prosecution to prove his guilt, was a step as unnecessary as it was unprecedented. . . . There was no example to suggest that the trial of a head of state was feasible.[34]

What this choice did, for the first time in modern history, was make a reigning king formally liable for the specifics of his misdeeds—not just to God in the hereafter, as the mirrors repeat, but to man, under law, in this life. A lever, based on defined legal principles, was being fashioned to provide redress.

Though it was man, not God, who would hold Charles accountable, the legal axioms used to convict him could have been taken from the pages of a number of mirrors. There was that oft-repeated adage, for example, that the guilt for subordinates' misdeeds lies with the ruler.

"The existence of iniquitous judges," wrote Jonas d'Orléans in 830, "is the sin of the prince."[35]

Or as fourteenth-century William of Pagula put it: "He takes on the guilt of the perpetrator who neglects to fix what he can correct."[36]

The principle of command responsibility was central to the prosecution brief against Charles: "The said Charles Stuart, hath *caused and procured* many thousands of the free people of this nation to be slain."[37]

Prosecutor John Cooke, in what would have been his closing argument, elaborated—with an explicit repudiation of the "rogue subordinates" thesis.

> Nor does the common objection "that the judges and evil counsellors, and not the king, ought to be responsible for such maladministrations, injustice and oppression" bear the weight of a feather in the balance of right reason. For, 1) Who made such wicked and corrupt judges? Were they not his own creatures? . . . *He that does not hinder the doing of evil, if it lies in his power to prevent it, is guilty of it as a commander.*[38]

This was exactly the type of guilt Afghans imputed to the United States for the Karzai government's misdeeds.

Cooke also pointed out that the king "had benefit of [the] illegal fines"[39]—was, in words that Afghans might have used, profiting from corruption, and by that means implicitly approved it.

And Cooke analyzed the way purchase of office, a feature of many modern kleptocracies, allows for the wholesale capture of government institutions. "For when a man shall give five or ten thousand pounds for a judge's place," and the king

> shall the next day send to him to know his opinion of a difference in law between the king and the subject and it shall be intimated unto him that if he do not deliver his opinion for the king he is likely to be removed out of his place the next day . . .

. . . and having gone into debt to buy that place, the man can't afford to lose it, then "the law was as the king would have it," and "that very act of his made the king at the least a potential tyrant."[40]

On the mesmerizing occasion of the trial, which transfixed the population of England and much of the Western world as accounts of it spread, the king refused to plead—to the great frustration of Cooke, who had counted on the legitimacy that a full, adversarial procedure would confer. The barrister produced enough evidence to take up two days of proceedings.[41] But he never did deliver that closing argument, because there was no one to argue against.

Under English law at the time, silence was considered a confession.[42] Charles I's judges found him guilty and, after deep and fearful deliberation, condemned him to death. The king was executed on a frigid January 30, 1649.

And so England, like Holland before it, woke up one morning a republic—though it did not stay that way for long. Even so, the effort of groping their way toward representative government forced the English to think the mechanics through. The ideas developed during those years would inspire the American experiment a century later.

Though it was immaterial to his case against Charles, for example, Cooke took up the argument against monarchy itself. In his view, even benevolent monarchs were nefarious, "for when kings are good, the people are never jealous of their liberties, and fair language and a few good acts . . . bring the people into a fool's paradise."[43]

Cooke's contemporary, John Milton, also writing just after Charles I's trial, made a more elaborate argument against monarchy. "All men naturally were born free," he took as his starting point, "born to command and not to obey." Only because of their propensity to commit violence did they gather in towns for protection and ordain a governing authority: "not to be their lords and masters, but to be their deputies and commissioners." Laws were made "that should confine and limit the authority of whom they chose to govern them," to subtract "as much as might be from personal errors and frailties."

But what if "the law was either not executed, or misapplied"?

The only remedy left them [was] to put conditions and take oaths from all kings and magistrates at their first installment . . . who upon those terms and no other received allegiance from the people. . . . And this ofttimes with express warning, that if the king or the magistrate proved unfaithful to his trust, the people would be disengaged. And they added also counselors and parliaments, not to be only at his beck, but with him or without him, at set times.

Thus did Milton, echoing the Dutch a century earlier, explicitly resolve the fundamental defect in the Mirrors for Princes: their failure to provide any recourse but God's judgment against a transgressing king. "For if the king fear not God—as how many of them do not—" then what are the people to do? "If [rulers] may refuse to give account, then all covenants made with them at coronation, all oaths are . . . mere mockeries, all laws which they swear to keep made to no purpose."

It follows, wrote Milton,

> that since the king or magistrate holds his authority of the people
> . . . for their good in the first place and not his own, then may the
> people as oft as they shall judge it for the best, either choose him
> or reject him, retain him or depose him, though no tyrant, merely
> by the liberty and right of free born men to be governed as seems
> to them best.[44]

Milton had described elective kingship, or a presidency. He had built the argument for democracy—as the best practical means of guaranteeing redress of legitimate grievances, the best means of appeal here on earth.

Writing forty years later, John Locke used the discipline of logic to advance this line of thinking, in two "Treatises of Government." He criticized monarchy, "where one man, commanding a multitude, has the liberty to be judge in his own case, and may do to all his subjects whatever he pleases, without the least liberty to anyone to question or control those who execute his pleasure." The very objective of government, Locke wrote, is "setting up a known authority to which everyone of that society may appeal upon any injury received."

He went on to discuss the best apportionment of governmental duties and modes of operation for branches carrying out different functions. The legislative power, he concluded, was best "placed in collective bodies of men, call them senate, parliament, or what you please." He discussed the need for majority rather than unanimous votes, why a legislature needn't remain in permanent session, while executive must be exercised continuously, and he began the intricate task of determining the relative supremacy of different branches of government.[45]

In this way did Locke and other political theorists of his day continue the work of replacing God, in ordering human affairs, with a mechanism devised by human reason. And they began sketching the shapes of the gears and rods that made up that reason-based contraption.

AMONG PARLIAMENT'S supporters during the English Civil War were seven of the ten young men who made up the first graduating class of Harvard College. They, along with many other Americans, sailed to England to take part in the struggle against absolutism. Some went on to take up key positions in the short-lived English republic.[46]

Americans avidly read Locke as well as later writers who expanded his ideas—notably the brilliant French philosopher Montesquieu, whose compendium *The Spirit of the Laws* shaped much of the colonists' exploration into how a rational government should be structured. The birth of the United States was deeply influenced by the previous two centuries' events in northern Europe.

In the context of the achievements of their Dutch and English forebears, the American's originality lay not so much in throwing off the yoke of monarchy, or in declaring all men equal and endowed with rights that they could not give up even if they wanted to. Those points had already been made. Where the American revolutionaries broke truly new ground was in the engineering work they did on the rational mechanism designed to promote those rights and ensure appeal against abuse. The delegates to the American constitutional convention seemed to have felt that if they could tool the gears of government just right, then justice, prosperity, and tranquility would *have* to ensue.

By the time their representatives met in Philadelphia to amend the Articles of Confederation that loosely bound the thirteen former British colonies, Americans had amassed a lot of experience in designing governments. Each of the states had drafted at least one constitution. They had tried unicameral and bicameral legislatures, different electoral procedures and lengths of office, and especially, different trade-offs between curbs on tyranny and means of forestalling anarchy (or too much egalitarianism).

The mere fact of holding elections, Americans already knew, was not sufficient to guarantee people's rights. That truth—that an election per se is less important than the architecture within which it takes place—played out in the painful struggles that took place in Arab Spring countries after their revolutions.

James Madison, a key proponent of a more "energetic" national government, saw elaborate, interlocking elements as the best protection against a strong government's potential excesses. "A government composed of such extensive powers," he wrote to George Washington on April 16, 1787, "should be well organized and balanced.

> The legislative department might be divided into two branches; one of them chosen every ___ years by the people at large, or by the legislatures, the other to consist of fewer members. Perhaps the negative on the laws [veto] might be most conveniently exercised by this branch. As a further check, a council of revision including the great ministerial officers might be superadded.[47]

For the next five months, such details and many more were probed and considered, modified and adopted or discarded.

As delegates broke out into two main groupings during the course of the debates, it was the "Antifederalists"—those suspicious of concentrated national power—who also recoiled at the elaborate devices Madison or John Adams favored as checks on concentrated power. One writer disagreed with the Federalists' presumptions of inherent human self-interestedness—the belief that government officials, as he put it,

> will ever be actuated by views of private interest and ambition, to the prejudice of the public good; that therefore the only effectual method to secure the rights of the people and promote their welfare is to create an opposition of interests [within the government].

For this Antifederalist, a better way to guarantee public integrity was through personal morality (and the absence of acute income inequality): "A republican or free form of government can only exist where the body of the people are virtuous, and where property is pretty equally divided."[48]

The Federalists' more jaundiced view of human nature won out. Indeed, the most widely accepted argument against the draft constitution was its lack of explicit safeguards of basic rights, such as those in the Dutch charters or the Magna Carta. With that vice remedied by the promise of a ten-article Bill of Rights, the Constitution was adopted.

AND IN THIS FASHION, over the course of about two centuries— with rich input from the great European revolution in thinking called the Enlightenment—a constitutional form of government was slowly hammered out. It was an alternative to rule by princes who claimed to be the incarnation of God's will on earth and therefore above challenge. A set of mechanisms based on "reason and right" had supplanted the principle of rule by God's chosen lieutenant, as a better guarantee of just, uncorrupt government.

The United States and other countries spent the next two centuries testing and perfecting these mechanisms—sometimes in bitter and bloody strife—and expanding the rights they guaranteed and the categories of people thought to be endowed with those rights. And though it developed in the West, this basic structure of government was adopted—at least in its outward forms—by many of the new nations in Asia and Africa when they won their independence from colonial powers.

But what if that finely tuned device is captured in turn by some tight-knit network, intent on its own enrichment? What happens if the careful contraption is repurposed to serve the interests of this criminal network, which has gained control of the levers of power that matter—the army or other security forces, the civil service, the financial system— and has reworded legislation that was designed to curb abuses to allow it to "circumvent law by law"?

Some people, in that case, are likely to discard that rational mechanism altogether. Some people will appeal for an "alternative, upright methodology, in which it is not the business of any class of humanity to lay down its own laws to its own advantage, at the expense of the other classes." And that infallible methodology, argued Osama bin Laden in a 2007 video, "is the methodology of God Most High."[49]

Some people, in other words, will turn back to God. Lured by militant advocates of a religious ordering of human affairs, they will seek to roll back four hundred years of political history.

And that is exactly what the great seventeenth-century political thinker John Locke predicted would happen.

> Where an appeal to law, and constituted judges, lies open, but the remedy is denied by a manifest perverting of justice, and the barefaced wresting of the laws to protect or indemnify the violence or injuries of some men or party of men, there it is hard to imagine any thing but a state of war: for wherever violence is used, and injury done—though by hands appointed to administer justice—it is still violence and injury, however colored with the name, pretenses or forms of law, the end whereof being to protect and redress the innocent, by an unbiassed application of it . . . ; wherever that is not bona fide done, war is made on the sufferers, who having no appeal on earth to right them, they are left to the only remedy in such cases, an appeal to heaven.[50]

CHAPTER THIRTEEN

Violent Extremists

Wait a second.

As I worked through this historical material, riveted by the saga of a carefully constructed mechanism coming to replace God as the main principle ordering government, I could not ignore one glaring fact: the people engaged in that process were practically all Protestants.*

Why Protestantism? What is the link between reformed religion and representative government as a device to ensure the redress of grievances? Searching for answers to that question, I discovered something else: a separate strand tying corruption to religious extremism. This strand is not bounded by the arc of specific historical events; it is remarkably consistent through time.

---

* The major exceptions, of course, were the Catholic French, whose reflections both inspired America and led to their own revolution. But even in France, Huguenots were the vanguard of the innovative thinking on sovereignty and the protection of rights. According to the Huguenot Philippe Mornay, kings "were raised to their dignities by the people and therefore they should never forget . . . in what a strict bond of observance they are tied to those from whom they have received all their greatness." Mornay sketched out the notion of separation of powers, writing that "officers of the kingdom receive their authority from the people in the general assembly of the states . . . to preserve the rights and privileges of the people, and to carefully hinder the prince." Philippe Mornay, "A Defence of Liberty Against Tyrants," in Hans Hillerbrand, ed., *The Protestant Reformation* (New York: HarperPerennial, 2009), pp. 261ff.

But to unearth it, I had to go back to the source:

"The Reverend Father Martin Luther, Master of Arts and Sacred Theology . . . intends to defend the following statements." So, legend has it, read a handbill that was tacked up on the carved wooden door of the Castle Church in Wittenberg, Germany, on October 31, 1517, inviting scholars to a public debate on a long list of propositions.

1. When our Lord and Master Jesus Christ said, "Repent" (Matthew 4:17), he willed the entire life of believers to be one of repentance.
2. This word cannot be understood as referring to the sacrament of penance . . . as administered by the clergy.

Luther's historic Ninety-Five Theses founded Protestantism, one of the most far-reaching intellectual and spiritual revolutions in human history. And these first two statements certainly sound theological in nature. Yet they were written in a temporal context—a context, it turns out, that had a lot to do with corruption.

In Luther's day, Christians who had sinned were expected to regret their misdeeds—to feel remorse or "repentance," the key word in the first thesis—and to prove their contrition by performing humbling acts such as fasting or almsgiving. Only then could they regain full membership in the community and ensure their salvation after death.

Accomplishment of difficult or humiliating deeds, and a priest's determination that they were sufficient to cancel out the sin, was "the sacrament of penance," the key phrase in Luther's second thesis. For many, the importance of performing these physical acts overshadowed that of the inward psychic reality of repentance.

People who died having confessed their sins but failed to perform penance were believed to incur a kind of debt, which they would have to pay off by suffering pain for some time in a limbo called purgatory. Lurid images in church windows and stonework, and the horrifying language of weekly sermons, frightened congregations with the agonies awaiting them should they die with accounts due.

Over time, church authorities began to offer people a dodge to avoid actually performing the penitential acts. They could purchase "indulgences" after confessing their sins. The vendors of these indulgences were eventually authorized to receive confession and administer absolution, though they were not priests.

In other words, just by handing over some money to buy an indulgence, a person could, in a single brief transaction, go through all the steps that guaranteed passage to heaven. Or even get a deceased loved one released from the torments of purgatory, by buying an indulgence in his or her name. The church had stumbled on a huge business. People started bankrupting themselves.

In 1515 a special indulgence was put up for sale in Germany. Cash-strapped Pope Leo X wanted to complete the construction of a magnificent church in Rome. The archbishop of Mainz—who had borrowed heavily to purchase his position, along with two other lucrative posts— was put in charge of the marketing campaign. Half the proceeds of the sale were earmarked for his creditor. So vital did the archbishop consider this mission that he ordered all other religious preaching to stop when vendors arrived in a town to hawk the indulgence.[1]

This was the context in which Luther composed his theses, which included:

27. They preach only human doctrines who say that as soon as the money clinks into the money chest, the soul flies out of purgatory. . . .
50. Christians are to be taught that if the pope knew the exactions of the indulgence preachers, he would rather that the basilica of St. Peter were burned to ashes than built up with the skin, flesh, and bones of his sheep. . . .
72. Let him who guards against the lust and license of the indulgence preachers be blessed.

Luther's theses—the genesis of the Reformation—were in large part an indictment of corruption.

So was a missive he wrote three years later, "To the Christian Nobility of the German Nation." Luther was a sensation by then; his theses, printed in Latin and German, had spread as far as Switzerland. They were drawing fervent applause from Germans of all ranks. The pope was threatening to excommunicate him.

Luther's response was an open rebuke to the Holy Father. "It is shocking to see the . . . vicar of Christ . . . going about in such a worldly and ostentatious style that neither king nor emperor can equal," he wrote. "This kind of splendor is offensive."[2]

In the twenty-first century, Afghans and Tunisians and Uzbeks found such ostentation offensive in their governing officials too.

Rome, wrote Luther, is full of "buying, selling, bartering, changing, trading, drunkenness, lying, deceiving, robbing, stealing, luxury, harlotry, knavery. . . . And out of this sea the same kind of morality flows into all the world."[3]

A stream is muddied from its source.

Luther castigated the practice of appointing one man to several ecclesiastical posts, "coupl[ing] together ten or twenty prelacies," so that "one thousand or ten thousand gulden may be collected," allowing a cardinal to live "like a wealthy monarch at Rome."[4]

He criticized the widespread purchase of office: "No bishop can be confirmed unless he pays a huge sum for his pallium." Legal cases over purely temporal matters are called to Rome, he complained, where judges are ignorant of local laws, justice (or injustice) is sold, and excommunication is used as a threat to blackmail people. Monasteries are given over to caretakers who appoint "some apostate, renegade monk," who "sits all day long in the church selling pictures and images to the pilgrims."[5]

And all this, Luther charged—in terms Egyptians and Tunisians echo today—was especially despicable because it was done under the color of law: "They have bound us with their canon law and robbed us of our rights so that we have to buy them back again with money."[6]

Obviously, the copious and profound teachings of Martin Luther cannot be boiled down just to a diatribe against corruption. His exploration of such doctrines as the physical presence of Christ in the host at communion, the importance of faith to salvation, and the role of priests as intercessors with God go far beyond such economic concerns. Still, many of the very elements of creed that he contested were used by the church to maintain a monopoly over the salvation of the faithful—a monopoly that made widespread extortion possible.[7]

LUTHER WAS hardly the first to lash out at the corruption of the Catholic Church. The twelfth-century mirror writer John of Salisbury reserved some of his choicest language for Rome:

> Scribes and Pharisees sit[ting] within Rome . . . accumulate valuable furnishings, they pile up gold and silver at the bank . . . delight in the plunder of churches and calculate all profits as piety. They deliver justice not for the sake of truth but for a price. . . . Even the Roman pontiff himself is burdensome and almost intolerable to everyone, since . . . he erects palaces and parades himself about not only in purple vestments but in gilded clothes. . . . They pick clean the spoils of the provinces as if they wanted to recover the treasures of Croesus.[8]

In the 1430s, an anonymous cleric probably living in Basel, where today's Switzerland meets Germany and France, conceived a far-reaching reform of the church and empire, purportedly on behalf of the Holy Roman Emperor Sigismund (d. 1437). From its terms, a detailed picture of the church kleptocracy emerges. Along with indulgences—"as I love God, terrible simony and sin"[9]—the text denounces multiple benefices,[10] the sale of papal seals for official documents,[11] and cardinals' large retinues.[12] The reform called for a fixed salary for all church officials and an end to clerics' demands of "gifts" for their work, or the sale of dispensations for their illegal activities (such as sleeping with their maidservants).[13]

In the latter half of the fifteenth century and the early sixteenth, a whole body of complaint literature grew up, collectively referred to as the "grievances of the German people against Rome." A treatise submitted to the Diet of Worms in 1521 listed one hundred and one specific complaints, including:

- Transfer of secular cases to Rome or ecclesiastical courts, under pain of excommunication,
- Transfer of benefices to Rome if a cleric dies there or on his way,
- High annual taxes ("annates") imposed on Germany,
- High confirmation fees for bishops, or the requirement that prelates buy or lease their benefices from Rome,
- Annulment of the local elections to church office to make way for the pope's cronies,
- Sale of absolution or dispensation from sins, even future sins,
- Penances made "so formidable that the sinner is obliged to buy his way out of them,"
- "Mendicant friars, relic hawkers, and miracle healers [who] go . . . through our land, begging, collecting . . . and extracting large sums of money"; permission to do so in return for a cut of the take,[14]
- Threat of excommunication or withholding of sacraments to extort money, collective punishment on whole villages, even for matters of debt,
- Appropriating a cut of pilgrims' offerings at shrines,
- Extortion of contributions for public processions,
- Extortion of payment for graves in the churchyard,
- Pressure on dying people to bequeath their property to the church instead of their kin.[15]

There was enough material in those complaints for a sketch of the kleptocratic structure of church in the early sixteenth century, along the lines of that whiteboard drawing at ISAF headquarters that depicted the structure of acute corruption in Afghanistan.*

Without doubt, the Reformation—which ignited wars and toppled kingdoms, in one of the most sweeping upheavals in Western history—was a revolution against kleptocracy.

---

* See Appendix.

WHERE THE new reformed religion and its rebellion against church kleptocracy intersects most dramatically with the origins of modern representative government is during the Dutch Revolt.* Key to that conflict was Phillip II's savage repression of Protestant religious practice.

In the spring of 1566, barred from building their own churches, adepts of the new faith began congregating outside city walls, amid the hedgerows and pastures, to listen to itinerant preachers.

"I must not fail to inform your Highness," wrote the governor of the city of Lille (now part of France) to King Philip II's regent in the Netherlands, "of two preachings that were held last night. The principal one . . . attracted about four thousand people." Reports from infiltrators he had placed in the crowd allowed the governor to quote some of the meeting's incendiary language: "Pray God that He destroy these idolatrous Papists, and have courage, for we are strong, but our time has not yet come."[16]

"Despair made those who dissented in religion more obdurate," wrote an eyewitness after the events, "and made them prefer to oppose the government openly and confess their belief frankly, rather than to remain for ever oppressed and subdued."[17] The lack of recourse was pushing Dutch Protestants to extremes.

Try as the local nobility might "to punish and curb this insolence and disorder of the sectarians," they could not keep the people from attending these "hedge sermons."[18] The crowds grew larger. Worshippers, returning home from the sermons, would clatter through town, "armed and be-cudgeled, and singing psalms."[19]

---

* Part of what makes this material conceptually challenging, at least for me, is the fact that a single episode epitomizes two apparently contradictory reactions to kleptocracy: the start of the process of elaborating a constitutional form of government on the one hand, and violent religious extremism on the other. The leadership of the Dutch revolt incarnated both tendencies. There is no current indication that Al Qaeda and its subsidiaries will evolve a new mechanism of representative government, the way the descendants of those early Protestant extremists did in the Dutch and short-lived English Republics, or in the United States. On the other hand, the tendency toward tolerance and representation is not Protestantism's only propensity. A strong undercurrent of dogmatic puritanism does persist and, though not often physically violent, is growing more powerful in places like Nigeria—and in some parts of the United States.

By July, Philip's regent was calling up soldiers, foot and horse.[20]

In mid-August, the Netherlands exploded.

The governor of Lille's August 16 report recounts that Protestants on their way to outdoor sermons suddenly veered off toward the towns of "Messines, Quesnoy, Warnenton, Commynes," where they "trashed, broke images, sepulchers, and made gigantic disorders at churches, hospitals, and cloisters."[21]

The appalled governor of Aire wrote of similar unthinkable scenes in his region two days later:

> I would not know how to express or spell out to Your Highness the great desolation that exists in Flanders, to see daily all the churches and chapels of the countryside devastated, ruined, and violated by the new evangelists. They carried out of the said churches all the furnishings for the holy sacrament, and played with them as with a bowling ball, and threw the very sacred consecrated host on the ground, broke the tables and altars, the figures and portrayals of the cross, of the virgin and the saints there represented, and set fires in several places. On top of that, they tore down the altars, shattering the stones of them, and also broke the baptismal fonts, tore up the books, and carried off all the ornaments and even all the cloths and other linen serving the said churches.[22]

On a quick-burning fuse, the riots leaped from the towns of the southern Netherlands to the north, leaving behind the smoking and amputated ruins of thousands of ecclesiastical buildings, and the torn and twisted remains of vestments, chalices, altars, statues, paintings, plate, candlesticks, books, and even kegs of wine and costly butter.[23]

It has been called "iconoclasm," and indeed, the rioters went after icons, or religious images, whose presence in a place of worship they considered idolatrous. But they did not attack just images. They fell upon all the manifestations of the wealth and riches that the church had been extorting for so long and parading before their eyes. The ferocity of the destruction speaks to the depths of the people's rage.

Those images—the painted statues of the saints or the Virgin Mary, the relics in their precious receptacles, even great crucifixes, were regularly taken out on procession, bedecked in brocades and furs, jewels at wrists and neck, while an impoverished public, assembled by the sides of the streets, gazed up at them.[24]

"They put robes of silk on their idols made of old wood," an anonymous complaint from the French-speaking southern Netherlands put it, "leaving us brethren of Christ naked and starving."[25]

Sometimes, armed with a candlestick or a stave, the iconoclasts would simply beat an object to pieces, hammering it blindly. But often there was a method to their vandalism. Statues were defenestrated, beheaded, their noses cut off. In one case, a Saint Nicholas was executed by hanging.[26] The rioters seemed to be acting out a ritual punishment upon the symbols of the church, in retribution for the crimes of the Roman kleptocracy.

And those early Protestants, in revolt against kleptocracy, can only be described as violent religious extremists.

SKIP NOW to 2012. Al Qaeda–linked rebels, garbed in Afghan-cut clothes and black turbans, fall upon the legendary Malian desert city of Timbuktu and—as they deal out savage shari'a law penalties—set about trashing dozens of historic shrines dedicated to Sufi saints. They reduce ancient mud-brick mausoleums to rubble, raze a fabled monument at the city gates, and smash modern statues. "Not a single mausoleum will remain in Timbuktu," a rebel proclaimed to Agence France-Presse. "God doesn't like it."[27] According to Human Rights Watch, "bars and hotels . . . associated with alcohol consumption and prostitution" were also targeted.[28] Later, fleeing the town ahead of French and Malian troops in January 2013, the militants set fire to the governor's office and libraries that have stored precious manuscripts for hundreds of years.[29]

The similarities between the early Protestants and today's Islamist extremists don't end with iconoclasm. The Puritans were famous for frowning on liquor, dancing, and festivities. They turned to the literal text of scripture for teachings on religious practice and the conduct of daily life. Where they could, they imposed their preferred practice on civilians by law, sometimes inflicting gruesome punishments on nonconformists.[30] They wore ostentatiously modest black and white clothes—

like those special Islamist veils—allowing adepts to recognize each other, whether they were Dutch or Huguenot or natives of Plymouth on the Massachusetts Bay.

And, as adamantly as today's Salafis, they flung the label of unbeliever at anyone who differed with their rigid doctrine. "Puritans," spat James I, in the preface to his mirror for Harry, imagine themselves "in a manner without sin, the only true church, and only worthy to be participant of the sacraments, and all the rest of the world to be but abomination in the sight of God."[31]

The other remarkable manner in which today's violent jihadis parallel the early Protestants is that they articulate their struggle, at least in part, as a reaction to the kleptocratic practices of local rulers—in the modern case, inspired and enabled by the United States.

Even to suggest such an equivalency—including the proposition that violence in both cases grew out of legitimate grievances—may seem offensive to many Americans. But more than a dozen years after 9/11, the events of that day are now entering the realm of history. And to subject them, as historical events, to the type of critical analysis that episodes from earlier times and more distant places receive, is not to dishonor or belittle the victims.

Abstracted from that painful psychological context, the resemblance between the language Al Qaeda uses to explain its violence, and that of the earlier Protestant insurrectionaries castigating the acute corruption of the Catholic Church and its royalist allies, is unmistakable.

In a video sent to the Al-Jazeera cable television network in late fall of 2004, for example, Osama bin Laden emphasized the kleptocratic practices of Arab rulers—and U.S. officials' emulation of them—as he sought to correct what he saw as Americans' misunderstanding of the motivation behind the 9/11 attacks.

"Even though we are in the fourth year after the events of September 11th," Bin Laden said, "Bush is still . . . hiding from you the real causes."[32] Among those causes, he listed U.S. support for the 1982 Israeli invasion of Lebanon and both Gulf wars. The aim of the 2003 war in Iraq, he emphasized, was "to replace [an old agent] with a new puppet to assist in the pilfering of Iraq's oil."

Then Bin Laden began analyzing the George W. Bush administration, which resembled, in his view, "the regimes in our countries, half of which are ruled by the military, and the other half . . . by the sons of kings and presidents." And those leaders—of Arab military dictatorships and Gulf monarchies alike—are "characterized by pride, arrogance, greed and misappropriation of wealth."

President George W. Bush's long friendship with these kleptocratic Arab rulers, Bin Laden told Americans, gave him an opportunity to observe their corruption, the impunity with which they were committing it, and the lack of any means of appeal or redress. Bush, Bin Laden suggested, "became envious of their remaining decades in their positions, to embezzle the public wealth of the nation without supervision or accounting."[33]

The theme of corruption also dominates a 2009 video interview disseminated by Al Qaeda's media division. Here Ayman al-Zawahiri, who succeeded Bin Laden at the head of the organization, declared:

> Regimes that are corrupt, rotten, and allied with the Crusaders
> . . . have tried to be secretive about the uprising and the jihadist
> anger. . . . [The uprising] defends the stolen Muslim rights and
> their honors that are being violated by those regimes every day.
> . . . Popular awareness is more convinced, now, that these corrupt
> and rotten regimes are the reason behind economic injustice and
> corruption, the political oppression, and social detachment.

Other Al Qaeda publications dissect the details of public corruption scandals, such as a 2006 Saudi deal to buy seventy-two Eurofighter jets, which allegedly included BAE Systems' gift of a lavish honeymoon for the daughter of Saudi Prince Bandar bin Sultan, then secretary general of the UN Security Council.[34]

Through application of the "command responsibility" principle that served as the basis for convicting King Charles I, that figures in so many Mirrors for Princes, and that explains why Afghans hold Washington responsible for the Karzai government's behavior, Bin Laden and other senior Al Qaeda figures blamed the United States for the corruption of their own rulers.

Abd al-Rahman Atiya, killed in a drone strike in 2011, conceded that the 9/11 attacks had been launched because of hatred for some aspects of Western culture, but the main rationale was the U.S. role enabling Arab kleptocracies.

> Yes we hate the corruptive financial lifestyle that does not please God . . . But . . . the more important reason is their . . . appointing collaborative regimes for them in our countries. Then they support these regimes and corruptive governments against their people, who demand freedom and want to abide by Islam.

This Western support for Middle Eastern kleptocracies was "the real reason that pushed the mujahideen to carry out these blessed attacks."

Atiya went on to blast the aspects of Western culture he deemed most objectionable—excesses that have seemed especially pronounced since the 1990s: "It is a corrupt, wayward, and unjust system . . . based on beastly behavior, and seven principles: greed, gluttony, injustice, selfishness, extreme materialism, abandonment of religion."[35]

In this context—and recalling the history of Dutch Protestants ransacking the physical manifestations of Catholic kleptocracy—the choice of the Pentagon and the Twin Towers, near Wall Street, as the target of the 9/11 attacks may take on an enhanced meaning. Perhaps Al Qaeda's main intent was not to kill large numbers of Americans so much as to visit a spectacular symbolic punishment upon the manifestations of what it saw as a criminal kleptocracy that controlled the most powerful instruments of force on earth. Perhaps Al Qaeda was in fact committing an act of iconoclasm: replicating the kind of sentences that the 1566 Protestants executed on churches and articles of devotion the length and breadth of the Low Countries.[36]

These roughly comparable instances, from different centuries and religions, exemplify a persistent relationship between corruption and religious extremism. In periods of acute, self-serving behavior on the part of public leaders, Christians and Muslims alike have often sought a corrective in strict codes of personal behavior derived from the precepts of puritanical religion. And they have imposed it, if necessary, by force.

Those who object to this remedy should look for other ways to cure the cause.

CHAPTER FOURTEEN

Remedies

Violent religious extremism is not the only menace to international security that systemic corruption can fuel. It is just the particular variety that dominated the imagination of most Western decision makers early in the twenty-first century. Massive popular uprisings leading to revolution, government collapse, and bloody or dangerous aftershocks constitute another potential peril rooted in kleptocracy. Events across the Arab world beginning in 2011 and in Ukraine in 2014 furnish clear examples. Iraq experienced a kind of hybrid of the two that year, as militant extremists, joined by non-jihadi locals, conquered much of the north and west of the country.

Other threats to world stability are also generated by intense, systemic government corruption. Unnoticed, like some odorless gas, it fuels these threats without attracting much policy attention.

When every government function is up for sale to the highest bidder, violations of international as well as domestic law become the norm. Do Iran and North Korea frighten the world with their nuclear ambitions? Both purchased the technology from officials at the Pakistan Atomic Energy Commission.[1] Are international sanctions regimes often too porous to contain targeted regimes? Corrupt governments help circumvent them.

Acutely corrupt governance doesn't just aid terrorist organizations by driving indignant citizens into their arms; it provides haven and logistical support for those very same groups, as officials avert their eyes in exchange for a bribe. Nairobi residents joke about the "Shebab bribe"—double the normal rate—that allowed attackers to infiltrate the Westgate Mall in September 2013, in a siege that claimed more than sixty lives. Trafficking rings that have secured safe passage past corrupt officials for migrants or sex slaves may also provide transit for mules carrying a dirty bomb. Some corrupt governments, like Algeria's or Pakistan's or Yemen's, may deliberately cultivate terrorist groups—even while simultaneously projecting themselves as counterterrorism allies, to tap into a continuing flow of military assistance dollars.

Trafficking rings, whether they deal in illicit drugs or substandard medicine, restricted resources such as protected wildlife, or weapons, or conflict minerals, can obtain their product of choice or move it without leaving tracks through highly corrupt environments. "In Zimbabwe," write two of France's most distinguished Africanists, Jean-François Bayart and Béatrice Hibou, "the traffic in ivory and rhinoceros horn has involved not only guerrilla movements but also the military authorities. In general, illegal diamond exports are not carried out by small-time diggers or traders, but by those at the highest reaches of power."[2] In some cases, the protections afforded humanitarian organizations may be wrongfully extended to trafficking networks that pose as NGOs.[3]

Where criminality is the norm, the systematic theft of proprietary information across borders is rewarded. "The scale of international theft of American intellectual property is unprecedented," a commission chaired by a former director of national intelligence and a former ambassador to China found in 2013. Losses add up to "hundreds of billions of dollars per year, on the order of the size of U.S. exports to Asia." China, one of the world's most corrupt countries, "is the world's largest source of IP theft."[4]

In Albania, Argentina, Bulgaria, Colombia, Honduras, Mexico, and Montenegro, among other acutely corrupt countries, public officials have entered into destabilizing alliances, even symbiosis, with transnational criminal superpowers: drug and weapons syndicates whose activities span continents. In these and other cases, some rival criminal network, often posing as a "Robin Hood," may mount a violent challenge to corrupt government networks. Such scenarios have exacted a shocking price from populations both inside and beyond national boundaries.[5]

Where conflict exists, corrupt governing networks may deliberately maintain the civil strife, to provide ongoing opportunities for extracting resources—including humanitarian aid—or for profiteering from the sale of necessities: "It is at the moment that a crisis becomes most evident that external finances flow most easily."[6]

The militaries in acutely corrupt countries make unreliable allies. As defense funding is siphoned off to the purses of the powerful, armies are often poorly trained and equipped, their rosters full of "ghost soldiers." Officers sell matériel, even to the same enemies they are supposed to be fighting. Military professionalism and capabilities are inadequate to protect borders, leaving such countries vulnerable to attack. In 2014, the militaries of Ukraine, Nigeria, and Iraq put every one of these ills on display. Kleptocratic governments cannot be expected to honor the conditions attached to the provision of military aid. Proliferation, forging of end-user certificates, and other types of fraud are likely to be the norm. And cooperation, like Pakistan's in allowing NATO to use its overland routes into Afghanistan, is often provided only for a price, which can be raised as soon as dependence is established.

Other corruption-related security threats burn on a slower fuse. Corrupt government practices contribute to severe economic distortions, threatening financial sector stability, for example, when banks are pillaged or fraudulent banking practices are widespread. Kleptocratic networks can also undermine the economic diversity of their countries, as they focus government effort on extracting natural resources whose returns they capture. Other economic sectors wither or are actively undermined by cheating on customs or other types of unfair competition. Economic opportunities dry up. Unemployment rises. And the distortions that result can have destabilizing impacts on entire economic ecosystems.

Acute corruption damages physical ecosystems just as indelibly. Kleptocracies don't care much about environmental degradation. Their policies—or lack of them—often exacerbate the impact of climate change and incapacitate efforts to curb it. Worsening environmental conditions, in turn, increase the suffering of populations, making them more likely to rise in revolt.[7] In climate-vulnerable countries—Haiti, for example, or the Philippines—the impact of natural disasters is compounded by corruption. And disaster relief, while on the face of it not a security issue, is a priority mission for the U.S. Marines.

Obviously, not even severe and structured corruption—nor any other single driver—can be solely blamed for such complex phenomena as insurgency, revolution, economic depression, or the partial capture of states by transnational criminal organizations. This book has emphasized acute corruption not because it is the sole driver but because it is a remarkably underappreciated one. The interplay of kleptocratic governance with other factors increases the likelihood of a severe international security event occurring at a given time.

Networks determined to exploit weaknesses lying nearby, such as Al Qaeda franchises that can capitalize on local grievances, or criminal superpowers on the hunt for leaders to co-opt, are one such factor. Preexisting separatist movements might be another, or high unemployment, or an ethnic or sectarian split, or severe local economic disparities caused by geographic or environmental factors, or a recent economic downturn, or an autocratic leader's advanced age.[8]

IT WOULD be wrong to imply that Western governments have been entirely insensible to the problem of corruption. Washington has led the drive to end businesses' habit of bribing government officials to gain access to markets. The Foreign Corrupt Practices Act and antibribery conventions modeled on it have revolutionized corporate behavior. As concern about terrorist financing and tax evasion has risen, efforts to combat money laundering and tax fraud have picked up momentum. The 2014 Ukraine crisis sparked further interest in the issue within the U.S. government. International institutions such as the Organization for Economic Cooperation and Development and the G-20 are helping tighten norms. Some European nations, such as Norway, have begun attaching strict conditions to foreign aid, including repayment requirements if the conditions are not met. And by funding their activities and providing at least a degree of implicit protection, international aid agencies provide lifelines to grassroots anticorruption activists.

Yet where Western governments are paying for anticorruption efforts out of one pocket, they are often paying off corrupt governments out of another—and far more lavishly, via budget support, military assistance, basing rights, international loans, major development projects, or covert cash handouts. Corruption is usually classified as a humanitarian aid problem, to be handled by donor agencies, not mainstreamed into overall foreign and defense policy. And while governments may support across-the-board efforts on a multilateral level, they almost never consider acute corruption as they shape their approach to specific countries. Human rights, religious freedom, protections for the LGBT community may enter the conversation, but corruption rarely does.

Tools to raise the cost of kleptocratic practices exist—in abundance. It's just a matter of finding the courage and finesse to use them. All the levers and incentives listed below can be further refined, and new ones imagined, in specific contexts. Particular corrupt officials or structures have unique vulnerabilities and desires; and timelines and windows of opportunity for effective action will be specific to individual cases and will suggest even more potential actions as they are examined. Many of the actions below can and should be routinized—folded into the everyday activities of relevant bureaucracies—so as to reduce the onus on leaders to sign their names to audacious and thus potentially career-threatening moves. But in other cases, a strategy may need to be carefully thought through and tailored to the specific conditions of a given country at a specific point in time.

Generically, the leverage might be organized in the following categories.

CHIEF OF STATE TOOLS

To provide officials with impetus and authority for taking steps listed below, chiefs of state should consider enunciating an anticorruption policy, with appropriate motivation, and directing their ministries or cabinet departments to make use of all relevant powers and resources to further it. In the United States, an executive order or presidential memorandum might be an appropriate mechanism. The chief of state should assign a staff member to follow up on implementation of the directive across government agencies.

Publicized face-to-face meetings with Western chiefs of state often serve as important status-enhancing events for corrupt leaders. Victims of corruption decry photo opportunities with the U.S. president as key enablers of their corrupt regimes. Such interactions should be agreed to and choreographed with care.

INTELLIGENCE TOOLS

INTELLIGENCE AGENCIES are driven by the questions their clients ask them. If they have not compiled much information on the security impacts of acute corruption to date, it is because few policy makers have pointed them at that problem. Systemic corruption should be explicitly included in the intelligence community's annual assessment of threats to U.S. national security, and similar such assessments regularly conducted by other Western governments. Intelligence professionals should be pulled off other tasks and assigned to study the structure and operations of kleptocratic networks as functioning systems. A framework for analysis should include such information as: the levers of power captured by the network, its favored revenue streams, its structure and manning, the degree of vertical integration, the internal and external enablers that reinforce it and facilitate its operations, its vulnerabilities, public attitudes toward corrupt practices, the other risk factors with which corruption interacts, the presence of constructive (popularly respected) actors inside or outside of the system, as well as the details of financial flows. Analysts and intelligence executives must design new collection requirements to fill knowledge gaps on these issues. Financial intelligence and information that helps pierce shell company or "beneficial ownership" smoke screens is particularly vital.

Given the different types of specialized knowledge required, "fusion cells," bringing civilian and military intelligence professionals together with colleagues from the Treasury Department or the FBI or their international equivalents, will increase efficiency.

A better understanding is needed of the ways Western governments actively enable acute corruption, especially when they in effect buy access to top officials or national territory, or intelligence, or counterterrorism cooperation, or when they retrograde matériel from or through systemically corrupt countries after a war.

A research agenda, both inside and outside government, aimed at better elucidating the interplay between acute corruption and other risk factors in provoking past security events would take this subject beyond the intuitive, toward a substantiated argument that could better influence policy debates. Further research into methods applied by countries that have successfully curbed acute corruption would also help policy makers.

Finally, it is critical that direct intelligence agency payments to "assets" be brought into line with Western governments' overarching policy priorities. Such decisions should be made through open debate at the cabinet level, in which other top government officials can weigh in with their own considerations. It is no longer acceptable for intelligence agencies to be able to hide from their colleagues in the cabinet—or even from the chief of state—the identities of the high-ranking foreign government officials they are paying.

DIPLOMATIC TOOLS

HOW A POWERFUL country engages with partner nations can influence their behavior and sends signals that are eagerly parsed by their populations. The United States and other Western governments should shape their diplomatic engagements with acutely corrupt governments in such a way as at least to avoid glorifying their practices. As is the case with chiefs of state, high-level publicized meetings with foreign ministers—or even overly cozy personal relationships—enhance leaders' status.[9] Corruption should figure among talking points for high-level bilateral meetings, including suggestions of detailed knowledge of partner government practices, and of potential repercussions, if concrete follow-up is actually likely. In cases of governments that prize international legitimacy, foreign ministers should call out acute corruption as often as they do the depredations of violent insurgents. But officials should beware of making threats if the political will to carry them out does not exist.

Diplomats should take greater pains to connect with populations in kleptocratic countries, without members of the government or their agents present. And they should protect their right to do so when such governments inevitably push back—as Bahrain's did by expelling U.S. Assistant Secretary of State Tom Malinowski in July 2014. They should avoid using government cutouts to conduct their everyday business—to interpret for them, or provide supplies or logistics solutions.

Visas for visits to or study in Western countries are highly prized in the developing world. As part of a strategized campaign targeting specific networks, visas should be denied or delayed to select kleptocratic figures. On the other hand, witnesses in cases against suspected offenders, local criminal investigators, prosecutors working such cases, and other constructive actors should be granted expedited visas and other facilitation. To date, the U.S. tendency has been to turn its back on financial or legal professionals who have taken a stand and suffered for it.

So long as international attention does not put them at risk, oversight bodies that prove their independence should receive support and capacity-building resources. So should individual legal or oversight professionals seeking to take a stand. They should receive encouragement and help in appealing to international professional bodies, such as the International Association of Supreme Audit Institutions.

Western countries can even help establish special judicial or oversight institutions within corrupt countries, if the environment allows, and provide international staff to bolster their independence. And Western officials can use their convening power and influence within multilateral bodies and institutions to ensure that acute corruption remains in the international policy spotlight.

An important function of foreign ministries is to promote bilateral investment and trade opportunities abroad for businesses of their own countries. Care should be taken in pursuing such efforts not to overlook hidden pay-to-play tollbooths, or otherwise inadvertently to reinforce corrupt ruling networks' control over key sectors of their nations' economies in the rush to capture economic "wins" for the home front.

It is the diplomatic toolbox that affords the most flexibility, the greatest ability to send messages subtly, with a concrete impact that can be camouflaged in delicate language. And yet in my own experience and according to senior U.S. civilian officials, U.S. diplomats typically resist holding the line on corruption. Their traditional role of cultivating relationships seems to trump other considerations.

FINANCIAL SYSTEM TOOLS

CURRENT anti-money-laundering rules—and in the United States, provisions under both the Patriot Act and Comptroller of the Currency authorities—provide for enhanced monitoring of the financial transactions of money-laundering suspects and "politically exposed persons." Those requirements can be focused on select kleptocratic officials—ideally, again, as part of a synchronized strategy.

Several U.S. financial sanctions regimes could similarly be used to target kleptocratic officials whose activities fall within the categories of wrongdoing they penalize. The Narcotics Kingpin[10] and Transnational Criminal Organizations[11] sanctions might be particularly relevant.

But given the severity and diversity of the security problems fueled by acute corruption, perhaps it is time to consider a new financial sanctions regime, enacted by executive order, that is explicitly aimed at significant corruption. The existence of such a regime does not automatically determine which individuals will be penalized. Those targeting decisions are made in interagency debate that weighs the political and diplomatic trade-offs on a case-by-case basis.

U.S. sanctions against Russia after its annexation of Crimea included a provision authorizing their application to officials

> responsible for, or complicit in, or responsible for ordering, controlling, or otherwise directing, acts of significant corruption in the Russian Federation, including the expropriation of private or public assets for personal gain, corruption related to government contracts or the extraction of natural resources, bribery, or the facilitation or transfer of the proceeds of corruption to foreign jurisdictions.[12]

Such language could serve as the basis for a broader executive order or legislation, and similar measures in other Western countries.

LEGAL TOOLS

FOREIGN CORRUPT PRACTICES ACT prosecutions—which have done so much to curb businesses' reflex to pay foreign officials for access to markets—could be selectively aimed at businesses suspected of bribing a particular kleptocratic official who is under the policy spotlight. Currently, the selection of targets is random, based on the ease of making a case. As part of such prosecutions, bribe payers should be encouraged to inform on bribe takers or other bribe payers. And their information should be collated and used as part of a strategized effort to reach targeted kleptocratic officials. Threat of prosecution to elicit such information should be part of that strategy.

Prosecutions under the Racketeer-Influenced and Corrupt Organizations (RICO) statute could also be mobilized, along with prosecutions under national legislation of Western countries where members of kleptocratic networks hold dual citizenship.

Prosecutions under U.S., U.K., and some other countries' civil law that allow for the forfeiture of assets connected to a crime—even if no individual has been convicted or even apprehended for committing it—should also be directed in a more targeted fashion at the assets of specific kleptocrats. In the United States, currently, an understaffed office in the Department of Justice makes what cases it can, with too few resources and without any connection to broader U.S. foreign policy. (In April 2014, Attorney General Eric Holder announced a new team of FBI investigators dedicated to this effort. The dozen personnel exponentially increased investigative manpower.)

Other asset tracing and recovery efforts aimed specifically at the proceeds of corruption should be expanded, not least when those proceeds are held in the form of prestigious real property in Western capitals.[13]

Reinforced and targeted searches and seizures of cash above a legal limit at airports that serve as hubs for transfer of illicit funds, such as Delhi, Dubai, or Frankfurt, could provide information as well as assets to return to countries in question.

Robust legal assistance should be provided to professionals living and working inside kleptocratic or transitioning countries, who are bringing cases within their own borders against corrupt actors or assets.

Consideration should be given to expanding the rights of victims to bring cases internationally against perpetrators of severe, structured corruption. Such expanded jurisdictions in humanitarian law have led to war crimes cases in third-nation courts against Chilean and Rwandan perpetrators. Creative ways to break down traditional resistance to cooperation between justice ministry officials and civil society or victims' organizations conducting nonstate investigations should be explored.

AID TOOLS

UPSTREAM of any changes in the way aid is delivered, Western countries and international organizations such as the World Bank and the IMF must gain a better grasp of how development assistance, including loans, millennium challenge assistance, grants by the global fund to fight AIDS, and capital for infrastructure improvements, becomes yet another "rent" that is captured by kleptocratic ruling networks. More research is needed into the ways kleptocratic networks use shell organizations such as GONGOs or contractors owned by a family member to monopolize international funds. Donor agencies should also actively collect information on contract and implementation irregularities, including by means of whistle-blower protections and rewards.

Contracting guidelines should direct aid officials to steer clear of implementing partners whose beneficial owners are members of corruption networks. When it seems impossible to do so, a rigorous cost-benefit analysis should be conducted to determine whether the beneficiary population might not be best served in the long run if the project were not carried out at all.

Contracts should be better tailored, stipulating conditions for the use of the money (rather than the endless paper formalities that are currently imposed to avoid fraud, but that often end up favoring network-linked implementers that command the working capital required to hire sophisticated grant-writing professionals). Provisions should stipulate—

as Norway's foreign assistance contracts do, for example—the reimbursement of aid money when conditions are not met. Future aid should be conditioned on remedial action.

To provide sufficient oversight for the millions of dollars in aid provided annually, independent monitoring and evaluation must be featured in every aid contract. Such monitoring activities should be considered integral to the program being funded—not part of "overhead," a budget line that donors constantly seek to minimize. Independent special inspector generals, such as those empowered to oversee U.S. aid to Afghanistan and Iraq, should become the norm, and their enforcement powers should be enhanced.

When planning assistance to anticorruption efforts abroad, Western governments should resist the temptation to think of corruption primarily as a technical problem, to be addressed by means of equipment or capacity building. Donor agencies should distinguish between countries in which a significant number of government officials who matter are making a bona-fide effort to address the problem—and where technical assistance might help them—and countries whose corrupt governments are extracting resources largely unchecked. In those cases, anticorruption assistance is likely to be captured as yet another rent—including by regime-affiliated nonprofits.

Legitimate civil society organizations cannot be expected to bear the whole burden of anticorruption efforts alone, especially if other Western interactions with the corrupt government tend to enable it. Civil society assistance should be provided with attention to the real power dynamics, to the risk activists incur, and to the types of support other than money that might give them more weight.

Transparency, while a good starting point, should not be thought of as a synonym for accountability; too often it has proved to be no such thing. Funding for transparency programs should seek those that make that link explicit. Alternatively, they should be focused on sectors or revenue streams most likely to expose external enablers, so Western activists can make use of the newly available information in support of local civil society efforts.

Finally, donor agencies should consider expanding the range of civil society institutions they support beyond the familiar set of issue-oriented

NGOs. Professional organizations, even labor unions, may have an interest in combating corruption, as well as the economic clout and institutional infrastructure needed to gain traction. Aid providers should also think more creatively in terms of innovative, broad-based, nonviolent citizens' movements.

SECURITY SECTOR TOOLS

IN JUNE 2014, President Obama announced a new counterterrorism approach that would place increased emphasis on cooperation with host-country militaries. "I believe we must shift our counterterrorism strategy . . . to more effectively partner with countries where terrorist networks seek a foothold," Obama argued, calling for a fund of up to $5 billion "which will allow us to train, build capacity, and facilitate partner countries on the front lines."[14] But recent fiascos in Libya as well as Iraq have illustrated the potential pitfalls of such a strategy.[15] Even—or especially—when short-term counterterrorism imperatives are at stake, host-country military units should not be seen as a substitute for a government that commands the respect of its people. Careful analysis of the structure of potential partner regimes, along the lines described in the "Intelligence Tools" section above, should inform any decision on whether and how to engage with host-country militaries. Anticorruption vetting procedures should be developed.

In general, U.S. military assistance tends to be supplied in standard packages: provision of funds that can be used only to purchase U.S. military hardware (which usually comes with certain conditions attached), training for units or educational opportunities for individual foreign officers, and the staging of joint exercises. But such packages should be more thoughtfully designed, taking the specifics of each country into account—the role different security branches play in the kleptocratic structure, the fungibility of money within recipient-country budgets, the desired, and likely, impact of expanded educational opportunities for officers in the United States, and other such factors. Much more effort should be devoted to imposing creative conditionality on the provision of military assistance, such as requiring remedial anticorruption efforts, or culturally sensitive companion outreach to the civilian population.

Western military units that are in fact deployed to play an "advise and assist" role, or special operations teams that are often the first to deploy into a potentially hostile environment—and tend, in their hurry, to forge alliances of convenience—must be made aware of the pernicious downstream effects of inadvertently enabling a kleptocratic network. Such considerations should be integrated into their doctrine and training. Once in a country, they must immediately assign intelligence resources to studying the linkages and practices of the locals they work with. They should be instructed to observe and report on their trainees' behavior and to intervene on corruption issues as necessary.

Guidelines, like those for donor agencies, should direct military contracting officers to study and avoid local security companies or service providers whose beneficial owners are members of corruption networks.

Western militaries often help implement disarmament, demobilization and reintegration programs for foreign militias when conflicts are winding down, or they provide assistance for reforms to security sectors in transitioning countries. These programs should also take corruption concerns into consideration. Often military forces, and especially the police, are the first government representatives the population encounters. So their behavior is particularly critical in shaping ordinary people's view of their young government. In these contexts, focus on corruption is perhaps the most vital of all.

In countries where the military is the most powerful governing institution, such as Algeria or Egypt or Pakistan, the chairman of the Joint Chiefs of Staff (CJCS)—not the secretary of state—plays the role of chief U.S. diplomat. It is his relationship with his counterpart that represents the U.S. government's channel to the real rulers. In that context, the CJCS must widen the aperture through which he regards the country, seeing well beyond the confines of a traditional military-to-military relationship. All of the tools listed in the "intelligence" and "diplomatic" sections above are critical to his interactions with those countries and to his reporting on them to his peers on the U.S. National Security Council.

MULTILATERAL TOOLS

MANY OF the suggestions included in the "Aid Tools" section above apply equally to international grant- and loan-making institutions. Forensic and 360 audits should be conducted on loans and assistance packages, together with rigorous due diligence on recipient governments and organizations, and the true necessity of projects to the population. Too many infrastructure loans provided by the IMF or other multilateral institutions, to pay for such white elephants as the port in Kelibia, Tunisia, or the Rabat-to-Casablanca high-speed rail line, have in fact served as cash cows for kleptocratic elites. Suffering populations, meanwhile, have had to foot the bill. Too often, multilateral organizations furnish technical or capacity-building assistance, seeing such support as apolitical. But, in the context of a captured state, economic or even capacity-building support is always political. Careful analysis of who is receiving such assistance (truly mid-level constructive actors who could launch wholesale reform in the future, as is often argued?), or what use the government intends to make of the enhanced capacities, should be undertaken before launching such programs.

Reporting requirements that exist, such as those covering extractive industries, should be enforced and tightened. Membership in such reporting associations should not serve as a whitewash for kleptocratic governments—or the multinational corporations that do business with them.[16] Data transparency rules should encompass the release of data to the public, not just to member governments. And international organizations themselves should be subject to the type of "access to information" rules that many Western governments have enacted at home, so beneficiary populations can see the use to which money provided their governments has been put.

International institutions should continue reducing the barriers to sharing financial intelligence and information that identifies beneficial owners of front companies. The IMF and the Asian Development bank, among others, can put pressure on kleptocratic countries to reform their banking practices holistically—not just to enforce minimums on capital reserves. For, as was the case in Ben Ali's Tunisia, central banks controlled by kleptocratic networks may recapitalize private institutions that have provided nonperforming loans to system cronies, thus in effect transferring wealth from the population to the network.

Existing international regulations on potential revenue streams, or facilitation services that enable kleptocratic practices, require enforcement. Such regulation covers extractive and financial industries as well as land registries. Less formal codes of conduct, applied to facilitators such as accountants and lawyers, should be tightened and enforced by professional associations.

Multilateral bodies must also ensure that enabling legislation called for in anticorruption conventions has indeed been passed and is being put into effect. Rigorous peer reviews could be part of that process. Or an independent international enforcement and monitoring body, along the lines of the Organization for the Prohibition of Chemical Weapons, which won the 2013 Nobel Peace Prize, might be appropriate.

Refusing to hold important multilateral meetings in targeted kleptocratic countries would help create an international climate of disapproval.

Finally, international institutions as well as bilateral lenders should consider canceling or reducing "odious debt"—particularly in cases where kleptocratic governments have been removed and transitioning countries are cash-strapped. In cases where the private capture of donor funds is patent, it is unfair to make a victimized population also pay for the criminality of its rulers. Forcing lenders to assume more of the risk might help induce them to choose the loans they will extend with greater care.[17] (Where a kleptocratic regime remains in place, on the other hand, debt-forgiveness may ease the economic pressure that gives populations some leverage over their political elites.)

BUSINESS TOOLS

THROUGH THE investments they make, their modes of operation, and the relationships they build (and how they build them) in host countries where they work, multinational corporations are themselves significant foreign policy actors. Their objectives and motivations may differ from those of their originating nations, but that distinction is often not discernible to host-nation populations.

Businesses, especially those that make significant capital investments, such as in the extractive industries, should reassess the time horizon they apply to their risk analysis. Actions that may seem to reduce short-term risk, such as paying off or cozying up to gatekeepers for the kleptocratic elite, may be exacerbating longer-term risks to company investments, by exciting popular indignation against the government and against its business enablers. (Attacks on oil company personnel in southern Nigeria are a case in point.) Businesses should use the framework suggested in the "Intelligence Tools" section above to analyze the business environment in such countries. They should use such analysis to inform their choices on where to invest, with whom to partner, and which branch of commerce or industry to select.

They can add to general knowledge—and facilitate curbs to the corrupt practices that both distort the business environment and threaten security—by systematically reporting to their home-country foreign or commerce ministries the bribe solicitations they have received.

They should understand that what are frequently referred to as "facilitation payments" are not as innocuous as often suggested. Distinguishing between such "petty" bribery and so-called "grand" corruption, or major pay-to-play requirements, is a flawed analysis in countries such as the ones examined in this book. These systems are vertically integrated, and "petty" facilitation payments enable and reinforce their structure and practices. While it may seem impossible to avoid paying such petty bribes, anecdotal evidence indicates that a flat refusal to do so—especially by apparently powerful or desired foreign partners, ideally acting in concert—usually succeeds, and may help alter the incentive structure. At least the collecting of detailed information (name of bribe-taker, position, amount, circumstances, relevant legal provisions, etc.) and lodging of complaints, as well as actively seeking redress, represents a first step toward breaking down systematic impunity.

In light of all the considerations above, businesses should consider expanding their notions of "corporate responsibility" to include their role in facilitating the development or survival of kleptocratic systems.

Such an expanded view is especially critical for direct enablers, such as banks and accountants, or PR or lobbying firms. Insofar as kleptocratic governments are functioning criminally, then their facilitators are accessories. They bear some of the moral—if not currently much material—responsibility, not just for the criminal behavior, but for the often dramatic and destabilizing and expensive reactions it sparks. And businesses will increasingly be held responsible: as home-country populations become increasingly sensitized to these issues and information becomes increasingly available, repetitional risk in encouraging such regimes will grow.

CITIZENS' TOOLS

PRIVATE CITIZENS in Western countries can assist anticorruption efforts by identifying grassroots organizations fighting corruption in foreign countries and—where the connection would not endanger them—supporting them and publicizing their work.[18] Citizens can also negatively spotlight enablers in their own countries—banks, or accounting firms, or legal professionals who provide their services to abusively corrupt officials in developing countries.

Similarly, just as citizens' campaigns have raised multinational corporations' awareness about the rights of workers producing their goods or the safety of their overseas factories, campaigns about the way companies enable corrupt practices can impact branding and employee pride. Light can be shed on the ways corrupt governments have attracted a particular company's investment—such as shutting down local competition, deactivating local regulations, or forgiving taxes. Or Western citizens can explain the inadequacy of "offsets" that corporations may publicize, such as providing mosquito netting in an African country where raw materials are extracted without guarantees that the revenues accrue to the population rather than to the kleptocratic rulers' private coffers.

Citizens can also expose purchases by members of kleptocratic networks of luxury goods in their countries and help shame the purveyors.

INCENTIVES

A STRATEGIC and synchronized campaign to reduce acute corruption must also include rewards and incentives for reform. Loans and grants, development assistance, provision of equipment, and valuable contracts are all potential incentives.

So are bilateral or multilateral trade deals, and membership in the World Trade or World Customs Organizations, or the European Union, or other multilateral "clubs" such as the Extractive Industries Transparency Initiative, or decisions to hold important international gatherings in a given country. Highly corrupt governments often long for an international seal of approval and the status associated with membership in such bodies. Such benefits should not be accorded lightly. They should be used to reward true reform.

TRADE-OFFS

POLICY DECISIONS are always the product of trade-offs between competing or even conflicting priorities or options, or policy preferences promoted by different government agencies. Some of the considerations weighing on policy makers that may conflict with an anticorruption agenda include the value of maintaining a given relationship, especially when it is seen as the "least bad" in a tough neighborhood or when the country in question has become a sole source of needed goods, facilities, or services. Other trade-offs include demand for natural resources a country might possess, its pivotal geopolitical position and relationships, or its presumed ability to do harm.

Targeted corrupt officials may be conscious of the other items on their partner's agenda and strike back in ways that threaten those other priorities. To deter punitive action, venally corrupt officials may close overland routes or airspace, for example, cut off energy supplies to neighbors, cease sharing intelligence, cease complying with international treaties, or refuse to assist diplomatically with other problem countries when crises arise. Pressure on such governments may precipitate instability in their countries—or their leaders may suggest that it will, presenting short-term kleptocratic stability as the only alternative to chaos.

Top decision makers in Western countries, moreover, are under staggering time pressures. Officials' time and bandwidth are as limited as budgets in an age of austerity, and policies that might help curb acute corruption place demands on all three. Short-term, crisis-driven decision making, of the type that prevails in Washington as in other capitals, favors work with whoever the current foreign partner happens to be and encourages focus on leaders in general, not on populations. It also reinforces risk aversion. And employing most of the leverage listed here entails political risks.

Without an accurate measure of those risks, however, or the true likely costs and benefits of all courses of action, policy trade-offs will be based on false premises, a skewed calculus.

Western governments must begin systematically analyzing the costs of *not* addressing corruption, which currently go unweighed in national security decision making. More time and effort should be spent identifying "least bad" alternatives to enabling alliances with kleptocratic rulers. International partners and proxies could be encouraged to play the role of "heavy" on corruption issues in specific cases; they should be identified and skillfully enabled.

Advocates for a tougher stance against acute corruption should be alert for windows of opportunity or strategic openings regarding specific countries, and be nimble enough to exploit them. They should acknowledge potential costs of the policies they promote to other national security objectives, and they should think through ways of reducing those costs. They should work on objectively quantifying the likely real value or impact of steps they advocate, including the chances they will in fact contribute to change. Or their value to national interests even if they don't—relieving the United States or other Western countries of "command responsibility," for example, by distancing them from the behavior of corrupt governments.

The political courage to make use of such leverage—absent a burning crisis and before one is even sure to burst out—is hard to muster. The most prudent tack so often seems to be leaving well enough alone. Crises, moreover, provide the inescapable rationale for dramatic action.

And yet the stakes are just too high not to try to intervene otherwise, and upstream of a visible white-water crisis. If Western countries wish to reduce the likelihood of extremist or revolutionary violence abroad, if they want to curtail their use of military force when emergencies erupt—with the staggering financial and human costs and uneven chances of success such use of force entails—they must be willing to take political risks ahead of time. They must work to create redress for legitimate grievances. They must show as much courage in deploying leverage as they have, to date, in deploying soldiers.

These tools should be thought of as prevention, worth the proverbial pound of cure. By helping damp down one key driver of dangerous insecurity, they represent alternatives to military action at some later date. They reduce the "command responsibility" of Western countries in enabling abusive corruption. And most important, these products of a constitutional order offer aggrieved citizens of captured states at least somewhere, on earth, to turn. They provide a measure of appeal.

Self-Reflection

The analysis in this book does not just apply to the extreme cases it has examined, where the whole of government has morphed into a criminal organization bent to no other business than personal enrichment, and has retooled the crucial gears of state power to that end. To highlight the problem of kleptocracy only in places like Nigeria and Afghanistan is to reinforce a tacit superiority complex: those populations, of the global south, are somehow unsuited to rational government. They are culturally prone to predation. Reform is not possible, only containment.

It is also to duck the significance of the global economic meltdown of 2008.

The analysis here applies, and strikingly, to countries closer to home, where governments have been dangerously encroached upon in recent years—even partially colonized—by what John Locke would call "some party of men."

As was devastatingly chronicled by Fintan O'Toole in his 2010 *Ship of Fools*, Ireland's economy was largely taken over by the 1990s by a kleptocratic network that wove together public officials, top banking executives, and real estate developers. The initial result was a country that seemed to shake its historical demons of poverty and backwardness to become a global example of prosperity, fueled by low taxes, low wages, a hyperactive financial services industry, debt, and a property boom. Growth rates hovered above 7 percent. Ireland was hailed as a "Celtic Tiger."

Until it imploded. In 2008 the Irish economy collapsed. Ghosts of the nineteenth-century Great Hunger seemed to awaken, to haunt anew the acres of abandoned houses that disfigured the moors, their doors creaking in a bitter wind, while thousands of Irish took the road of exile, once again, to try to earn their keep abroad.

O'Toole emphasizes the impunity that Irish political wrongdoers enjoyed during these years, and banking regulators' narrow focus on the level of assets that financial institutions could declare on paper as counterweight to their obligations. He examines the unwillingness of Irish citizens to confront the manifest criminality that surrounded them, evoking "the idea of disassociation in psychiatry, where, in response to trauma, the mind distances itself from experiences that it does not wish to process. This mechanism was at work in relation to corruption." Irish politicians, writes O'Toole, mastered this mechanism

> with a clarity approaching genius. Instead of hiding the vast wealth for which an innocent explanation was impossible, [they] flaunted it, relying on the capacity of the public at large both to know that [they] must be corrupt, and somehow to confine this knowledge to a dark corner of the brain where it remained inert and irrelevant.[1]

A similar unwillingness to confront the corruption in their midst seems to afflict the citizens of other Western countries.

More explicitly than many, O'Toole explores the interplay of morality and economics that underlies the ambiguity of the word "corruption." In Ireland, he points out, a culture prevailed that "saw sex, rather than money, as the currency of sin."[2]

> There has to be a general recognition that this crisis is moral as well as economic. It is, indeed, a perfect illustration of the economics of morality—the absence of a sense of propriety, of restraint and of right and wrong, was not just obnoxious, it was economically disastrous.[3]

Iceland was another example of a model northern European market-driven democracy that fell prey to partial capture by a tight-knit network of government officials and banking executives. A revolving door seemed to spin between the top reaches of government and the banking sector, as the longest-reigning prime minister, David Oddsson, departed government only to take up the reins of the central bank.

As was the case in Tunisia or Egypt, a financial sector that was rapidly privatized around 2000 fell into the hands of ruling party cronies. Regulation was lax, and borrowing—both institutional and personal—epic. Tiny Iceland's banks made loans totaling some 900 percent of GDP.[4] As in Ireland, real estate speculation fueled a bubble. Officials also ceded public land for such controversial foreign investments as a sprawling, futuristic project to harness the energy of three rivers in the island nation's fragile northeastern wilderness for the purposes of firing an Alcoa aluminum smelter.[5] The environment minister waved away severe adverse environmental impacts detailed in studies submitted by the developers themselves. Questions mounted as to the advisability, but also the propriety, of the deals.

When an acute liquidity crisis began crippling the international financial system in late summer 2008, followed by a run on banks, Iceland's economy gave way.[6] The gigantically overleveraged banks proved "too big to bail" and had nowhere to go but under. "There is a real danger," Prime Minister Geir Haarde told his fellow citizens, "that the Icelandic economy . . . could be sucked into the whirlpool, and the result could be national bankruptcy."[7]

The ingredients of Iceland's poisonous stew sound familiar. But the antidotes the nation's—albeit tiny—population selected broke new ground. Though they were imperfect and ultimately derailed by the networks they targeted, Iceland's initial responses to its crisis suggest ways forward for other Western nations that have strayed dangerously close to kleptocratic governance themselves.

After the failure of Iceland's top three banks, thousands took to the streets of Reykjavik in a din of clanging casseroles and frying pans. The first demand of this "kitchenware revolution" was accountability. Prime Minister Haarde was forced to resign and became the first Icelandic minister ever to be indicted for official misconduct. Some citizens worried he was being scapegoated, and the parliamentary court eventually whittled the charges against him down to the trivial.

In a March 2012 *Guardian* op-ed, economics writer Alda Sigmundsdóttir acknowledged that Haarde would likely beat the charges, that it might not be fair to hold a single man accountable for the multiple failings that led to the meltdown. Yet, she argued,

> the trial is necessary. The Icelandic collapse was not just an economic collapse—it was also a moral collapse. It was a collapse of the people's trust in its country's politicians, institutions and financial system. It revealed to the vast majority of us that we'd had no idea of the extent of the political corruption and neglect that lurked beneath the surface of our society for decades.[8]

Haarde was the only Western leader to be made answerable in any way for deeds connected with the 2008 economic crash.

But Icelanders did not stop with drumming their prime minister out of office and putting him on trial. To address the underlying weaknesses in Iceland's governing framework and democratic procedures, they demanded a sweeping revision of their nation's constitution.

The approach they adopted was remarkable. Nine hundred and fifty citizens were drawn at random from the national register to form a constitutional assembly. Within a day of convening, the body agreed upon the need for a substantially new constitution, and defined priorities to guide the efforts of those who would actually draw up the document.

Twenty-five drafters posted versions of their work online, soliciting feedback from the public via social media, among other formats. The resulting provisions restructured the oversight relationships between the legislative, executive, and judicial branches of government, revamped the rules governing elections, and declared that natural resources not then privately owned were the "joint and perpetual property of the nation," which could only be leased, not permanently acquired.[9]

In the end, as Iceland pulled out of its economic slump, public pressure waned, and parliament never put the draft to a vote. Instead, it changed the rules for passage, so as to require a more substantial majority, thus making adoption of the draft even less likely. The new constitution languished.[10]

Still, Icelanders' instincts were right. They understood that their political leaders had to be held to account. They realized that the contraption that had ordered their government for decades needed maintenance and retooling if it was to continue to serve its purpose. And they knew that the governed had the right to roll up their sleeves and play mechanic.

Americans might learn from their Icelandic neighbors.

The politicians and bankers in Ireland and Iceland, the real estate speculators, the property developers, the investors, loan sharks, and advertising consultants, not just in Europe but in Egypt and Tunisia and other outlandishly corrupt countries, gained inspiration from a common source: the United States. Ideas on the benefits of quick privatization, the harmfulness of financial and environmental regulation, the ability of markets to self-regulate, the virtue of making a killing and flaunting it, the acceptability of corporate payoffs to politicians via outsized campaign contributions, all have their origins here.

Too many excellent books have been written about the failings of U.S. governance that prompted the global financial meltdown of 2008 for me to hazard a summary of that tale here.[11] But a few quotes make the key points. In *13 Bankers*, Simon Johnson and James Kwak suggest that the kleptocratic capture of U.S. institutions may even have been more significant or insidious than it was in the type of countries this book has covered—partly because it was nearly invisible.

> Between the revolving door and the competition for regulatory "business," there was a confluence of perspectives and opinions between Wall Street and Washington that was far more powerful than emerging-market-style corruption. Wall Street's positions became the conventional wisdom in Washington; those who disagreed with them . . . were marginalized as people who simply did not understand the bright new world of modern finance. This group-think was a major reason why the federal government deferred to the interests of Wall Street repeatedly in the 1990s and 2000s.[12]

During that period and later, those who represented the particular interests of Wall Street monopolized the top government positions that oversaw their area of activities. This "party of men" was able to design "villainous laws that circumvent law by law," so as to render their corruption legal.

"A lot of that stuff wasn't necessarily illegal," President Barak Obama opined on October 6, 2011. "It was just immoral or inappropriate or reckless."[13]

Others disagree.

"We are not talking about walking out of a store absentmindedly and forgetting to pay," writes the documentary filmmaker Charles Ferguson, whose *Inside Job* won the 2010 Academy Award for best documentary,

> or littering, or neglecting some bureaucratic formality. We are talking about the deliberate concealment of financial transactions that aided terrorism, nuclear weapons proliferation, and large-scale tax evasion; assisting in major financial frauds and concealment of criminal assets; and committing frauds that substantially worsened the worst financial bubbles and crises since the Depression. . . .
>
> Tolerance of overtly criminal behavior has now become broadly, structurally embedded in the financial sector, and has played a major role in financial sector profitability and incomes since the late 1990s. . . . The absence of prosecution gradually led to a deeply embedded cultural acceptance of unethical and criminal behavior in finance. And . . . it generated a sense of personal impunity.[14]

Ferguson goes on to list the prosecutable offenses most likely committed during the lead-up to the crisis, including securities and accounting fraud, bribery, perjury, RICO offenses, and personal conduct offenses.[15]

"If . . . the Great Recession was in material part the product of intentional fraud," wrote Judge Jed Rakoff, of the formidable Second District Court of New York, in early 2014, "the failure to prosecute those responsible must be judged one of the more egregious failures of the criminal justice system in many years."

Federal prosecutors, Rakoff suggests, may have been focused on different priorities. But the main explanation he offers for the lack of prosecution is "the government's own involvement in the underlying circumstances that led to the financial crisis."[16] With their government helping create conditions favoring criminality, the people of the United States had no effective means of appeal.

And it's not just the financial industry that has enjoyed a uniquely symbiotic relationship with U.S. government officials. Add the defense industry, the energy sector, and the health care industry, and it becomes clear that just a few "classes of men" have held inordinate sway over the functioning of Washington in the past several decades. Something systemic is wrong.[17]

The American state is not entirely captured yet. But to stop its drift into the hands of our own criminalized networks—and to forestall the extremism that is born of desperation—it is time to consider revision of the venerable clockwork that has ordered our polity and provided redress for more than two centuries. It is not potential improvements to its workings that we lack. It is clear-sightedness about the gravity of the danger we court, and the courage to dare to design them.

APPENDIX

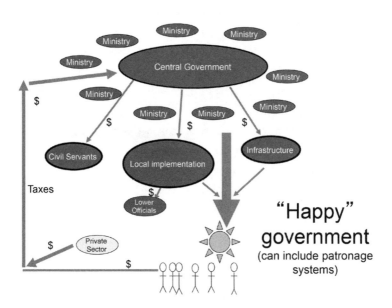

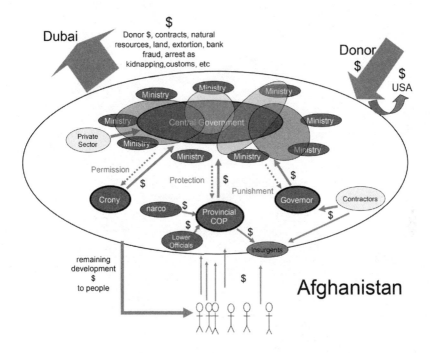

The critical distinction between these two diagrams is the direction of the money flow. In patronage systems, as in healthy modern governments (*p. 212*), resources are drawn from the population to the center, but then are largely distributed back downward within the system, in the form of patronage, or else infrastructure, public services, decent salaries for public officials, and so on. In today's Afghanistan, the money is moving upward within the system and is largely sent outside Afghanistan altogether. ("Dubai" is a placeholder for offshore financial havens.) The revenue streams captured are listed on the top left. In return, the government provides free rein ("permission") to extract resources, protection from repercussion, and punishment of officials with too much integrity. The bounceback arrow on the top right represents the contractors' profits and other overhead spending that never reaches Afghanistan at all. ("USA" is a placeholder for the international community.) Note the absence of any arrow representing taxation.

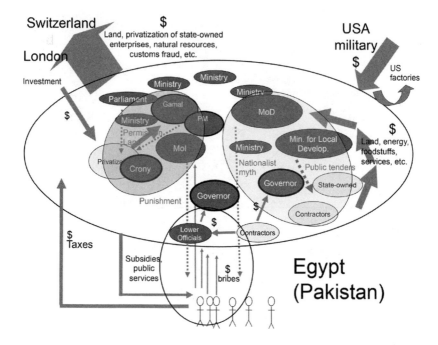

Mubarak's Egypt had two main—and largely separate—kleptocratic systems, which were only beginning to compete late in the first decade of the twenty-first century. The oval on the left represents Gamal Mubarak's crony-capitalist network, and the levers of state power it captured, while the lighter oval on the right represents the military-kleptocratic network. More money is distributed downward in Egypt, in the form of public services and so on, than in Afghanistan.

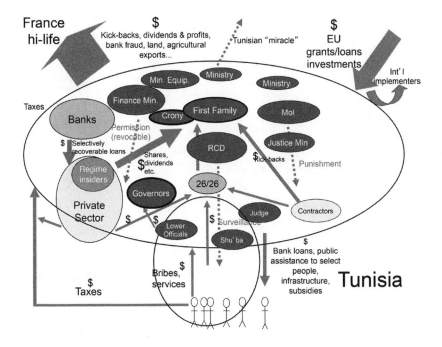

Note the important role of the private sector and especially the banking system in Tunisia's kleptocratic structure. "RCD" was the ruling party, which infiltrated the entire country via its local and professional "cells." "26/26" was a purportedly voluntary charity fund controlled by the Ben Ali clan.

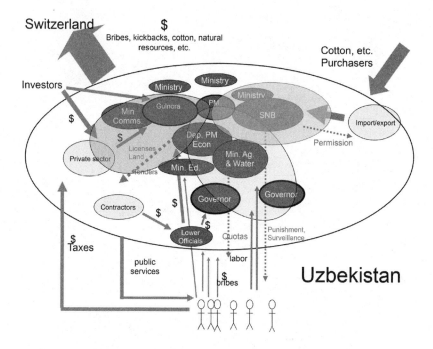

In Uzbekistan, at least up through 2013, there seemed to be three primary kleptocratic networks. Gulnora Karimova's, which focused primarily on "pay-to-play" authorizations for foreign investments, especially in the telecommunications sector, is depicted on the left. The middle oval represents the huge cotton sector. And the oval at the top right is the National Security Service (SNB), whose principal revenue stream is trafficking and customs fraud. The right-hand arrow indicates money into the system as a whole, not specifically to the SNB network's revenue stream.

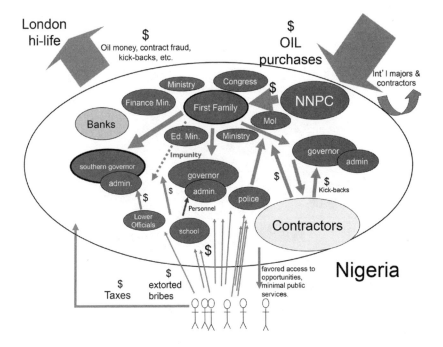

The most significant difference between Nigeria's structure and the others depicted is the degree of downward distribution that occurs within the system. Large blocks of oil revenues are sent downward from the center to state governors, in what remains to a significant degree a patronage system. Pressure to provide redistributive patronage remains strong in lower echelons of society, and in complex ways conflicts with—and reinforces—the extractive corruption of the elites. Upward extraction by way of extorted bribes remains rampant, however, and a key feature of the system. Public funds are siphoned away from the national and state budgets by way of contract fraud perpetrated by civil servants, who gain access to their positions by way of the education system. As in colonial times, public schooling is thus seen by many as an intake valve to the corrupt system.

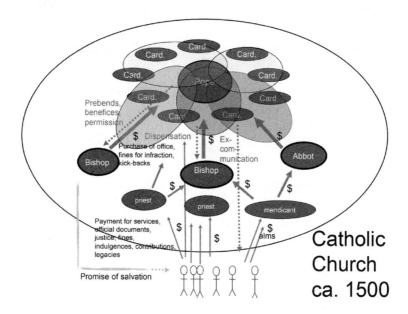

In the late medieval Catholic Church, priests and mendicant friars paid a cut of their take up the line. The money traveled in a similar fashion all the way up the vertically integrated system to the Vatican. In return for the vast kickbacks, Rome sent benefices and dispensations to subordinate officials, as well as an implicit license to extort money from parishioners, or threatened them with excommunication (punishment) if they got in the way. At the lowest level, money was extracted from ordinary people by means of the Church's monopoly over a desperately desired commodity: salvation.

ACKNOWLEDGMENTS

ACKNOWLEDGEMENT PAGES are a conundrum. It's sort of like wedding invitations. Either you invite everyone, and the party's too loud and the value of the invitation declines, or you don't, and people are offended. In that spirit, those of you whose names escaped this list, please accept true apologies for my absentmindedness, or please feel snubbed, or relieved, depending on your worldview.

Thanks to the Carnegie Endowment for International Peace, whose remarkable collegiality took my breath away when I first walked through the doors. President Jessica Mathews, of course, of abiding insight; Tom Carothers, a rigorous thinker and admirable manager and role model; Marwan Muasher; George Perkovich; and next-door friend and incisive observer of India, Milan Vaishnav. Along with my peers, I have learned enormously from our dynamic junior fellows—experts all at "managing up." Reedy Swanson, ostensibly assigned to the South Asia program, enthusiastically plunged into literature and leads on Uzbekistan. Mokhtar Awad's acute powers of observation and rigorous analysis opened my eyes in Egypt. Yusuf Ahmed was invaluable in helping me prepare for and think through Nigeria. He has also been a mainstay of the Corruption and Security Initiative related to this book. Program Assistants Tiffany Joslin, Molly Pallman, and Anisha Mehta have raised the team's bar on fun, professionalism, and intellectual content. Crack librarians Keigh Hammond and Chris Lao-Scott unearthed treasures, including pamphlets in strange typeface from the Library of Congress—unusual fare for a policy think tank. Wise Mr. Gill has kept me grounded in plain reality.

The U.K.'s Department for International Development is remarkable for its investment in deep thought and analysis that can contribute in creative ways to the improved delivery of foreign assistance, and foreign policy writ large. Grateful thanks for its support of Carnegie's Democracy and Rule of Law Program.

Along with treasured others, deep and abiding appreciation goes to:

Penetrating Kathy Anderson. Anyone who needs a literary agent, if you have something worth writing, call Kathy. She will look inside you and find the core of it.

Norton's Tom Mayer. I can't thank him enough—not just for his editing, but most importantly for having the imagination to believe in this book.

The inimitable Sally Donnelly. Yes, there it is, your name spelled out in the daylight. Many of the events recorded here would never have transpired without Sally.

Adm. Mike Mullen, most abidingly for his friendship. Also for precious intellectual collaboration. And for being a prince and tolerating my jagged shards of mirror.

Abd al-Ahad, Fayzullah, Nurallah, Pashtoon, Sarwar, Shafiullah, and Sultana, who shared their country and their hearts with me.

Jeff Dressler, the finest Junior 'Scope.

My sisters, Eve and Angelica, irreplaceable fellow-travelers, literally as well as figuratively. Eve plunged into the Arab Spring with me, her artist's eye and profound intuition fraying a path, and helped me hash out many of the core ideas in this book. Angelica's wonder at Uzbekistan stoked mine. Her general insight, lifelong, is unparalleled. All the best thinking arises in that rich space in the middle that we populate together.

And, of course, my brilliant, indomitable, ever-evolving Sainted Mother.

Finally, thanks to my father, and to his memory. For, among other things, shedding a guiding light on what constitutes a well-lived life.

NOTES

Chapter One: "If I See Somebody Planting an IED . . ."

1. See Sarah Chayes, *The Punishment of Virtue: Inside Afghanistan After the Taliban* (New York: Penguin, 2006).

Chapter Two: "Lord King, How I Wish That You Were Wise"

1. See, for example, Miles Unger, *Machiavelli* (New York: Simon & Schuster, 2011).
2. Niccolò Machiavelli, *The Prince*, trans. (into French) Marie Gaille-Nikokimov (Paris: Librairie générale française, 2000) chap. 19, p. 131.
3. Ibid., chaps. 17 and 19, especially pp. 125–26 and pp. 131–32. See also Machiavelli, *Discourses on Livy*, trans. Harvey C. Mansfield and Nathan Tarcov (Chicago: University of Chicago Press, 1996), bk. 3, chap. 6, p. 219.
4. Machiavelli, *Prince*, chap. 15.
5. Allen Gilbert, *Machiavelli's Prince and Its Forerunners* (Chapel Hill: Duke University Press, 1938), p. 4.
6. For example, one passage reads:

> Tell him, it is through the truth of the ruler that plagues, great lightnings
>   are kept from the people.
> It is through the truth of the ruler that he judges great tribes, great riches.
> It is through the truth of the ruler that he secures peace, tranquility, joy,
>   ease, comfort.
> . . .
> It is through the truth of the ruler that abundances of great tree-fruit of
>   the great wood are tasted.
> It is through the truth of the ruler that great milk yields of great cattle
>   are maintained.
> It is through the truth of the ruler that abundance of fish swim in streams.

7. In the end, a different son, Charles, succeeded James on the English throne. He was tried and beheaded as a tyrant in 1649. See Chapter 12.

8. James VI and I, "Basilicon Doron," in *King James VI and I: Political Writings*, ed. Johann Sommerville (Cambridge: Cambridge University Press, 1994), p. 1.

9. Nizam al-Mulk, *Traité de gouvernement*, ed. and trans. (into French) Charles Schefer (Paris: Sindbad, 1984), pp. 36, 379ff.

10. Ibid., p. 90.

11. Ibid., p. 64.

12. Ibid., p. 87.

13. Ibid., p. 44.

14. Ibid., p. 45.

15. Ibid., p. 59.

16. Crimes "were ordered, committed, or condoned by government personnel in Afghanistan . . . who would not have come to power without the intervention and support of the international community." Human Rights Watch, *Killing You is a Very Easy Thing for Us* (2008), p. 9. ISAF officers in contact with Taliban detainees reported that the activities of the Afghan national security forces were at least indirectly attributed to ISAF, leading to growing sympathy for militant attacks against ISAF personnel and facilities.

17. Jonas d'Orléans, *Le métier de roi ("De institutione regia")*, ed. and trans. (into French) Alain Dubreucq (Paris: Éditions du Cerf, 1995), pp. 42, 49, 199–201.

18. Ibid., pp. 209, 199.

19. Ibid., pp. 191, 213.

20. John of Salisbury, *Policraticus*, trans. Cary J. Nederman (Cambridge: Cambridge University Press, 1990), bk. 4, chaps. 1 and 2, pp. 28, 30.

21. Ibid., title of bk. 8, chap. 20.

22. William of Pagula, *The Mirror of Edward III*, in *Political Thought in Early Fourteenth-Century England: Treatises by Walter of Milemete, William of Pagula, and William of Ockham*, ed. and trans. Cary Nederman (Tempe: Arizona Center for Medieval and Renaissance Studies, 2002), pp. 81–82

23. Ibid., p. 86.

24. Ibid., p. 89.

25. Ibid., p. 109.

26. Erasmus, *Education of a Christian Prince*, ed. Lisa Jardine (Cambridge: Cambridge University Press, 1997), pp. 40–41.

27. Ibid., p. 85.

28. "Care must be taken, meanwhile, that discrepancies in wealth are not excessive: not that I would want anyone to be forcibly deprived of his goods, but some system should be operated to prevent the wealth of the many from being allocated to the few." Ibid., p. 75.

29. Ibid., p. 34.

30. Machiavelli, *Discourses*, bk. 3, chap. 6.

Chapter Three: Hearing the People's Complaints

1. As was the case in Tunisia and Egypt, after their dictators were overthrown in 2011.

2. Nizam al-Mulk, *Traité de gouvernement*, ed. and trans. (into French) Charles Schefer (Paris: Sindbad, 1984), pp. 46–47.

3. Ghazali, *Book of Counsel for Kings (Nasihat al-Muluk)*, trans. F. R. C. Bagley (London: Oxford, 1964), p. 95.

4. *The Sea of Precious Virtues: A Medieval Islamic Mirror for Princes*, trans. Julie Scott Meisami (Salt Lake City: University of Utah Press, 1990). See also Jonas d'Orléans, *Le métier de roi ("De institutione regia")*, ed. and trans. (into French) Alain Dubreucq (Paris: Éditions du Cerf, 1995): "In ancient times, judges held court at the city gates so that no citizen would have difficulties accessing them, or suffer violence or calumny" (p. 207).

5. Nizam al-Mulk, *Traité*, p. 47.

6. See, for example, Thomas Carothers and Marina Ottoway, eds., *Uncharted Journey: Promoting Democracy in the Middle East* (Washington, D.C.: Carnegie Endowment for International Peace, 2005).

7. John of Salisbury, *Policraticus*, trans. Cary J. Nederman (Cambridge: Cambridge University Press, 1990), bk. 5, chap. 10, pp. 85–86.

8. Paula Loyd, then working alongside soldiers as a member of a Human Terrain Team, died in 2009, after suffering a gruesome attack in a village west of Kandahar. A local she was interviewing suddenly drenched her with gasoline he was carrying and lit her on fire. She succumbed to the burn wounds weeks later at the Brooke Army Medical Center. Paula, her life, and its end are chronicled in *The Tender Soldier*, by Vanessa Gezari (New York: Simon & Schuster, 2013). Family and friends established the Paula Loyd Foundation (www.paulaloydfoundation.org) in her name. It is dedicated to the education of Afghan girls, future leaders of their country.

Chapter Four: Nonkinetic Targeting

1. William of Pagula, *The Mirror of Edward III*, in *Political Thought in Early Fourteenth-Century England: Treatises by Walter of Milemete, William of Pagula, and William of Ockham*, ed. and trans. Cary Nederman (Tempe: Arizona Center for Medieval and Renaissance Studies, 2002), pp. 76, 94. John of Salisbury concurred: "If a person knows something and does not act upon it, he is accused not by reason of ignorance, but by reason of malice." *Policraticus*, trans. Cary J. Nederman (Cambridge: Cambridge University Press, 1990), bk. 5, chap. 11, p. 92. So did Nizam al-Mulk: "People will say . . . 'If [the king] is informed [about the exactions that take place in the kingdom] and makes no effort to end them, he is no different from the oppressors, and he approves the tyranny.'" *Traité de gouvernement*, ed. and trans. Charles Schefer (into French) (Paris: Sindbad, 1984), p. 118. References to this principle are frequent throughout the Mirrors for Princes literature.

2. Jed Rakoff, "The Financial Crisis: Why Have No High-Level Executives Been Prosecuted?" *New York Review of Books* 61, no. 1 (January 9, 2014), p. 4.

3. It blamed "not only a resilient and growing insurgency; there is also a crisis of confidence among Afghans—in both their government and the international community—that undermines our credibility and emboldens the insurgents." The new strategy the controversial assessment outlined defined its call to "prioritize responsive and accountable government—that the Afghan people find acceptable—to be on a par with, and integral to, delivering security." Stanley McChrystal, "Commander's Initial Assessment," August 30, 2009, http://wapo.st/1lLh5HI. Four years later, outgoing ISAF commander General John Allen briefed President Obama that "corruption is *the* existential, strategic threat to Afghanistan." His successor, General Joseph Dunford, initiated a study on corruption whose first words are: "Corruption directly threatens the viability and legitimacy of the Afghan state. Corruption alienates key elements of the population, discredits the government and security forces, undermines international support, subverts state functions and rule of law, robs the state of revenue, and creates barriers to economic growth." (U.S. Joint Staff, Joint and Coalition Operational Analysis, "Operationalizing Counter/Anti-Corruption Study," Washington, February 28, 2014.)

4. Ghazali, *Book of Counsel for Kings* (Nasihat al-Muluk), trans. F. R. C. Bagley (London: Oxford, 1964), p. 76.

5. In early July 2014, with large swathes of Iraq conquered by Islamist militants allied with disenfranchised Sunnis, Prime Minister Nuri Kamal al-Maliki appealed to the same logic. He rebuffed international calls for a government expanded beyond the confines of his tightly-knit ruling network. "The battle today is the security battle for the unity of Iraq," he said in a speech broadcast on state television. "I don't believe there is anything more important than mobilizing people to support the security situation. Other things are important, but this is the priority." (Quoted in Rod Nordland, "Iraqi Premier Places Unity Second to Fighting ISIS," *New York Times*, July 2, 2014.)

6. Paul Fishstein and Andrew Wilder, "Winning Hearts and Minds? Examining the Relationship Between Aid and Security in Afghanistan" (Medford, MA: Feinstein International Center, Tufts University, 2012), http://bit.ly/1eTl3z5.

7. Colin Camerer, *Behavioral Game Theory: Experiments in Strategic Interaction* (Princeton: Princeton University Press, 2003), pp. 42–81.

8. Rakoff, "Financial Crisis," p. 6; David Gomez, "Spies Like Them: How Robert Mueller Transformed—For Better and for Worse—The FBI into a Counterterrorism Agency," *Foreign Policy*, May 31, 2013, http://atfp.co/1gCLlna; Sarah Chayes, "Blinded by the War on Terrorism," *Los Angeles Times*, July 28, 2013.

9. Major General Mike Flynn challenged the intelligence community to begin addressing this gap. See Major General Michael T. Flynn, Captain Mike Pottinger, and Paul D. Batchelor, *Fixing Intel: A Blueprint for Making Intelligence Relevant in Afghanistan* (Washington, D.C.: Center for a New American Security, 2010), http://bit.ly/1qPUjSw.

10. Erasmus, *Education of a Christian Prince*, ed. Lisa Jardine (Cambridge: Cambridge University Press, 1997), p. 65.

11. The list of targeted insurgents was called the Joint Prioritized Effects List (JPEL).

Chapter Five: Vertically Integrated Criminal Syndicates

1. For conventional wisdom, see former State Department senior adviser Barnett Rubin's *Afghanistan from the Cold War Through the War on Terror* (Oxford: Oxford University Press, 2013), which contains passages such as "Politics is highly personalized, tending to crystalize around powerful men and their patronage networks" (p. 299), and "Reforms based on professionalism and merit will take years to create effective security agencies and ministries for service delivery. In the meantime there are only two alternatives to fill the gap: international provision of security and services, and reliance on mechanisms of patronage that became strengthened and took on new forms during decades of war" (p. 177).

2. On July 9, 2014, U.S. Special Representative to Afghanistan and Pakistan James Dobbins suggested "that the new [Afghan] government will continue to rely on patronage, in the manner of Afghan President Hamid Karzai, to stabilize the fault lines in Afghan society. 'You had a country with very weak institutions that didn't project much beyond the capital, and [Karzai] had a country that was divided into two languages, different religious structures, different tribal and ethnic structures, and he held it together very successfully through a process of distributing patronage.'" Joshua Rosenfeld, "US Envoy: Candidates' Support of 'National Unity' Is Key to Next Afghan Government," Asia Society, July 10, 2014, http://bit.ly/1rGbpn5. And: "Karzai's best asset is that he knows how his country works, with loyalties transacted on the basis of kinship, faith and cash," according to Alex de Waal, "The Price of Peace," *Prospect*, November 17, 2009, at http://bit.ly/1kFBlua. A senior U.S. official is quoted saying Karzai and Secretary of State Hillary Clinton "have a very good relationship, they can speak together as politicians and they can talk in terms of not just the policy dimensions of things, but also the political ramifications," in Kim Ghattas, "Will Hillary Clinton's Gamble on Karzai Pay Off," BBC News, November 20, 2009, http://bbc.in/1jltmkf.

3. Alissa Rubin, "Karzai Vows Corruption Fight, but Avoids Details," *New York Times*, November 3, 2009.

4. This expression contains religious overtones: to pray, a Muslim must be wearing clothes that are ritually clean, untouched by blood, urine, or feces or by such impure animals as dogs or cats. The expression suggests the conceptual convergence between corruption and ritual impurity evoked throughout this book.

5. John of Salisbury, *Policraticus*, trans. Cary J. Nederman (Cambridge: Cambridge University Press, 1990), bk. 6, chap. 1, p. 108.

Chapter Six: Revolt Against Kleptocracy

1. Erasmus, *Education of a Christian Prince*, ed. Lisa Jardine (Cambridge: Cambridge University Press, 1997), pp. 34, 74–75.

2. *The Sea of Precious Virtues: A Medieval Islamic Mirror for Princes*, trans. Julie Scott Meisami (Salt Lake City: University of Utah Press, 1990), p. 298.

3. Erasmus, *Education*, p. 28, 74. See also John of Salisbury's description of the pope: "The

Roman pontiff himself is burdensome and almost intolerable to everyone, since . . . he erects palaces and parades himself about not only in purple vestments but in gilded clothes." John of Salisbury, *Policraticus*, trans. Cary J. Nederman (Cambridge: Cambridge University Press, 1990), bk. 6, chap. 24, p. 133.

4. Niccolò Machiavelli, *The Prince*, trans. (into French) Marie Gaille-Nikodimov (Paris: Librairie générale française, 2000), p. 131.

5. By 2014, the pattern was even visible to the mainstream *Economist* Magazine. See "Our Crony Capitalism Index: Planet Plutocrat," March 15, 2014.

Chapter Seven: Variation 1

1. Shana Marshall and Joshua Stacher, "Egypt's Generals and Transnational Capital," Middle East Research and Information Project 262: Spring 2012.

2. Robert Springborg, Naval Postgraduate School professor, quoted in Cam Simpson and Mariam Fan, "Egypt's Army Marches, Fights, Sells Chickens," *Bloomberg Businessweek*, February 17, 2011, http://buswk.co/1mh6qaN.

3. For a rare example of a dispute, see Merrit Kennedy, "A Big Battle over a Tiny Isle in the Nile," NPR, March 9, 2013, http://n.pr/1dak1xX.

4. Zaineb Abul-Magd, "The Generals' Secret: Egypt's Ambivalent Market," *Sada*, December 24, 2012, http://ceip.org/1gKA6FE.

5. Information from multiple interviews in Cairo, July 2013. See also Yezid Sayigh, *Above the State: The Officers' Republic in Egypt* (Washington, D.C.: Carnegie Endowment for International Peace, August 2012).

6. Syria's ruling crony-capitalist network resembles that branch of Egypt's dual civilian-and-military kleptocracy. Bashar al-Assad, who actually did succeed his father rather than just being poised to do so, plays the role of Gamal Mubarak. He abruptly liberalized Syria's economy in the 2000s, with his network—which included some of the Sunni business elite as well as his own Alawites—getting privileged access. Syria, however, lacks the separate and competing military kleptocratic structure, and it features a critical sectarian divide, amounting to minority rule, shared with Bahrain, but not Egypt.

7. U.S. Embassy cables are generally supportive of privatization, only rarely highlighting the favoritism and lack of transparency.

8. "Egypt Labor Strikes Break Out Across the Country; Protesters Defiant," AP/*Huffington Post*, liveblog, February 9–May 25, 2011, at http://huff.to/1cVBjOS and similar coverage for the role of factory strikes in fueling the 2011 revolution's momentum. "The destructive practice of privatization, in particular, often promoted as 'modernization' or 'liberalization,' has been a source of mass discontent in Egypt for years; widespread disapproval of this policy . . . played a significant role in the revolt that toppled the Mubarak government. For example, in 2003–2004, Gamal Mubarak, President Mubarak's son, sought to 'modernize' Egypt's economy by undertaking a secretive privatization campaign which many Egyptians claimed was rife with corruption. Multiple companies were sold at a fraction of their values to foreign investors. Gamal took over the Economic Policy Committee of his father's party, the National Democratic Party, and . . . began modernizing,

or *privatizing*, Egypt's economy." (And see the specific example of the Omar Effendi retail chain in the rest of the blog.) Michael Termini, "Egypt Privatization and the Sordid Tale of World Bank Managing Director Mahmoud Mohieldin," Government Accountability Project, August 10, 2011, http://bit.ly/1pSStlC.

9. Erasmus, *Education of a Christian Prince*, ed. Lisa Jardine (Cambridge: Cambridge University Press, 1997), p. 79.

10. John of Salisbury, *Policraticus*, trans. Cary J. Nederman (Cambridge: Cambridge University Press, 1990), bk. 5, chap. 10, p. 88.

11. Nathan Brown, "Why Do Egyptian Courts Say the Darndest Things," *Washington Post*, March 25, 2014.

12. Gamal Amin, *Egypt in the Era of Hosni Mubarak* (Cairo: American University in Cairo Press, 2011), p. 8.

13. "Underlying the movement's economic views is a conviction that the old order was run on the basis of corruption at all levels: crony capitalism at the top seeping down to lower-level coping mechanisms of those left out of the scramble to exploit state resources for private ends. What the Brotherhood offers as a remedy is virtue." Nathan J. Brown, *When Victory Becomes an Option: Egypt's Muslim Brotherhood Confronts Success* (Washington, D.C.: Carnegie Endowment for International Peace, January 2012), p. 15. A BBC interviewee described the Muslim Brotherhood as "untainted by sleaze, corruption, and cronyism" in "Egypt Election Results: Your Views," BBC, June 24, 2012, http://bbc.in/Ot5ORd. See also U.S. Embassy cable, "MB Platform Calls for 'Mixed' Public-Private Economy," August 26, 2011, http://bit.ly/OyES29.

14. Ayman al-Zawahiri, "The Facts of Jihad and the Lies of Hypocrisy" al-Saheb, August 4, 2009, at http://bit.ly/1gCR5ol.

15. Interview conducted by Mokhtar Awad.

16. Sarah Chayes, "The Egyptian Restoration," Carnegie Endowment for International Peace, August 1, 2013, http://ceip.org/1icUq6R; Rick Gladstone, "Cairo Attacks Were Intended to Provoke, Some Say," *New York Times*, August 17, 2013; Robert Zaretsky, "Egypt's Algerian Moment," *Foreign Policy*, August 20, 2013; Daniel Byman and Tamara Wittes, "Now that the Muslim Brotherhood Is Declared a Terrorist Group It Just Might Become One," *Washington Post*, January 10, 2014. See also Dominic Tierney, "Bashar al-Assad and the Devil's Gambit," *The Atlantic*, July 16, 2014.

Chapter Eight: Variation 2

1. "Tunisia, under your leadership, is fully engaged in modernity, benefiting from the riches that are at the foundation of progress, what is known as 'The Tunisian Miracle,' for over fifteen years," observed French president Jacques Chirac. "Discours de Jacques Chirac à Tunis," Voltairenet, December 3, 2003, http://www.voltairenet.org/article11464.html. See also Francisco Rodriguez and Emma Samman, "The North African Miracle," in *UNDP Let's Talk Human Development*, November 12, 2010, http://zunia.org/post/the-north-african-miracle.

2. David D. Kirkpatrick, "Behind Tunisia Unrest, Rage over Wealth of Ruling Family," *New York Times*, January 13, 2011; Elaine Ganley and Jenny Barchfield, "Leila Trabelsi,

Former Tunisian First Lady, Despised by Nation," *Huffington Post*, January 17, 2011, at http://huff.to/1p84CoA.

3. Lotfi Ben Chrouda, *Dans l'ombre de la reine* (Neuilly-sur-Seine: Michel Lafont, 2011), p. 43.

4. Walter of Milmete, *On the Nobility, Wisdom, and Prudence of Kings*, in *Political Thought in Early Fourteenth-Century England: Treatises by Walter of Milemete, William of Pagula, and William of Ockham*, ed. and trans. Cary J. Nederman (Tempe: Arizona Center for Medieval and Renaissance Studies, 2002), p. 47. And according to the mid-twelfth-century Persian *Sea of Precious Virtues*: "Whoever takes more than [what is required to seek a wife, build a dwelling, and obtain a mount] from the public treasury, to make a separate stable for his horses or a chamber for his slaves, or to seek cups of gold and silver, brocades, and silks, or to amass silver, He will come to God on Judgment Day burning and gasping." *The Sea of Precious Virtues: A Medieval Islamic Mirror for Princes*, trans. Julie Scott Meisami (Salt Lake City: University of Utah Press, 1990), p. 112. The trusty John of Salisbury advised against appointing "those who cannot, or indeed disdain to, be content with a little," for they will commit the worst extortions. John of Salisbury, *Policraticus*, trans. Cary J. Nederman (Cambridge: Cambridge University Press, 1990), bk. 5, chap 10, p. 87. See also Crystia Freedland, *Plutocrats: The Rise of the New Global Super-Rich and the Fall of Everyone Else* (New York: Penguin, 2012). For a powerful description of money addiction from someone who suffered it, see Sam Polk, "For the Love of Money," *New York Times*, January 19, 2014.

5. On the African Peer Review Mechanism, see: http://aprm-au.org/

6. Béatrice Hibou, *La force de l'obéissance: économie politique de la répression en Tunisie* (Paris: Éditions la Découverte, 2006), p. 79. For an in-depth study on how the Trabelsi family's manipulation of investment laws and other business regulations advantaged their private sector investments, see Bob Rijkers, Caroline Freund, and Antonio Nucifora, "All in the Family: State Capture in Tunisia." The World Bank, Policy Research Working Paper #6810, March 2014.

7. Hibou, *La force de l'obéissance*, p. 34.

8. Ibid., p. 35, 44.

9. Ibid., p. 50.

10. Ben Chrouda, *Dans l'ombre*, pp. 43–47, 54, 84–92, 94–95ff.

11. Hibou, *La force de l'obéissance*, pp. 197–98.

12. "The representatives of the central power did not hesitate to use the banking sector to transmit their messages of disapproval or their punishment of groups or individuals suspected of independence." Ibid., p. 81.

13. John of Salisbury, *Policraticus*, bk. 5, chap. 14, p. 95.

14. Hibou, *La force de l'obéissance*, pp. 125–30.

15. John of Salisbury, *Policraticus*, bk. 6, chap. 1, p. 105. And Erasmus wrote: "Many laws have been introduced quite justifiably, but have been put to the worst uses by the corruption of officials." *Education of a Christian Prince*, ed. Lisa Jardine (Cambridge: Cambridge University Press, 1997), p. 86.

16. A number of leading Islamists, including members of the government elected in 2012, were castrated in prison.

17. Interview conducted by Mokhtar Awad.

Chapter Nine: Variation 3

1. Sultan Zahir ud-Din Muhammed Babur, *The Baburnama*, Wheeler Thackston, ed. and trans. (New York: Modern Library, 2002), p. 3.

2. Human Rights Watch, *"Bullets Were Falling Like Rain": The Andijan Massacre, May 13, 2005* (June 2005), p. 30, http://bit.ly/OyHZHi. Among the best accounts of the massacre are this report; OSCE/ODIHR, *Preliminary Findings on the Events in Andijan, Uzbekistan 13 May 2005* (Warsaw, June 20, 2005), http://bit.ly/1lLqmzs; Galima Bukharbaeva, "Blood Flows in Uzbek Crackdown," Institute for War and Peace Reporting, May 13, 2005, http://bit.ly/1fWFVno; Galima Bukharbaeva, "No Requiem for the Dead," Institute for War and Peace Reporting, November 20, 2005, http://bit.ly/1qQ6xdS; and International Crisis Group, *Uzbekistan: The Andijan Uprising*, Asia Briefing No. 38 (Brussels: May 25, 2005), http://bit.ly/Nr5X6v. For an analysis that places the events in a broader context, see Sébastien Peyrouse, "Tensions sociales et politiques en Asie Centrale: Retour sur l'insurrection du 13 Mai 2005 en Ouzbékistan," in Marlène Laruelle and Sébastien Peyrouse, eds., *Islam et politique en ex-URSS* (Paris: L'Harmattan-IFEAC, collection Centre-Asie, 2005).

3. Human Rights Watch, *"Bullets Were Falling Like Rain,"* p. 14.

4. OSCE/ODIHR, *Preliminary Findings*, p. 15.

5. Human Rights Watch, *"Bullets Were Falling Like Rain,"* p. 25. "People had waited for this moment for so long . . .We were waiting for the officials to come to the meeting, we wanted this so badly . . . Finally, after all this time [the people] could express their problems. The whole population had been waiting for this moment" (p. 22). Bukharbaeva, in "No Requiem for the Dead," quotes a leaflet she picked up from the scene of the protest: "Let the region's governor come, and representatives of the president too, and hear our pain. When we make demands, the authorities should hear us."

6. Jonas d'Orléans, *Le métier de roi ("De institutione regia")*, ed. and trans. (into French) Alain Dubreucq (Paris: Editions du Cerf, 1995), p. 211.

7. Nizam al-Mulk, *Traité de gouvernement*, ed. and trans. (into French) Charles Schefer (Paris: Sindbad, 1984), pp. 87, 95, 59. And Jonas warned: "If he doesn't do so . . . it will be proof of his negligence and lack of justice. People will say: 'It's six of one, half dozen of the other. Either the king knows, or doesn't know about the disorder and exactions that take place in the kingdom. If he is informed and makes no effort to make them go away, he is no different from the oppressors, and he approves the tyranny. If he doesn't know what's going on, he's feckless and ignorant.'" *Le métier de roi*, p. 118.

8. On Bloody Sunday in 1905, St. Petersburg protesters were shot while attempting to submit a petition to Tsar Nicholas II. The episode is seen as one of the events that led to the Russian Revolution.

9. Akram Yuldashev, *Yimonga Yul* ("The Path to Faith"), Russian translation from Uzbek, http://bit.ly/PMk606.

10. Human Rights Watch, *Burying the Truth: Uzbekistan Rewrites the Story of the Andijan Massacre* (September 2005), p. 13, http://bit.ly/1fWJs58.

11. OSCE/ODIHR, *Preliminary Findings*, p. 9.

12. Islam Karimov, "Press Conference by the President of the Republic of Uzbekistan on Events in Andijan," Tashkent, May 14, 2005, http://bit.ly/1iAoHtL.

13. OSCE/ODIHR, *Preliminary Findings*, p. 12. Bukharbaeva, in "No Requiem for the Dead," further quotes the leaflet recovered from the scene: "If you have a government job, your salary is not enough to live on. If you earn a living by yourself, they start envying you and putting obstacles in your way."

14. Human Rights Watch, *"Bullets Were Falling Like Rain,"* p. 19.

15. Alisher Ilkhamov, "The Phenomenology of 'Akromiya': Separating Facts from Fiction," *China and Eurasia Forum Quarterly* 4, no. 2 (2006), p. 42, http://bit.ly/1hx0chb.

16. Human Rights Watch, *"Bullets Were Falling Like Rain,"* p. 7.

17. "They used money from a mutual support fund that they had set up to engage in charitable work, and regularly transferred savings to children's homes and schools. . . . These Islamic businessmen had calculated the actual minimum living wage in Andijan (which turned out to be equivalent to 50 U.S. dollars, or almost ten times the official minimum wage) and had agreed to pay their employees a higher wage than that." Igor Rotar, "Uzbekistan: What is Known About Akramia and the Uprising?" *Forum 18 News Service,* June 16, 2005, http://bit.ly/1eORuZw.

18. Human Rights Watch, *"Bullets Were Falling Like Rain,"* p. 8. "The independence of the group, detached from state control and patronage, is most likely to be the key concern for the authorities." Ilkhamov, "Phenomenology," p. 42. Human rights investigators concur that the crackdown and the subsequent torture and interrogation of members of the group and other Andijan residents were directed by officials from the capital, Tashkent, not by local officers.

19. U.S. Embassy in Tashkent, "Uzbekistan: Gulnora Karimova's Geneva U.N. Appointment May Reflect Concerns About the Future," September 18, 2008, WikiLeaks, http://bit.ly/1dauvNN.

20. Camille Polloni, "La justice française s'intéresse a la fille du dictateur ouzbek," *Le nouvel observateur,* July 31, 2013, http://bit.ly/1p8bF9D.

21. John Davy, former Ucell CFO, on Swedish Public Television's *Uppdrag granskning* (Mission Investigate), broadcast May 22, 2013, http://bit.ly/1loLa8I. See among other cables, "Skytel Scandal: Fiasco in the Making," WikiLeaks, February 24, 2005, http://bit.ly/1hx3AZc

22. U.S. Embassy cable, "Gulnora Karimova Provides Grants in Hope of Improving Image," November 3, 2005, http://wikileaks.org/cable/2005/11/05TASHKENT3019.html. In February 2013, when I was in Tashkent, U.S. officials and major donor agencies attended a gala event organized by Karimova for one of these organizations, the Fund Forum.

23. U.S. Embassy cable, "First Daughter Lola (Karimova) Cuts Loose," November 26, 2004, http://wikileaks.org/cable/2004/11/04/TASHKENT3180.html.

24. The 2010 liquidation of the Karimova-controlled conglomerate Zeromax, with significant energy holdings, may indicate competition by the SNB for the natural resource sector.

25. "Corruption is used on a systematic basis as a mechanism of direct and indirect administrative control over higher education institutions. Informal approval of corrupt activities in exchange for loyalty and compliance with the regime may be used in the countries of Central Eurasia for the purposes of political indoctrination." Ararat Osipian, "Feed

from the Service: Corruption and Coercion in the State-University Relations in Central Eurasia," October 1, 2007, MPRA paper no. 10818, http://bit.ly/1fFnIpu.

26. John of Salisbury, *Policraticus*, trans. Cary J. Nederman (Cambridge: Cambridge University Press, 1990), bk. 5, chap. 10, pp. 86, 93. He also wrote that "among the ancients it was considered among the forms of sordid behaviour if one did for a price that which ought to be free on the basis of obligations of office. Also, they broadened the interpretation of this 'price' to the extent that it encompassed not only all kinds of money, but also all services and works that were not otherwise owed." Ibid., bk. 5, chap. 15, pp. 94–95.

27. Nizam al-Mulk, *Traité de gouvernement*, ed. and trans. (into French) Charles Schefer (Paris: Sindbad, 1984), p. 73.

28. Reliable figures are extremely hard to derive because of the lack of transparency of the Uzbek economy in general and especially this sector, which is a main revenue stream for the kleptocratic networks. Nodir Djanibekov, Inna Rudenko, John P. A. Lamers, and Ihtiyor Bobojonov report 13 percent in "Pros and Cons of Cotton Production in Uzbekistan," in Per Pinstrup-Andersen and Fuzhi Cheng, eds., *Food Policy for Developing Countries: Case Studies* (Ithaca, N.Y.: Cornell University Press, 2010), http://cip.cornell.edu/dns/gfs/1279121771. For the higher estimate, see Alisher Ilkhamov, "Uzbekistan's Cotton Sector: Financial Flows and Distribution of Resources," Open Security Foundations, 2014 (draft, cited with permission of the author), p. 9.

29. William of Pagula, *Mirror of Edward III*, in *Political Thought in Early Fourteenth-Century England: Treatises by Walter of Milemete, William of Pagula, and William of Ockham*, ed. and trans. Cary Nederman (Tempe: Arizona Center for Medieval and Renaissance Studies, 2002), pp. 78, 83.

30. "A significant factor that differentiated the 2012 cotton harvest from previous years was the reduction in state-sponsored forced labor of children under the age of 15. . . . The scale of coercive mobilization of high school students increased compared to previous harvests. . . . During the 2012 cotton harvest, the government shifted a significant share of the burden of the cotton harvest to citizens over the age of 18, by forcing greater numbers of university students, government employees, private sector businessmen and low-income residents to contribute to the harvest." Uzbek-German Forum for Human Rights/Cotton Campaign, *Review of the 2012 Cotton Harvest in Uzbekistan* (UGF, December 20, 2012), p. 4, http://bit.ly/1g7hx3u. Workers at the GM plant also had to go, or risk losing their jobs if they refused, according to an unpublished Cotton Campaign interview with a GM worker. See also *Le travail forcé des enfants en Ouzbékistan: des changements mais sans amélioration* (Grenoble: École de Management, Centre d'Études en Géopolitique et Gouvernance, March 2012); and U.S. Embassy cable, "Uzbekistan: UNICEF Shares Results of Child Labor Assessment," October 30, 2008, WikiLeaks, http://bit.ly/1nBlstt. For a surreal assessment of the Uzbek cotton industry, in which no mention is made of forced labor, see Stephen MacDonald, *Economic Policy and Cotton in Uzbekistan* (Washington, D.C.: U.S. Department of Agriculture, Economic Research Service, October 2012), http://1.usa.gov/1cVUh84. See also Ilkhamov, "Uzbekistan's Cotton Sector," pp. 22–25.

31. See also Ilkhamov, "Uzbekistan's Cotton Sector," pp. 16–22.

32. In fact, according to Ilkhamov, "Uzbekistan's Cotton Sector," the entire profit from cotton production and sales is not transparent, as "profits are appropriated not simply

by the government, but by a single government fund, the *Selkhozfond* of the ministry of finance, an entity which . . . is only accountable to a narrow circle within the leadership." The estimated $640 million in annual profit from the sale of cotton is entirely off budget. "An analysis of available data shows that the state budget receives practically nothing from cotton export earnings or from the sale of cotton except for taxes on land use." Pp. 7, 37.

33. http://www.hizb-uzbekistan.info/index.php/yangiliklar/zbekiston/913-g-karimovaning -onga-sajokhati-kha-ida, accessed April 2014.

Chapter Ten: Variation 4

1. U.S. Department of State, media note, "Terrorist Designations of Boko Haram and Ansaru," November 13, 2013, http://1.usa.gov/1dc2sMu, and special briefing, "Background Briefing on Designation of Boko Haram and Ansaru as Foreign Terrorist Organizations and as Specially Designated Global Terrorists," November 13, 2013, http://1.usa .gov/1j1ywlx.

2. International Crisis Group, *Northern Nigeria: Background to Conflict* (International Crisis Group, December 20, 2010), p. 36, http://bit.ly/1gAfkbh; Andrew Walker, "What Is Boko Haram?" U.S. Institute of Peace, June 2012, p. 4, http://bit.ly/1g0qwm7; and John Campbell, "To Battle Nigeria's Boko Haram, Put Down Your Guns," *Foreign Affairs*, September 9, 2011. See also Kyari Mohammed, "Matters Arising from the Boko Haram Crisis," n.d., http://bit.ly/1eS3mds.

3. Human Rights Watch, *"Everyone's in on the Game": Corruption and Human Rights Abuses by the Nigeria Police Force* (August 2010), pp. 24, 25, http://bit.ly/1l73Qnk.

4. Ibid., pp. 29, 32–39, 42–54.

5. Daniel Jordan Smith, *A Culture of Corruption: Everyday Deception and Popular Discontent in Nigeria* (Princeton, N.J.: Princeton University Press, 2008), p. 63.

6. *The Sea of Precious Virtues: A Medieval Islamic Mirror for Princes*, trans. Julie Scott Meisami (Salt Lake City: University of Utah Press, 1990), pp. 83, 120, 138.

7. See United Nations Development Program, *Human Development Report, 2013: International Human Development Indicators*, http://bit.ly/OxsVdf

8. Oil-producing states get an extra 13 percent, and oil companies such as Chevron build much of the local infrastructure, schools, and hospitals in the states where they operate.

9. "Nigeria's NNPC Must Account for $10.8 billion oil revenue: finance minster," Platts McGraw Hill Financial News, January 20, 2014, http://bit.ly/1gQBcj9.

10. "Transcripts from Senate Hearing on Missing Funds: Sanusi, Iwealla, Diezani and Yakubu (Opening Remarks)," Press Release Nigeria, February 13, 2014, http://bit.ly/ 1doFusA; and Adam Nossiter, "Nigerians Ask Why Oil Funds Are Missing," *New York Times*, March 10, 2014.

11. Tim Cocks, "UK Police Probing Shell, ENI Nigerian Oil Block Deal," Reuters, January 24, 2013, http://reut.rs/1gbzVIA.

12. Benoît Faucon, "Nigerian Oil Theft Prompts Shell to Act," *Wall Street Journal*, April 12, 2013.

13. Christina Katsouris and Aaron Sayne, *Nigeria's Criminal Crude: International Options to Combat the Export of Stolen Oil* (Chatham House, September 2013), http://bit.ly/1n7lMKW. Though the report leads with the dramatic statement that "Nigerian crude oil is being stolen on an industrial scale," (p. 1) critics complain that the published version was sanitized, to focus primarily on small-scale bunkering, rather than on the wholesale involvement of the Nigerian oil sector and the highest reaches of government.

14. "Nigeria: An Open Letter From Mutiu Sunmonu," Shell Sustainability Report, 2012, http://bit.ly/1j4ms06.

15. The pattern is unique neither to Nigeria nor to oil. "Since they specialize in the export of a small range of primary products, African countries are particularly susceptible to a management of their main economic resources [that] is highly politicized and centrally controlled. This is particularly the case with regard to mining and oil production. The extraction of minerals in enclave centres of production, sometimes offshore, enables the political authorities to negotiate royalties and other agreements directly with major companies." Jean-François Bayart, Stephen Ellis, and Béatrice Hibou, *The Criminalization of the State in Africa* (Bloomington: Indiana University Press, 1999), p. 84. The authors report that African countries, on average, retain a measurably lower proportion of the revenues than do OPEC countries.

16. John Campbell, *Nigeria, Dancing on the Brink*, updated ed., Council on Foreign Relations (Lanham: Rowman and Littlefield, 2013), p. 15; Adam Robert Green, "Agriculture is the Future of Nigeria," *Forbes Magazine*, August 8, 2013; and "We Will Grow Nigerian Agriculture," the agriculture ministry's own brief to top Nigerian economic officials, September 2011, reproduced by the Nigerian investment firm Dorneo Partners, http://bit.ly/1dqAclg.

17. Human Rights Watch, *Criminal Politics: Violence, "Godfathers," and Corruption in Nigeria* (October 2007), pp. 17–30, http://bit.ly/1lPCQpR.

18. Ibid., pp. 33–40.

19. Ibid.; Ike Okonta, *The Fire Next Time: Youth, Violence, and Democratization in Northern Nigeria* (Wuse II Abuja, Nigeria: Friedrich Ebert Stiftung, December 2012), http://bit.ly/1j7ljrn; and European Union Election Observation Mission, *Nigeria: Final Report: General Elections, April 2011*, http://bit.ly/OxzsVv.

20. When I began researching prices after this incident, I discovered that similar practices prevail in the United States. See Nina Bernstein, "How to Charge $546 for Six Liters of Saltwater," *New York Times*, August 25, 2013.

21. Smith, *Culture of Corruption*, pp. 80ff.

22. That comment made me think back to Qayum Karzai, the brother of the Afghan president, and the NGO I ran for him. I remembered how irritated his half-brother Ahmed Wali was that we were not "getting enough contracts."

23. See the thoughtful discussion of the ambiguous dynamic between social obligation and corruption, and its evolution toward a one-way, extractive dynamic in Smith, *Culture of Corruption*.

Chapter Eleven: Up a Level

1. The best public account of the Kabul Bank case is Dexter Filkins, "The Afghan Bank Heist," *The New Yorker*, February 14, 2011.

2. "This Week Transcript: Karzai, Khan and Levitt," ABC News, August 15, 2010, http://abcn.ws/1j4qn4i.

3. William of Pagula, *The Mirror of Edward III*, in *Political Thought in Early Fourteenth-Century England: Treatises by Walter of Milemete, William of Pagula, and William of Ockham*, ed. and trans. Cary J. Nederman (Tempe: Arizona Center for Medieval and Renaissance Studies, 2002), p. 76. The other mirror writers concur. "If a person knows something and does not act upon it," wrote John of Salisbury, "he is accused not by reason of ignorance but by reason of malice." *Policraticus*, trans. Cary J. Nederman (Cambridge: Cambridge University Press, 1990), bk. 5, chap. 11, p. 92. "If [the king] is informed [of the exactions that take place] and makes no effort to end them," wrote Nizam al-Mulk, "then he's the same as the oppressors and approves the tyranny." *Traité de gouvernement*, ed. and trans. Charles Schefer (Paris: Sindbad, 1984), p. 118.

4. Petraeus did follow our suggestion to enlarge the original Anti-Corruption Task Force and place it under independent, high-level command. He called on a long-time protégé, General H. R. McMaster, to head what was renamed Task Force Shafafiyat (Transparency). McMaster launched a lengthy, formal planning process, but his style shattered the fragile collusion that had existed between the mutually suspicious civilian and military officials. Within a few months, it was evident that Shafafiyat's main purpose was not actually to challenge the grip of kleptocratic networks over Afghanistan's government but to help Petraeus persuade members of Congress that he was "working" the corruption problem. Over the years, young, dedicated officers did make some inroads on the military mindset—the need to collect intelligence on host government officials, for example, and to pay attention to the way money was spent. For "if money is a weapon system," as Lieutenant Colonel Jodi Vittori put it, "then it can shoot you in the foot just as easily as any other, if it's used inappropriately or aimed in the wrong direction."

5. Bob Woodward, *Obama's Wars* (New York: Simon & Schuster, 2010).

6. Robert W. Komer, *Bureaucracy Does Its Thing: Institutional Constraints on U.S.-GVN Performance in Vietnam*, Rand, Defense Advanced Research Projects Agency (August 1972), p. vi, http://bit.ly/1gQNfgB.

7. During the notorious 2009 debate over U.S. Afghanistan policy, the key question was eventually asked. To inform one of the Principals Committee meetings, the National Security Staff (NSS) sent out a query as to whether it was possible to defeat an insurgency on behalf of a government seen by its people as illegitimate. Working in McChrystal's headquarters at the time, I was stunned at the very idea. It took me awhile to come up with more than a one-word answer: "No." Eventually I drafted an argument that I sent directly to Admiral Mullen. After a few days, the same question came down from the NSS, phrased differently. And then another version. It was as though "no" were a simply unacceptable answer, and the decision makers thought that if they could reword the question just the right way, perhaps they could change reality.

8. Carl Forsberg, *Power and Politics in Kandahar*, Afghanistan Report 5, Institute for the

Study of War (April 2010), http://bit.ly/0xAMYp, and abundant international press coverage of Ahmed Wali Karzai.

9. Adam Entous, Julian Barnes, and Siobhan Gorman, "US Shifts Afghan Graft Plan," *Wall Street Journal*, September 20, 2010.

10. Matthew Rosenberg, "With Bags of Cash, C.I.A. Seeks Influence in Afghanistan," *New York Times*, April 28, 2013.

Chapter Twelve: Forging an Appeal on Earth

1. See, for example, Frans de Waal, *The Age of Empathy* (New York: Three Rivers, 2009), pp. 158–200.

2. William of Orange, "A missive in the form of a supplication to His Royal Majesty of Spain, on behalf of the prince of Orange, the States of Holland and Zeeland, etc., 1573," in E. H. Kossman and A. F. Mellink, eds., *Texts Concerning the Revolt of the Netherlands* (Cambridge: Cambridge University Press, 1974), p. 107.

3. Ironically, as kings were claiming God's support for extending and consolidating their power, they were showing less concern about God's judgment for their misdeeds.

4. Martin van Gelderen, *Political Thought of the Dutch Revolt* (Cambridge: Cambridge University Press, 1999), p. 30. "Many rancors had built up under the government of [Charles] the Bold, over, in particular, the violation of local and regional privileges, a consequence of centralizing reforms." Maurice-A. Arnould, "Les lendemains de Nancy dans les 'Pays de par deca' (Janvier-Avril 1477)," in W. P. Blockmans, ed., *Anciens pays et assemblées d'états*, vol. 80, *Le privilège général et les privilèges régionaux de Marie de Bourgogne pour les Pays-Bas* (Kortrijk-Heule: UGA, 1985), p. 13.

5. J. A. Fernandez-Santamaria, *The State, War, and Peace: Spanish Political Thought in the Renaissance, 1519–1559* (Cambridge: Cambridge University Press, 1977), p. 264.

6. Charles V, "Instructions de Charles-Quint a l'Infant Don Philippe, son fils," in Charles Weiss, ed., *Papiers d'état du cardinal de Granvelle, d'après les manuscrits de la bibliothèque de Besançon* (Paris: Imprimerie Royale, 1842), pp. 3:268, 270.

7. John Lynch, *Spain Under the Habsburgs*, vol. 1, *Empire and Absolutism, 1516–1598* (New York: Oxford University Press, 1964), pp. 171, 180. For rule via a tight circle of informal advisers, see A. W. Lovett, *Early Habsburg Spain* (Oxford: Oxford University Press, 1986), p. 122.

8. Lynch, *Spain Under the Hapsburgs*, p. 174. See also Kossman and Mellink, *Texts Concerning the Revolt of the Netherlands*, p. 3.

9. Lynch, *Spain Under the Hapsburgs*, p. 180. See also Van Gelderen, *Political Thought of the Dutch Revolt*, p. 32.

10. Peter Arnade, *Beggars, Iconoclasts, and Civic Patriots: The Political Culture of the Dutch Revolt* (Ithaca, N.Y.: Cornell University Press, 2008), p. 49, and the description of an engraved double portrait Philip had published, of him and Christ side by side. The inscription quoted I Peter 2:13–15: "For the sake of the Lord, accept the authority of every social institution: the king as the supreme authority, and the governors as commissioned by him . . .Such is God's will." Thus, argues Arnade, did Philip establish a "direct linkage

of Church, Crown, and political authority," pp. 171–72. See also Lynch, *Spain Under the Hapsburgs*, pp. 172–73.

11. "Avis de ceux des châtellenies d'Ypres, de Cassel, Bailleul, Warneton, etc., sur l'Acte de Modération," in I.L.A. Diegerick, ed., *Archives d'Ypres, Documents du XVI* siècle, vol. 3, *Documents concernant les troubles religieux* (Bruges: Aime de Zuttere, 1876), p. 76.

12. "Avis émis par les états de Flandre sur l'Acte de Modération," ibid., p. 85.

13. "Address and Opening to Make a Good, Blessed and General Peace in the Netherlands, and to Bring Them Under the Obedience of the King, in Her Old Prosperity, Bloom, and Welfare," in Martin van Gelderen, ed., *The Dutch Revolt* (Cambridge: Cambridge University Press, 1993), p. 93. Said William of Nassau: "I have only the following objectives in this war: . . .*that state affairs shall be discussed in the States of the provinces in accordance with the custom of our ancestors. *That political matters will be dealt with by the king himself and by the States which are chosen in every province and not be dispatched secretly by hired foreigners." "Remonstrance of William of Nassau, prince of Orange etc., redeemer of the freedom of the Netherlands, to the States and the people, 1572," in Kossman and Mellink, *Texts Concerning the Revolt of the Netherlands*, p. 96.

14. "Political Education Containing Various . . . Arguments and Proofs," ibid., pp. 183–86.

15. "Address and Opening," ibid., p. 85; "A Defense and True Declaration of Things Lately Done in the Low Country," ibid., p. 20.

16. Ibid., pp. 85–86. "The princes as well as the subjects of the country have always had to commit themselves by a formal contract and to swear a solemn oath that they would maintain these rights and realise them. The inhabitants therefore owe obedience to the rulers only on condition that the freedoms are maintained." "The Prince of Orange's Warning to the Inhabitants and Subjects of the Netherlands, 1 September, 1568," ibid., p. 84. See also Van Gelderen, *Political Thought*, p. 129.

17. "Edict of the States General . . . by which they Declare that the king of Spain has forfeited the sovereignty and government of the afore-said Netherlands," in Kossman and Mellink, *Texts Concerning the Revolt of the Netherlands*, pp. 216–17.

18. Simon Schama, *The Embarrassment of Riches: An Interpretation of Dutch Culture in the Golden Age* (New York: Vintage, 1997).

19. "The prince of Orange's warning to the inhabitants and subjects of the Netherlands," in Kossman and Mellink, *Texts Concerning the Revolt of the Netherlands*, p. 84.

20. Wim Blockmans, "L'histoire parlementaire dans les Pays-Bas et la Belgique XIIe–XVIIe siècles," in *Las Cortes de Castilla y León, 1188–1988. Actas de la tercera etapa del Congreso Científico sobre la Historia de las Cortes de Castilla y León* (Valladolid: Cortes de Castilla y León, 1990) pp. 173–92; Arnade, *Beggars, Iconoclasts*, p. 33; Van Gelderen, *Dutch Revolt*, p. xiv.

21. "Privilège de Marie de Bourgogne pour les états de Namur," in Blockmans, "L'histoire parlementaire," pp. 244–52. The most important text in this regard is the Great Privilege of February 11, 1477.

22. Raymond Fagel, "Immigrant Roots: The Geographical Origins of Newcomers from the Low Countries in Tudor England," in Nigel Goose and Lien Luu, eds., *Immigrants in Tudor and Early Stuart England* (Brighton: Sussex Academic Press, 2005), p. 48.

23. King James VI and I, "Basilicon Doron," in *King James VI and I: Political Writings*, ed. Johann Sommerville (Cambridge: Cambridge University Press, 1994), p. 1. I have modern-

ized the spelling. For James's theory of divine right absolutism, including the idea that the king is bound to the law only by his good will, and is the master of the lives and possessions of his subjects, see also "The Trew Law of Free Monarchies," ibid., pp. 62–85.

24. King James VI and I, "Speech in the Star Chamber," ibid., pp. 206, 211.

25. King James VI and I, "Basilicon Doron," ibid., p. 21.

26. King James VI and I, "Speech in the Star Chamber," ibid., p. 213.

27. Note that a similar process of centralizing and solidifying royal authority, based on a divine right argument, also preceded the French Revolution in the following century.

28. "The Petition of Right," in Samuel Gardiner, ed., *The Constitutional Documents of the Puritan Revolution, 1625–1660* (Oxford: Clarendon Press, 1906), pp. 67, 69.

29. *The Humble Petition and Advice of Both Houses of Parliament With XIX Propositions and the Conclusion Sent Unto His Majestie, the Second of June, 1642* (London: Hunscott and Wright, 1642).

30. Charles I, *His Majesties Answer to the XIX Propositions of Both Houses of Parliament* (London: Robert Barker, 1642).

31. Geoffrey Robertson, *The Tyrannicide Brief* (New York: Pantheon, 2005), p. 68.

32. "That by the authority of the divine book it is lawful and glorious to kill public tyrants . . ." John of Salisbury, *Policraticus*, trans. Cary J. Nederman (Cambridge: Cambridge University Press, 1990), bk. 8, chap. 20, pp. 206–10.

33. "Openness was part of the Anglo-Saxon legal inheritance: a trial . . . was akin to a rather ill-conducted public meeting, involving members of the local community as witnesses, jurors and spectators. . . .The open justice rule had not been applied to treason trials of other alleged royal miscreants, like Anne Boleyn and Mary Queen of Scots, which were for that reason alone legally questionable." Robertson, *Tyrannicide Brief*, p. 132.

34. Ibid., p. 133.

35. Jonas d'Orléans, *Le métier de roi ("De institutione regia")*, ed. and trans. (into French) Alain Dubreucq (Paris: Éditions du Cerf, 1995), p. 210

36. William of Pagula, *The Mirror of Edward III*, in *Political Thought in Early Fourteenth-Century England: Treatises by Walter of Milemete, William of Pagula, and William of Ockham*, ed. and trans. Cary Nederman (Tempe: Arizona Center for Medieval and Renaissance Studies, 2002), p. 82. William continued: "For in this way do many from your household behave, seizing the goods of others against their will, and knowing that their servants have committed these sorts of extortions and robberies throughout the land, nor do they apply any remedy. Wherefore, one who does this is guilty, when he is able to correct the situation and neglects to amend it." (p. 76). And: "For one who permits anything to take place that he is able to impede, even though he has not done it himself, has virtually done the act himself if he allows it" (p. 94).

37. "The Charge Against the King" in Gardiner, *Constitutional Documents of the Puritan Revolution*, p. 373; italics mine.

38. John Cooke, *King Charls his Case* (London: Peter Cole, 1649), p. 13; italics mine.

39. Ibid., p. 14.

40. Ibid., p. 11.

41. Including the testimony of royalist soldiers who had witnessed Charles taking command of troops and ordering the plunder of civilian properties, and captured letters he

sent abroad to obtain foreign military support for his cause. Robertson, *Tyrannicide Brief,* pp. 173–74.

42. Ibid., p. 164.

43. John Cooke, *Monarchy, No Creature of God's Making* (Waterford: Peter de Pienne, 1651). He plunged into an ongoing debate about the meaning of a story in the first book of Samuel, in which the elders of Israel ask Samuel for a king. Samuel warns then in lurid detail. "He will take one tenth of your flocks and you shall be his slaves." And he predicts: "In that day you will cry out because of your king, whom you have chosen for yourselves; but the Lord will not answer you in that day." For King Charles's father James I, that last clause proved that it would never be lawful afterward to revolt against a king, for the Israelites "renounce[ed] forever all privileges." Cooke argued the reverse, that the passage proves that if a nation accepts the rule of a king, "God is angry with them for giving away that liberty which he would have them keep." It was a scriptural debate that would continue to preoccupy political thinkers for decades, and is the reference for the "inalienable rights" clause of the Declaration of Independence—rights that the Israelites or anyone else could never cede, and certainly not in perpetuity, even if they wanted to.

44. John Milton, "The Tenure of Kings and Magistrates," in Martin Dzelzainis, ed., *Milton: Political Writings* (Cambridge: Cambridge University Press, 1991) pp. 8–13.

45. John Locke, "The Second Treatise of Government," in Ian Shapiro, ed., *Two Treatises of Government and a Letter Concerning Toleration* (New Haven, Conn.: Yale University Press, 2003), pp. 102–5, 138, 141, 142, 164.

46. Robertson, *Tyrannicide Brief,* pp. 68–69.

47. James Madison, "James Madison to George Washington (April 16 1787)," in Ralph Ketcham, ed., *The Anti-Federalist Papers and the Constitutional Convention Debates* (New York: Mentor, 1986), p. 34.

48. "'Centinal,' Number 1 (October 5, 1787)," ibid., p. 227.

49. Counterterrorism Blog, "Transcript of the Latest Bin Laden Video," *Counterterrorism Blog,* September 7, 2007, http://bit.ly/1iDRHDK.

50. Locke, "Second Treatise," pp. 108–9.

Chapter Thirteen: Violent Extremists

1. Diarmaid MacCulloch, *The Reformation* (New York: Penguin, 2004), pp. 121–23; Martin Brecht, *Martin Luther, His Road to Reformation,* trans. James Schaaf (Minneapolis: Fortress Press, 1985), pp. 176–82; and Richard Marius, *Martin Luther: The Christian Between God and Death* (Cambridge: Harvard University Press, 1999), pp. 128–39.

2. Martin Luther, "Letter to the Christian Nobility of the German Nation," trans. Charles Jacobs and James Atkinson, in *Three Treatises* (Philadelphia: Fortress Press, 1966), p. 26.

3. Ibid., p. 41.

4. Ibid., pp. 27–28.

5. Ibid., pp. 35, 48–49, 36–37.

6. Ibid., p. 75.

7. "The Augustinian disciples of Luther denied that the pope was de jure divino [by

divine law] head of the church and asserted that Peter's primacy among the apostles, and hence that of his successors, was based solo jure humano [only on human law]: consequently, the pope had no authority to compel Christians to obey man-made ordinances on pain of mortal sin." Alastair Duke, *Reformation and Revolt in the Low Countries* (London: Hambledon and London, 2003), pp. 41, 46.

8. John of Salisbury, *Policraticus*, trans. Cary J. Nederman (Cambridge: Cambridge University Press, 1990), bk. 6, chap. 24, p. 133.

9. "Reformatio Sigismundi," in Gerald Strauss, ed. and trans., *Manifestations of Discontent in Germany on the Eve of the Reformation* (Bloomington: Indiana University Press, 1971), p. 6.

10. "When corruption overtakes the head, it must spread to all the other members. Once the pope had allowed cardinals to hold plural benefices, bishops followed suit, and after that the monasteries, and following them everyone else in the church." Ibid., p. 10.

11. Ibid., p. 9.

12. "If an order sees that one of its members is a cardinal, it plagues him with requests for favors, so the cardinal bends the pope's ear day and night, offering gold and silver in return for privileges." Ibid.

13. Ibid., pp. 12, 14.

14. The Dutch were particularly incensed at such extortionate mendicants. See Duke, *Reformation and Revolt in the Low Countries*, pp. 35, 61.

15. "Statement of Grievance Presented to the Diet of Worms in 1521," in Strauss, *Manifestations of Discontent*, p. 52. I have condensed and paraphrased the items.

16. "Lettre de Maximilien Vilain de Gand, baron de Rassenghien, gouverneur de Lille-Douai-Orchies, à Marguerite de Parme (30 Juin 1566)," in Solange Deyon and Alain Lottin, *Les "Casseurs" de l'Été 1566* (Paris: Hachette, 1981), p. 215. "Lettre du Conseil de Flandre aux Magistrats d'Ypres," in Diegerick, *Archives d'Ypres, Documents du XVIe siècle*, vol. 3, *Documents concernant les troubles religieux* (Bruges: Aime de Zuttere, 1876), p. 3:92.

17. "The description of the events which happened in the matter of religion in the Netherlands," in E. H. Kossman and A. F. Mellink, eds., *Texts Concerning the Revolt of the Netherlands* (Cambridge: Cambridge University Press, 1974), p. 67.

18. "Deuxieme requête présentée à la régente par les nobles confédères," in Diegerick, *Archives d'Ypres*, p. 101.

19. "Lettre des Magistrats d'Ypres à leurs députés a Bruxelles," ibid., p. 120.

20. "Acte de la régente," ibid., p. 94.

21. "Lettre de Maximilien Vilain de Gand, baron de Rassenghien, gouverneur de Lille-Douai-Orchies a Marguerite de Parme, 16 August 1566," ibid., p. 217.

22. "Lettre de Jean de Morbecque, gouverneur d'Aire, a Marguerite de Parme, 18 August, 1566," ibid., p. 218.

23. "A heavy blow to the more than century-long quest by the Valois and Habsburg Burgundian princes to consecrate their authority through managing the sacred." Peter Arnade, *Beggars, Iconoclasts, and Civic Patriots: The Political Culture of the Dutch Revolt* (Ithaca, N.Y.: Cornell University Press, 2008), pp. 93, 171. According to Arnade, this linkage to royal authority was made explicit by the choice of targets (p. 103).

24. Deyon and Lottin, *Les "casseurs" de l'été 1566*, p. 118.

25. Quoted in Arnade, *Beggars, Iconoclasts*, p. 99.

26. Arnade, *Beggars, Iconoclasts*, p. 113. See also Deyon and Lottin, *Les "casseurs" de l'été 1566*, pp. 200–201.

27. "Mali Fighters Destroy More Timbuktu Tombs," *Al Jazeera*, December 23, 2012, http://aje.me/1gbLeQY.

28. Human Rights Watch, *Mali: War Crimes by Northern Rebels* (April 30, 2012), http://bit.ly/OCsM8l.

29. Luke Harding, "Timbuktu Mayor: Mali Rebels Torched Library of Historic Manuscripts," *Guardian*, January 28, 2013, http://bit.ly/1emwo7W. The UNESCO accounting of the damage is in *State of Conservation: Timbuktu* (UNESCO, 2013), http://bit.ly/1pcmZSi, and in "Damage to Timbuktu's Cultural Heritage Worse than First Estimated, Reports UNESCO Mission," UNESCO Media Services, http://bit.ly/PMw61S.

30. The Salem witch trials are a notable American example.

31. James VI and I, "Basilicon Doron," in *King James VI and I: Political Writings*, ed. Johann Sommerville (Cambridge: Cambridge University Press, 1994), pp. 5, 6. The Arabic word for the practice is *takfir*, meaning designating someone a *kafir* or "unbeliever." The practice was outlawed in Tunisia's 2014 constitution.

32. "Bin Laden Addresses the American People on the Causes and Outcome of the 9/11 attacks," Al Jazeera, November 1, 2004, http://aje.me/1gR13HU.

33. Ibid. Bin Laden suggested that Bush copied those rulers by having his son installed as a governor and committing electoral fraud.

34. "Grand Salaam! Eurofighter Flies Off With Saudi Contract," *Defense Industry Daily*, August 8, 2013, http://bit.ly/1l4AjLa.

35. "Al-Sahab Video Discusses Economic Crisis, Arab 'Corruption,' Torture, Part 1," *Al-Fajr Media Center*, September 23, 2009, http://bit.ly/1nhCjR5.

36. Discussion of the Reformation in a Muslim context is hardly new. See, for example, Michaelle Browers and Charles Kurzman, eds., *An Islamic Reformation?* (Lanham, Md.: Lexington Books, 2004). Often, however, the notion of "Reformation" is understood broadly as "reform" or as almost synonymous with the Enlightenment and its expansion of scientific inquiry, tolerance, and secularism—not the fundamentalist extremism of the Reformation's first years. One article in Browers's and Kurzman's volume compares the Afghan Taliban with the early sixteenth-century Anabaptists of the German town of Münster but considers only this very narrow comparison, and only in a context of religious crisis (not economic injustice).

A significant body of literature, moreover, is devoted to explaining modern extremist, or violent political, Islam, in other terms than I am suggesting here. Much of it posits an almost intrinsic difference between Muslim and Western societies, due to fundamentally divergent cultures or models of civilization and of the role of religion in society. See, for example, Samuel Huntingdon, *The Clash of Civilizations and the Remaking of World Order* (New York: Touchstone, 1996), and Bernard Lewis, *The Crisis of Islam: Holy War and Unholy Terror* (New York: Random House, 2004.) A more nuanced analysis looks to the dislocation and assault on identity imposed by rapid twentieth-century modernization; Gilles Kepel, *The Trail of Jihad* (New York: Belknap Press, 2003). Olivier Roy is perhaps the leading scholar of political Islam to emphasize political grievances alongside sociological upheaval. See his *The Failure of Political Islam* (Cambridge: Harvard University Press,

1998), and *Globalized Islam: The Search for a New Umma* (New York: Columbia University Press, 2004).

Chapter Fourteen: Remedies

1. "Corruption and Nuclear Proliferation" in *Corruption, Global Security, and World Order* (Cambridge, Mass.: World Peace Foundation and American Academy of Arts and Sciences, 2009), pp. 124–67

2. Jean-François Bayart, Stephen Ellis, and Béatrice Hibou, *The Criminalization of the State in Africa* (Bloomington: Indiana University Press, 1999), p. 89. See also Jeffrey Gettleman, "Elephants Dying in Epic Frenzy as Ivory Fuels Wars and Profits," *New York Times*, September 3, 2012.

3. Bayart, Ellis, and Hibou, *Criminalization*, p. 100.

4. Dennis Blair, Jon Huntsman, et al., *The IP Commission Report* (National Bureau of Asian Research, May 2013), http://bit.ly/1jgEEX6, pp. 1–2.

5. Kevin Casas-Zamora, ed., *Dangerous Liaisons: Organized Crime and Political Finance in Latin America and Beyond* (Washington, D.C.: Brookings, 2013)

6. Bayart, Ellis, and Hibou, *Criminalization*, p. 93. See also Linda Polman, *The Crisis Caravan: What's Wrong With Humanitarian Aid* (New York: Metropolitan Books, 2010).

7. Thomas Friedman examined this relationship with respect to Syria in "The Other Arab Spring," *New York Times* April 7, 2012. Note, similarly, the acute water and resource shortages in the north of Nigeria, where Boko Haram is most tolerated.

8. See Sarah Chayes et al., "Corruption: The Unrecognized Threat to International Security," Carnegie Endowment for International Peace, June 2014.

9. French foreign minister Michèle Alliot-Marie resigned under intense criticism after vacationing in Tunisia as the 2011 revolution was breaking out and accepting transport in a private plane belonging to a member of the Trabelsi inner circle. Kim Willsher, "French Foreign Minister Resigns," *Guardian*, February 27, 2011.

10. U.S. Department of the Treasury, Resource Center, Counter Narcotics Trafficking Sanctions, http://1.usa.gov/1eZ7uIH.

11. U.S. Department of the Treasury, Press Center, Fact Sheet: New Executive Order Targets Significant Transnational Criminal Organizations, July 25, 2011, http://1.usa.gov/1ditGT7.

12. H.R. 4728, "An Act to Support the Independence, Sovereignty, and Territorial Integrity of Ukraine, and for Other Purposes," title 2, sec. 203(c)(1), pp. 33–34.

13. "It is the sense of Congress that the Administration should provide expedited assistance to the Government of Ukraine through appropriate United States Government and multilateral programs, including the Department of Justice's Kleptocracy Asset Recovery Initiative, the Egmont Group, the Stolen Asset Recovery Initiative, the Camden Asset Recovery Inter-Agency Network, and the Asset Recovery Focal Point Initiative, to identify, investigate, secure, and recover assets missing from the Government of Ukraine or linked to purported acts of corruption by former President Viktor Yanukovych, members of his family, other former or current senior foreign political figures of the Government of

Ukraine, and their accomplices in any jurisdiction." Ibid., title 1, sec. 108(a), pp. 18–19. See also Andrew Marshal, "What's Yours Is Mine: New Actors and New Approaches to Asset Recovery in Global Corruption Cases" (Washington, D.C.: Center for Global Development, 2013), http://bit.ly/1fMbHi7.

14. "Remarks by the President at the United States Military Academy Commencement Ceremony," May 28, 2014, http://1.usa.gov/1qC4fyS.

15. See Sarah Chayes and Frederic Wehrey, "Obama's Dangerous New Terror War," *POLITICO Magazine*, June 18, 2014.

16. Matt Mossman, "Big Dig: How to Hold Miners—and the Governments They Work with—Accountable," *Foreign Affairs*, January 29, 2014, http://fam.ag/1ezQhob; and Nicholas Shaxson, "Nigeria's Extractive Industries Transparency Initiative: Just a Glorious Audit?" (London: Chatham House, 2009), http://bit.ly/1jjFq43.

17. Working Group in the Prevention of Odious Debt, *Preventing Odious Obligations: A New Tool for Protecting Citizens from Illegitimate Regimes* (Washington, D.C.: Center for Global Development, 2010), http://bit.ly/NzW72e.

18. The rising wave of repression against local civil society organizations and against foreign efforts to support them is highlighted in Thomas Carothers and Saskia Brechenmacher, *Closing Space: Democracy and Human Rights Support Under Fire* (Washington, D.C.: Carnegie Endowment for International Peace, 2014).

Epilogue: Self-Reflection

1. Fintan O'Toole, *Ship of Fools: How Stupidity and Corruption Sank the Celtic Tiger* (New York: Public Affairs, 2010), p. 183.

2. Ibid., p. 217.

3. Ibid., p. 221.

4. "Iceland: Cracks in the Crust," *Economist*, December 11, 2008.

5. Sarah Lyall, "Smokestacks in a White Wilderness Divide Iceland," *New York Times*, February 4, 2007.

6. Daniel Chartier, *The End of Iceland's Innocence* (Ottawa: University of Ottawa Press, 2011); and Roger Boyes, *Meltdown Iceland* (New York: Bloomsbury, 2009).

7. Quoted in Boyes, *Meltdown*, p. 2.

8. Alda Sigmundsdóttir, "The Trial of Iceland's Prime Minister Is About Democracy, Not Money," *Guardian*, March 5, 2012. See also Harry Wilson, "Ex-Iceland PM Geir Haarde to Escape Punishment Despite Guilty Verdict Over Banking Collapse," *Telegraph*, April 23, 2012.

9. Stórnlagaráo, "A Proposal for a New Constitution for the Republic of Iceland," March 24, 2012, http://bit.ly/1gFFBEX.

10. Thorvaldur Gylfason, "Democracy on Ice: A Post-Mortem of the Icelandic Constitution," *Open Democracy*, June 19, 2013, http://bit.ly/1mcTIbl.

11. Among the best are Simon Johnson and James Kwak, *13 Bankers* (New York: Random House, 2010); Charles Ferguson, *Predator Nation: Corporate Criminals, Political Corruption,*

and the Hijacking of America (New York: Crown Business, 2012); Neil Barofsky, *Bailout* (New York: Free Press, 2012); and Laurence Lessig, *Republic Lost: How Money Corrupts Congress—and a Plan to Stop It* (New York: Twelve, 2011).

12. Johnson and Kwak, *13 Bankers*, p. 97.

13. The White House, Office of the Press Secretary, News Conference by the President, October 6, 2011, http://1.usa.gov/OEB7Zk.

14. Ferguson, *Predator Nation*, pp. 160, 186.

15. Ibid., p. 190.

16. Jed Rakoff, "Why Have No High-Level Executives Been Prosecuted?" *New York Review of Books* 61, no. 1 (January 9, 2014).

17. See Lessig, *Republic Lost*. See also the narrow definition of corruption expounded in U.S. Supreme Court jurisdiction, most recently in *McCutcheon v. Federal Election Commission*, 572 U.S. 2, April 2, 2014:

> We have said that government regulation may not target the general gratitude a candidate may feel toward those who support him or his allies, or the political access such support may afford.

Or p. 19:

> [W]hile preventing corruption or its appearance is a legitimate objective, Congress may target only a specific type of corruption—*"quid pro quo"* corruption. As *Buckley* explained, Congress may permissibly seek to rein in "large contributions [that] are given to secure a political *quid pro quo* from current and potential office holders." 424 U.S., at 26. In addition to "actual *quid pro quo* arrangements," Congress may permissibly limit "the appearance of corruption stemming from public awareness of the opportunities for abuse inherent in a regime of large individual financial contributions" to particular candidates. *Id.*, at 27; see also *Citizens United*, 558 U.S., at 359 . . . Spending large sums of money in connection with elections, but not in connection with an effort to control the exercise of an officeholder's official duties, does not give rise to such *quid pro quo* corruption. Nor does the possibility that an individual who spends large sums may garner "influence over or access to" elected officials or political parties.

See also p. 14:

> When an individual contributes money to a candidate, he exercises both of those rights [political expression and political association]. The contribution "serves as a general expression of support for the candidate and his views" and "serves to affiliate a person with a candidate." *Id.* [*Cohen v. California*, 403 U.S.], at 21–22. Those First Amendment rights are important

regardless whether the individual is, on the one hand, a "lone pamphleteer or street corner orator in the Tom Paine mold," or is, on the other, someone who spends "substantial amounts of money in order to communicate [his] political ideas through sophisticated" means. *National Conservative Political Action Comm.*, 470 U.S., at 493. Either way, he is participating in an electoral debate.

INDEX

Page numbers in *italics* refer to diagrams.